Foot Soldier

FOOT SOLDIER

A Combat Infantryman's War in Europe

ROSCOE C. BLUNT JR.

SARPEDON
Rockville Centre, NY

Published by
SARPEDON
A Division of Combined Publishing

ISBN 1-885119-72-0

Parts of this work were published in 1994 as
Inside the Battle of the Bulge.

MANUFACTURED IN THE UNITED STATES OF AMERICA

Contents

I would like to express very special thanks to my devoted wife, Beatrice S. Dudley-Blunt, who, soon after we were married more than half a century ago, deciphered and typed hundreds of pages of my wartime chronicles and my dictation while the memories were still fresh. Without her talent, dedication and patience, this book would not have been possible. Whatever I am today comes from her love, support, guidance and intuition.

Preface

Not a day goes by in my life that my thoughts don't return to 1944–45. Few are the nights whey my head hits the pillow in a darkened bedroom that the sights, the sounds and the faces don't return to disturb me. It has become obvious to me that if these psychological, emotional scars have not healed in more than half a century, they are never going to. Robbed of my hearing by countless artillery barrages and the pounding punishment of an M-1 rifle fired thousands of times snuggled against my right cheek, and with a still painful inability to walk normally, a result of frozen feet during the Ardennes winter campaign, physical reminders also remain. As is so with countless other combat veterans, I am still paying the price for those dark years.

War memories are still triggered easily. Incoming fire is evoked by the snap of an ice-coated tree branch during a storm; the low, throaty chugging sound of a V-1 "buzz bomb" when a diesel truck rumbles by; burning Autumn leaves sometimes reflect the pungent, unforgettable smell of burning human flesh. Flashbacks are usually momentary. But they are always there.

Combat veterans of all wars are iressistibly drawn back to the scene of "where it all happened." Just as my paternal grandfather had returned to the Civil War battlefield at Cold Harbor where his left arm had been blown off by a Confederate "mini ball," during the early 1990s I retraced my military odyssey through Scotland, England, France and, especially, Belgium. In 17 Ardennes villages I walked the fields and forests trying to recognize even a single familiar hillside, stand of ttrees, farm building or muddy road intersection. I found only one, in Grand Menil, where I had gone one-on-one with a German King Tiger tank. Practically all signs of the terrible conflict have been erased by time. Not a single bullet-pocked scar remains on battlefield buildings, though farmers told me they still uncover German and American relics of the conflict when they plow their fields. One gave me a rusted-out German M-42 helmet unearthed the year before.

As I returned to the sites of numerous atrocities committed against innocent civilians, tears of remembrance flowed, exorcizing some of the demons that have been part of my existence these many years.

World War II veterans returning to Belgium today are treated with open adoration, bordering on love. Fresh flowers adorn both simple and impressive monuments to American valor beside practically every roadside. In rebuilt Houffalize, long-stemmed roses have been placed every day on a large monument to American troops by a small group of now-elderly women. A ribbon reads "Houffalize remembers."

I have never attended an 84th Infantry Division reunion. I am not a backslapping, let's belly up to the bar and relive the war type. My memories have seldom been verbalized. My squad was not a closely-bonded unit. In fact, I would be hard pressed to name them. None have ever contacted me and I have only tried to contact one, Joe Winston Everett of Oklahoma. I looked him up in 1967 but he had died two years before.

I have been told on several occasions there is a certain sadness to my voice. Perhaps so, for the war just won't go away. I now accept the reality that it never will. Again, part of the emotional price so many of us are still paying for our combat experience. But there is, at the same time, a bright side. As I age, I am increasingly proud and aware of the tremendous contribution our violent and tragic performance made to the history of our grand country, and, in fact, the entire world.

This book will, I hope, offer my three sons, Roscoe III, a communications consultant; Randie, an award-wining business executive; and Cmdr. Richard D. Blunt, a U.S. Navy "airdale," a special insight into who their father was before they knew him. To Roscoe III, I offer special thanks for guiding me through the many revisions necessary to make this book a reality.

Roscoe C. Blunt Jr.
September 2000

1

The Beginning of an Odyssey

The whistle blew. Instantly, pandemonium exploded as hundreds of men grabbed cumbersome, bulging barracks bags, backpacks, rifles, gas masks, travel orders and personal possessions, and stumbled out of the tar paper–covered temporary barracks and onto the "company street."

It was 0400, September 19, 1944, almost a year from the day of my induction at Fort Devens. It was drizzling slightly and depressingly chilly for mid-September. As the ungainly mob milled about, sleepily trying to form straight formations, all thoughts of Talladega Mountain maneuvers—snakes, swamps, chiggers, 35-mile forced marches and scantily-dressed front-gate camp followers—were pushed into the background. The "real thing," we all inwardly knew, was about to unfold.

As I bounded out of the hut, I was ready. I wanted part of the action fighting the Germans, for I envisioned myself a Don Quixote, or at least an intrepid knight who, through courageous exploits, would make my loving family back home proud of me. As I peered into the black, unyielding, mist, I didn't understand why so many of my older companions, men leaving wives and children behind, did not share my youthful enthusiasm.

These were men, I now realize, who had no desire to die alone in some war-ravaged foreign country for a cause that was not—at that time—clear to any of us. Little could we know, as we stood shivering in the pre-dawn darkness trying to wipe the sleep from our eyes, what lay ahead. For too many, death awaited. For the survivors, a lifetime of tortured memories would be the only reward for patriotic service. Each of us stood silently with our private thoughts waiting for our officers' next command. Moments later we were ordered to move out and the silent, almost sullen, column of men started to shuffle along, only gradually picking up the pace.

After a quarter-mile route step march, the pack straps started cutting into my shoulder blades and soon splotches of skin were rubbed raw by my itchy wool uniform, now drenched as the drizzle accelerated to lightly falling rain. When carrying a 40-pound pack, 10-pound rifle, gas mask and helmet, and dragging a 40-pound barracks bag along the ground, no amount of prior body building can prevent the pain and injury of improperly adjusted pack straps.

The pulsating ache in my shoulders intensified until I thought my arms were being pulled out of their sockets as the two-mile march to the troop train siding continued. Bunched-up lines of uniformed men, burdened and bent by the gear they they were toting, stretched from the doors of the transport trains at the Camp Kilmer, New Jersey railroad siding as far back as the eye could see before dissolving into the mist.

As I shuffled from foot to foot waiting for my turn to board the soot-stained transport train, I thought of the months of training I had received and had then taught to others as a cadreman. I wondered whether the training would protect me in combat and guarantee my safe return. There was no way I could have known while standing on that train platform in New Jersey that practically none of what I had been taught and then passed on to others applied to reality—that most of it was only untested and untried theory. No one had informed me, in training or elsewhere, that Army manuals are best thrown out the window on the first day of combat and that the odds of self preservation—the most basic of all human instincts—improve only if a warrior learns quickly to protect his own ass. No training manual is going to do it for him.

Eventually, we were all boarded, the first ones into seats; those who followed, in the aisles and on the car platforms, sitting, sprawling, sleeping or grumbling on disarrayed mountains of military gear. Seventy-five men were crammed into each car that was originally built to accommodate 48.

With repeated jerking and considerable metallic impact, the string of cars irritatingly lurched forward and backward with neck-snapping abruptness, coupling car after car until finally settling into the steady, roughly swaying rhythm of motion typical of passenger trains in the '40s. Some men peeled back the blackout shades trying to catch a glimpse through grimy windows of the countryside passing in the darkness or the occasional lights of sleeping upper New Jersey towns. Others tried to read letters from home, knowing full well the letters would be the last direct contact they would have with loved ones for many months to come, perhaps forever.

The world wasn't awake yet and neither were we. I tried to push my thoughts aside and sleep but it wouldn't come. The cattlecar conditions were too disorganized, uncomfortable and smelly. Cinder particles from the coal-powered engine filtered through closed, loose-fitting train windows, adding to the gritty discomfort of our sweat-soaked uniforms. Repeatedly, I cleared my nose or spat out inhaled cinder particles. About an hour into the move, the train slammed to a halt with the same abrupt violence it had begun with at Camp Kilmer.

"Let's go. Let's go Let's go. Line up in formation on the platform," a voice bellowed from the darkness outside our car windows. The voice was answered by a chorus of profanity from within our car. This brought laughter and more swearing, for the non-com outside couldn't possibly identify those who had yelled back at him. It was a small victory for us all, and in the Army small victories were important and to be savored. Men pushed and shoved, trying to find their gear as each fought for the platform doors, impatient to be rid of the train and out into what had to be cooler, fresher air.

We had no idea where we were, having been told only that we were soon to embark on a ship headed for the European Theater of Operations (ETO) to face the Germans. But how, when and where were secrets still locked in the minds and briefcases of the brass.

Eventually, the dim appearance of the Manhattan skyline informed us we were on the New Jersey side of New York harbor. The old army axiom, "Hurry up and wait," had not been left behind at Fort McClellan, Alabama or Camp Claiborne, Louisiana, my Army homes before Camp Kilmer. It had followed us all the way north to New Jersey, because once outside the wheezing train, we stood around and waited and waited, and then waited some more.

After what seemed an interminable length of time, small groups of us were loaded onto a ferry where we were able to test our sea legs. As the dirty and malodorous harbor oozed along behind us, we could make out a dock fingering its way out at us through the fog and drizzle. An hour of shifting from one foot to the other passed before a gray, overcast dawn broke. I found myself miniaturized by a huge, ramshackle, sheet metal warehouse on one side and the most gigantic ship I had ever seen on the other. I read the paint-peeling name on the prow: *Edmund B. Alexander.* The 786-foot troop transport, commissioned in 1928 and considered the largest of its class, was manned by a merchant marine crew.

The *Alexander* had been pressed into emergency wartime transport service and the neglect of maintenance caused by such urgent, nonstop usage showed everywhere. Expansive steel plates, mostly buckled and dented in need of repair or replacement, formed the ship's hull. Looking at the rusted corrosion, I wondered about the ship's seaworthiness. The anchor chain was also heavily coated with rust, giving the once-trim ship the appearance of an oversized tramp steamer straight out of a Humphrey Bogart movie. A volunteer group of Red Cross women wended their way through our ranks, dispensing hot coffee and doughnuts in an attempt to bolster our now sagging morale.

The milling crowd of GIs, more a mob than an orderly formation, inched its way forward, one step at a time, toward a steeply angled gangplank emerging from the drizzle. Finally, my turn came. Struggling to carry or drag all my gear, which had become heavier every hour, I eventually made it to the top of the gangplank to be greeted by a stone-faced Army clerk with a clipboard and an endless printed list of names and company designations.

"Blunt, Roscoe C. Jr., Company L, 333rd Regiment" (84th "Railsplitter" Infantry Division), I gasped. Like a robot, an emotionless voice barked out my sleeping quarters assignment, gave me a meal ticket that had to be punched at every meal, and then I was directed below deck. Bulling myself along the rail toward the stern of the ship, I hoped I could remember the directions I had been given. As I repeated them over and over in my mind, the GI behind me gave me a nudging shove. I, in turn, did the same to the bewildered GI in front of me.

The line wormed its way around a large hatch nearby like a flock of lost sheep trying to find its way back to the pen—in this case, our assigned sleeping quarters. Looking closer, I could see the line wrapped around the hatch at least six deep; any thought I might have entertained about getting to a bunk soon evaporated.

The line soon emptied into a passageway and a network of several flights of near-vertical maritime ladders as we worked our way lower and lower into the ship's bowels. Navy boot camp, I'm sure, trained sailors how to navigate these iron pipe ladders effortlessly while weighted down with arms full of gear, but Army basic training didn't.

The easiest way was to drop your gear and weapons down the stairs to the deck below, where they landed with a clanging thud, and then scramble down and retrieve them before some sergeant, or worse still, a lieutenant, saw what you had done. At this point, fast approaching sheer exhaustion, the last thing I needed was an ass-chewing from some Mickey Mouse officer. The trick, I learned, was to hold onto your gear long enough so you didn't drop it on some hapless GI below you.

As I struggled down one of the ship's ladders, someone above me accidentally lost his grip and a full, heavy barracks bag crashed down on my helmeted head, knocking me down the remaining stairs where I landed on top of my gear. Profanity vied with apologies, but neither helped my now almost hopeless frustration. Recruiting officers never told us about the conditions we were now encountering. If they had, some of us might have defected right then and there to the Air Corps. But it was too late now. We were all committed and, in fact, trapped on this huge steel, floating bilge palace.

We were told that 6,500 men were being crammed aboard into smelly, temporary living quarters with hammocks and crude bunks strung from ceilings and bulkheads. Everywhere there was mass confusion as men fought for the most comfortable accommodations they could find. Too exhausted to care, I took what was left: the floor. With my steel helmet as a pillow, my numb body, drained by exhaustion, was mercifully asleep almost instantly.

When I awoke about six hours later and settled myself in, I became aware of sounds I had never heard before: the heartbeat of creaks and groans, throbbing turbines and the grinding of stretching metal would be my orchestral accompaniment for the next 13 days. The nauseating stench of diesel fuel permeated our sleeping quarters, a smell we would have to live with, but never really get used to, for the remainder of the trip.

While I slept, the ship had gotten underway. I was disappointed I had missed the passing of the Statue of Liberty as we sailed out of the harbor. I soon became aware of the subtle pitch and roll of a ship at sea. My first sea voyage started September 20th, but I was soon to find out its physical effects on me would make me pray it would be my last time on a ship.

Rested somewhat, I felt my excitement level rise again but it soon became apparent that the years had washed away an important childhood memory: my susceptibility to seasickness. The last time I had suffered from this malady was on my junior high school class trip from Boston to Provincetown six years previously.

Hunger reminded me we had not been fed for many hours. In the ship's dining room, I sat down to a merchant marine meal far superior to anything the Army had ever offered. Too bad it would stay with me for only a few minutes. Real seasickness, I can attest, is one of the few times in life when you actually hope you will die.

Between trips to the rail to vomit, I managed to survive on a few Saltine crackers each day. Calls of nature were kept to a minimum, for to stand up was to swoon. I couldn't even-make the mandatory daily lifeboat drills, I was so sick. Flat on my back, about all I could manage was to scratch out a few lines in letters home and a journal I tried to keep each day. This private time helped pass the hours that I hoped would bring the ship eventually to harbor and me to land.

Several days into the voyage, during a brief catnap, the ship was suddenly wracked violently by a series of explosions. Panicky word spread throughout the billeting area that we had been torpedoed and were sinking. Seasickness be damned as many of us scrambled for our lives toward the upper deck with Mae West life jackets under our arms. Why hadn't I made those life boat drills, I chastised myself as I struggled top deck. I hadn't even learned how to put the damn thing on.

Sheepishly, the excited mob of GIs forged out into the open only to be faced with the ship's gun crews practicing their anti-aircraft proficiency at an open sky. I hadn't even noticed the gun emplacements on the ship before and it was a secure feeling to know we were armed, even it it was only with anti-aircraft capability. If it is possible for a face green with seasickness, to change to red from embarrassment for having been part of the panic-stricken exodus, mine did. As innocuously as possible, I tried to melt back into the steel gray labyrinth of the ship.

To this day, a half century later, I vividly remember the two weeks of constant seasickness experienced between the States and Europe. It was a torturous experience that no one should have to endure. I can only think back now that my indoctrination to sea travel must have occurred before the advent of anti-motion sickness pills, for we were never offered any. Even when I ventured on deck, thinking that fresh sea air might help, the debilitating nausea intensified and left me barely able to stand up, much less walk.

I endured each monotonous, seemingly endless day by reading, crawling evenings to an improvised movie theater, listening to canned music, or sitting on the fantail watching the ship's wake as we steamed eastward. And also there was the added burden of daily inspections— in the Army, inspections never ceased, even when those being inspected were near death. They were a way of life but it always puzzled me how the inspection team non-coms and brass never seemed to be afflicted with seasickness as the rest of us were.

In the distance, I could see a phalanx of other troop transports, unarmed merchant supply vessels and the protective U.S. Navy destroyers that guarded our convoy stretching to the distant horizons on both sides and to our stern. Even with the Navy protection, I still felt naked for I knew the German wolfpack submarines were out there searching for us. I had not mentioned it to the others but I had been watching the ship's crew who were on constant alert with binoculars for submarine periscopes or, as I feared, torpedo wakes.

Toward the voyage's end, I was able to keep down some meatless bullion, dry cheese and an occasional apple or orange. If I hadn't, I'm sure the bodily effects of this unprepared-for malnutrition would have been far more severe. I was still too weak to make it unassisted to the galley but there were always a few kind souls not given to seasickness who would bring some small snacks back to the less fortunate.

The sameness of each day was broken up slightly one morning when green cloth Red Cross ditty bags were distributed, containing shaving equipment, playing cards, cigarettes, and other sundry items intended to make our suffering more tolerable. Some nights I tried sleeping on deck, hoping the cold air would suppress my nausea, but I soon learned that lying on my back watching the ship's masts gyrat-

ing around and around only intensified the sickness. A sympathetic
merchant mariner who took pity on me suggested I watch the horizon,
or better still, the sky. I very gratefully found out his suggestion helped
somewhat.

On the twelfth day, while lying on a deck in the hole enduring my
discomfort, I became aware of an excited buzz emanating from the
upper decks. Never one to be left out of any action, even in sickness,
I managed to wobble and pull myself up several flights of passageway
steel stairs from the dankness of the lower compartments and into
brilliant sunlight.

Overhead, an antiquated, World War I, canvas-covered, open-
cockpit bi-plane emblazoned with British Royal Air Force (RAF)
insignia was circling protectively overhead. The plane, a relic of a
bygone era, was still serving a purpose in Britain's defense as a coastal
observation plane and, in doing so, was preserving its own niche in the
combined war effort. We all waved furiously at this first symbol of the
real war. The pilot and his "back seater" observer-gunner, their tradi-
tional white scarfs whipping in the prop wash, waved back and then,
as quickly as they had appeared, were gone again. Still flush with the
excitement of something new in our lives, we hung over the rail watching the tiny plane disappear over the eastern horizon, back to the
safety of its airfield. "We must be getting close to England," I mused
to myself before staggering back below to resume my siege of illness.

One day I asked a member of the ship's crew why a normal three-
day voyage was taking so many days.

"U-boats. We have to take evasive action all the way across," he
answered matter-of factly before returning to his duties. I learned later
we had been zigzagging across the ocean trying to avoid patrolling
German "wolf pack" submarines, well-known for their destructive
proficiency sinking Allied shipping from the Azores to the Caribbean,
and especially along the heavily traveled North Atlantic shipping
routes between the United States and Europe.

For several days, unseasonably warm weather had allowed us some
sundecking time, a wonderful respite from the foul-smelling hole
where we were quartered. The warmth of the sun also moderated the
dismal effects of my queasy stomach. A crew member told me we were
passing through an area west of the British Isles where the water and
climate were warmed by the Gulf Stream coursing its way northward

from the Gulf of Mexico and the Caribbean. For a few hours, it was almost like lounging on a cruise ship.

One morning, I awakened to find the *Alexander* rolling more violently than usual and even though there had been no solid food in my stomach for more than a week, my heaving and gagging became much more frequent. Hanging on to railings for dear life, I clumsily made my way to the upper desk and was almost knocked over by gale-force winds. A dungaree-uniformed mariner scurried by, swaying deftly with the ship's seasawing motion, bracing himself against the wind. Seeing my surprised expression, he said, "We're entering the Irish Sea. It's always like this."

As I stood mesmerized by mountainous swells, threatening, it seemed, to inundate the *Alexander,* the ship veered north, rolling sharply onto its starboard side as it did so. I hung onto a rail, wondering whether it was a desperate maneuver after a submarine sighting. But it had not been anything as dramatic as that; it was only a last-minute course change away from Le Havre and Cherbourg, France's two major seaports on the English Channel, where heavy Luftwaffe bombing and submarine activity had been reported. Cherbourg had been our intended destination but now, we were informed through the rumor factory, we would disembark in Scotland instead. For once, the rumor mill proved accurate. Other units of the 84th Division were also diverted away from France and were heading for Liverpool and Southampton in England. Eventually, the division would reassemble in the countryside surrounding the English city of Winchester, inland from Britain's Channel coast.

The ship cautiously slowed its passage northward through the outer reaches of St. George's Channel, past Bristol Channel, southwestern England's most important commercial shipping lane, and finally the Isle of Man before entering the southern extremity of the Irish Sea. In almost two weeks, the ship had covered about 3,300 miles.

Now, for all practical purposes, we were out of effective Luftwaffe range and we could relax a little. The submarine threat still existed but English aerial patrols were so intensive, we were told, that U-boats seldom ventured this close to the channels. Hours later, the ship passed between Donaghadee, Ireland on the port side and Drummore, Scotland on the starboard. The land masses were so distant on the horizon, however, they looked like indistinguishable islands on each side of the ship.

On the thirteenth day, I awakened to find land in sight off the starboard bow of the ship. Now I knew how Christopher Columbus must have felt after so many days of landless sailing. I celebrated by running to the ship's galley and eating an entire meal and, for the first time, I was able to keep it down.

It was Sunday morning, October 1, and the weather cooperated perfectly as the ship slowed its forward passage toward land. The pastoral Scottish landscape was breathtaking. A splendid quilted patchwork of stonewalled pastures, bordered by thin stands of thickly-foliaged trees and hedges enclosing herds of grazing cattle and sheep offered, to me, the ultimate serenity. A natural afghan of multi-hued, gently sloping farm lands gave way gracefully to cloud-enshrouded mountain ranges above them. An occasional farmer or shepherd waved from the hills and displayed their country's flag, receiving, in turn, a thousand railside responses.

Picturesque villages extended along the seaside at the foot of the hills and pastures. Here and there, an occasional sand-colored medieval castle could be seen nestled snugly against lush hills. Couples walked along the nearly deserted waterfronts, probably, I assumed, on their way to Sunday services. I realized it would probably be a long time, perhaps forever, before I would again be privy to such total tranquility.

So engrossed was I with the scenery and my thoughts of what lay ahead, I was unaware the ship had quietly stopped and dropped anchor beside one of these small villages.

I was able to get a good night's sleep, for we were told we would not be disembarking until the next day. Bright and early, I was up again to enjoy the peaceful Scottish landscape from railside. My reverie was soon shattered by a loudspeaker announcement that boomed throughout the ship: "Now hear this. Now hear this. Prepare to disembark. Return to quarters to disembark." I glanced at my wristwatch, a going away present from my parents. It was 0930, October 2, 1944. I scrambled below and assembled my gear.

I was about to find out that trying to bull-strength half a ton of army gear up four ship deck ladders is even more fun than depositing it below deck. But, as with most adversities in life, most anything can be accomplished with enough sweat, know-how, determination and luck.

Back on deck, I soon had my first opportunity to foster some international goodwill when a motor launch drew alongside the ship and its crew boarded the *Alexander*. I struck up a conversation with one of the Scotch mariners from the port but soon learned I could not fathom his rolling burr. I was the butt of the launch crew's humor as they laughed good-naturedly at my difficulty.

"We can understand you. How come you can't understand us? We're both speaking the same language," one joshed. Quickly resorting to a combination of pigeon-English and sign language, I gave the joker some American coins which he enthusiastically accepted, and I was given, in return, a copy of the Glasgow, Scotland Sunday newspaper and a "thruppennybit" souvenir.

The paper was filled with casualty lists and news from the front. As my eyes scanned the names and addresses, I realized, in a figurative sense, my war had arrived. Standing at the ship's rail reading the long lists of British dead had a strangely sombering effect on me; such newspaper listings were something I had never seen in America, where the war had been so far away and impersonal. I looked across the harbor at the peaceful village framed by resplendent beauty, and somehow I couldn't reconcile the two. Death, which had become almost a daily way of life for the people of the British Isles, was still strange to me, something with which I had never before had to contend.

As I basked in the warmth and brilliance of that early October sun, my young mind was slow to grasp that in only a matter of a few short weeks, death would become my own constant, terrifying companion.

2

The British Isles

The amorphous mob of hunched-over olive drab uniforms milling around the deck toting bulging equipment bags eventually defined itself into a single file that disappeared down the gangplank to a flotilla of military landing craft and Scottish tug boats bobbing on the tide beside the ship.

These makeshift ferries chugged back and forth across the harbor like so many ants taking us, a few at a time, across the surge to Greenock harborside, at the western mouth of Glasgow port. Again came the struggle with our gear as we disembarked from our rising and falling, pitching and rolling conveyances onto rickety gangplanks resting against the town's 12-foot-high wharves. Fortunately for many of us, the trip was only about a hundred yards, scarcely far enough for seasickness to reoccur. The reassuring solidness of a few steps on land, especially after a long sea voyage, quickly reacclimates one to a world where everything is not in constant motion.

GIs clambering off the makeshift ferry boats were piled on top of each other, turning the town's small dock into a mass of confused humanity until someone funneled off a few hundred men toward a railroad station some distance away. Amidst the several thousand GIs, four female American Red Cross workers were hawking hot coffee and doughnuts to as many as could crowd around their mobile wagon.

"Anyone here from Texas?" one yelled out shrilly. On a boatload of 6,500 men, there were bound to be a few from America's second largest state, and almost instantly she was surrounded by grinning soldiers, all anxious to reminisce about home—especially with a good-looking American woman.

The only sour note to the whole scene, and one I would hear referred to many times for years afterward, was that the Red Cross, supposedly a non-profit charitable organization, charged the GIs 15 cents for the Java and doughnuts. I declined their offer, if in fact it even was an offer, and so did many others in the crowd.

After sitting on our barracks bags along the waterfront for more than an hour, some ragged lines eventually formed and we were shunted along the town's narrow, cobblestoned streets toward a railroad station, dragging our duffle bags along as best we could. The streets were lined on both sides by multi-storied masonry homes and stores, many of them decorated attractively in Tudor style, the English architecture of the 1500s. But what became instantly apparent as we walked through the town was, in sharp contrast to the United States, how shabbily dressed the townspeople were, a reflection of the war's effect on this tiny seaport community.

As we stumbled over the cobblestones, toting our gear and trying at the same time to look military, the townspeople, for the most part, went about their business as if we weren't even there. A few of the older men, perhaps old former soldiers themselves, stood against the buildings smoking their pipes and nodding approvingly at us as we ambled by. Or, perhaps they only saw us as more cannon fodder to reduce the length of Britain's casualty lists.

Again, it was a long march to the waiting troop train but the bright and sunny weather was in our favor and the trek was infinitely more pleasant than the rain-soaked march two weeks earlier in New Jersey. The ensuing 16-hour train trip, culminating the next day in south central England, was an adventure in itself. We filed into compartmentalized cars about two-thirds the size of standard American Pullman cars and tried to make ourselves as comfortable as possible. We had been told it would be a two-day journey. Each car consisted of six to eight compartments that comfortably accommodated four passengers, two each facing one another. In Europe, passengers exit trains by the compartment doors rather than platform doors at the end of each passenger car as in America. Because of their reduced size, English passenger cars were uncomfortable and tended to sway and be noisier than their American counterparts.

The train labored out of the station and within minutes was swallowed up in valleys carved out of majestic hillsides. With each passing kilometer, the beauty of the pastures and gently sloping hills magnified Scotland's magnificence. The normal rowdiness of Army troops being transported was surprisingly absent as we continued southward toward England, for many of the passengers were gripped by their compartment windows watching the panorama slipping by.

K-rations were issued to everyone on the train and we got our first taste of combat field rations: a sealed packet of lemon powder, a small can of dry cheese containing ham flecks (or sometimes hash), four dog biscuits, eight small caramel candies, four Wings cigarettes, a stick of gum, and a book of matches.

Less than an hour after the train chugged its way out of Greenock, we arrived in Glasgow. The initial sights were culturally distressing; many of the buildings we saw were decrepit and often in shambles. Small knots of sallow, hollow-cheeked children, malnourished to a degree I had never seen in America, ran along the tracks beside the train waving victory signs with their hands and yelling "Any gum, chum?" Most of us threw what we could—cigarettes, candy, K-rations, gum, American money—out the train windows, causing furious scrambles of children fighting with the intensity of those determined to survive.

Everything I observed in Glasgow outside the compartment windows was uniform, starkly gray. Occasionally on the city's streets, triangular concrete forms covered with sandbags were constructed against buildings. These were the first bomb shelters I had seen. The war was becoming more real with each passing minute.

A fleeting rail sign passing in the darkness announced that we had reached Edinburgh. Again, everything looked the same: barren and dilapidated. The shabbiness along the way was broken occasionally by autumn foliage on the hillsides. Scotland's much-heralded tranquil lakes teased us momentarily and then were gone again. The brilliant reds and purples of the setting sun, much like the work of a careless painter, spilled from nature's pallet onto glistening, ribbon-like rivers, gorges and forests. One moment this beauty was at my fingertips and then it danced playfully away into my memory. I remember wishing I had been clever enough to steal this enchanting example of nature's splendor and transpose it onto canvas for those at home to enjoy some day. Each passing scene was truly a moment of exquisite beauty.

I had no way of realizing at the time how unfair it was to be offered these tantalizing landscapes and then have them so abruptly replaced with the visions of war's atrocities, filth and deprivation that I would soon encounter on the European mainland.

As the train crossed the English border and continued southward, the landscape became flatter and less scenic. It was almost as if fate and distance were trying to visually recondition us, to transpose us from one of nature's supreme triumphs to one of its abject failures.

The countryside was beginning to feature a certain uniformity of brick, stone or stucco structures—standardized housing, architecturally speaking. At Newcastle Upon Tyne, in North Umberland County and just in a few kilometers from the North Sea, the train stopped to refuel and all American troops were given chickenless chicken pie by the British Red Cross. At first taste, the meal seemed sparse but in food-starved England, this was a generous gesture. After we devoured the meal, the train continued its monotonous journey southward through the cities of Leeds, Sheffield, Birmingham, and eventually into London.

It was in that historic, fabled city that we finally saw for the first time the ravages of Hitler's saturation "blitz" bombing aimed at bringing the British people to their knees. As the train slowed within the city's limits, fires continued to burn under mountains of rubble on both sides of us, and skeletal buildings defiantly remained standing, like the English people, refusing to crumble. The acrid smell of a once majestic city burning itself into oblivion filtered into the rail cars, giving us still another taste of what lay ahead.

As we looked out the train windows, armies of women and older men struggled to clear streets of debris by hand, one stone, one brick at a time. Others poked through the ruins trying to retrieve lost treasures or something from the their past to hang on to for moral strength. It was almost with a sense of relief that the train pulled away from this utter destruction and continued southward through the untouched countryside. Being a somewhat casual observer of so much carnage and suffering in London prompted a guilt-like emotion, for we had just left an unmarred homeland where not a single bomb had, or would, fall.

The English people, I would soon learn, were allies but not overly friendly toward us. They seemed to resent that the "colonies" had twice in the past three decades plucked their hot chestnuts out of the fire for them. It was not uncommon to ride in a train compartment with British civilians for hours not hearing them utter a word—just watching you out of the corner of their eye—always reading or knitting for the war effort, anything to keep from engaging in conversation. English reserve is well known and generally accepted as fact, but I found their lack of civility akin to rudeness. During the month I was on English soil, I never fully adjusted to being snubbed so often by so many.

On the other hand, British "tommies" swaggered around the streets, chests thrown out, heads held high with heels clicking exaggeratedly on the pavements. A proud bunch they were, compared to the somewhat disheveled, rag-tag appearance of the average GI—a reflection, I presume, of the two nations' lifestyles.

It was 0400, 16 bone-weary hours later, before we finally pulled into Newbury, Berkshire, a town of about 5,000. I was learning that nothing in the military, especially the Army, is done at civilized hours. A fleet of one-ton, six-by-six trucks awaited our arrival and two miles later, we were all dumped out into a muddy apple orchard at an Air Force glider base dotted with drab-looking camouflaged pyramidal tents. These luxurious living conditions were capped off with wooden plank floors, wire spring, steel-pipe bunks and straw-filled ticking.

Eager for sleep, we settled in, eight men to a tent. I had experienced my share of mud at Fort McClellan and Camp Claiborne and even at home in the spring, but never anything like Newbury. We were constantly in ankle-deep mud. To venture outside to the mess facility—a circus-like tent pitched in another mud bog—or the latrine was to literally "walk the plank" and pray that no one was coming in the opposite direction at the same time. If so, it meant stepping off the wooden path and into the muck if the person approaching outranked you or was bigger than you. We made no attempt to keep uniforms or boots clean.

Our food was slopped into our mess kits by KP personnel in one homogeneous mess—most of which usually splattered onto our uniforms or field jackets—and was eaten only because to do otherwise was to go hungry. When it rained, and it did nearly every day in Britain, the garbage in the mess kit became soup. It was apparent from the first day in England where the army term "mess slop" came from. Hadn't they heard that an army travels on its stomach and that good food was important if soldiers were to be molded into successful fighting machines?

My first night at the glider base was spent in a sleeping bag smothered by several blankets, and still I shivered all night. The foggy, drizzly fall climate in England was the most consistently foul weather I had ever experienced.

Nearby pastures were cluttered with camouflaged OD (olive drab) American troop-carrying CG-4A gliders and huge, black, stubby-nosed British Horsa gliders. Word spread through the campsite that we were to be converted to glider troops and flown into battle in the CG-4As but this plan, if true, never materialized.

Still, despite the living standard to which we had been reduced in this quaint English countryside, the nearby town of Newbury had its pleasant aspects with narrow winding streets, neighborhood soccer games, movies and peaceful countryside walks. It was quite a paradox that such a tranquil setting was actually a staging area for men and equipment that would eventually wreak havoc, the likes of which the world had never seen, on the European continent and its peoples.

Planeloads of brass were being flown in almost continuously in C-47s; it was obvious that something big was in the works. The air of secrecy we sensed everywhere was intensified when our questions to higher-ups produced only vague and indirect answers. The only thing that was a certainty was that we were soon to cross the English Channel but where, how and why remained speculation. We were to eventually face the Germans and that, we were forced to accept, was all that we actually had to know.

After a week of Newbury's quagmire orchards, we were mercifully transferred to Barton Stacy camp, an abandoned British army facility outside Andover, about 15 miles southwest by truck. With wooden barracks, tarred parade ground, a PX (post exchange) and even a town nearby showing 25-year-old movies, this was more like home. Together with the 507th, 513th and 517th airborne units we were to stay there for three weeks in relative comfort.

But the improved living conditions were a cleverly disguised army trade-off: comfort for a return to military spit and polish, more commonly known in GI lingo as "chicken shit." We were rolled off our cots at 0600 each day for refresher training and our day usually ended only after a series of intensified nighttime field exercises. Full field pack cross-country forced marches were the order of the day and it quickly became obvious the Army was doing its damnedest to get us into top physical shape as quickly as possible—and for only one reason—combat, and soon. Hampshire dust clogging our mouths and throats while crawling through English countryside maneuvers tasted no better than Alabama red clay. And body bruises from a half-mile crawl on our bellies in England were just as painful as those we felt doing the same thing in Louisiana.

During one of the six-a-day orientation or training lectures we were forced to sit through on the parade ground, an unfamiliar non-com appeared and interrupted a class on the nomenclature of the M-1, air-cooled, light machine gun by asking for volunteers for a dangerous assignment, no questions asked. Volunteers, he said, would be transferred to a different outfit immediately. The first person to jump to his feet was Blunt. I couldn't afford to pass up a chance like this to become a hero at last. Or perhaps my impetuous action was just an attempt to cast aside the sheltered life I had led as a musician and college student back home.

The first dozen men to stand up were chosen and the transfer, as the non-com had promised, took place the same day. The cloak-and-dagger manner in which the whole episode took place made me wonder what I had gotten myself into. Our gear was collected in about half the normal time and we were whisked away in "six-bys" to an undisclosed location that I estimated to be about 20 miles away. It was the first time I had not been subjected to the long-established "hurry up and wait" army tradition. Everything had been meticulously planned and there would be no SNAFUs that day.

After about an hour, the truck transporting the volunteer group braked violently to a stop before a stately English mansion—Bentworth Hall in Alton, Hants. Without a word, we were quickly ushered inside, still having no idea what was in store for us. Our mood became more somber as we started to worry about our previous eagerness to get involved in a mysterious, so-called secret "high-risk assignment."

After being processed by a T-5 clerk who kept looking first at our orders and then up at us, and then back at the orders in the foyer of the 30-room estate, we were told to wait for further instructions. As I stood there, studying the ornately tiled fireplaces that were the focal point of every room, I wondered what nobility had previously lived there. The floors, ceilings, walls, and stairways were elegantly tiled in bright, regal-colored stone.

Although the mansion had been stripped of all its furnishings, the original grandeur was still evident. Thirty-five-foot-high ceilings and 50-foot-long rooms gave the mansion a castle-like, but nevertheless forlorn, appearance. A GI complement billeted there had rigged up portable electrical and heating systems for cooking and lighting. Wires were strewn everywhere in disarray and smoky stoves had smudged walls and ceilings with films of soot.

When the clerk finally finished processing our transfer orders, we were taken to a dining room and served a sumptuous meal on china-ware and linen-clothed tables. Still, no one had offered a clue about our new assignment. Could this be the last supper we had just been served? But if the gourmet food continued, perhaps this new assignment, whatever it was, might not be so hard to take after all.

Eventually, a buck sergeant showed up and escorted us to our quarters, a row of Quonset huts, each partitioned into two four-man rooms, and each equipped with a potbelly stove to hold back the cold English nights. The luxury of mattressed beds was another indication that something special, something important, was in our future. After we each selected bunks and stowed our gear, the sergeant walked us back to Bentworth Hall for what we hoped would be an orientation briefing. The suspense mounted. I was still unable to figure out what type of clandestine operation I had volunteered for.

As I passed through the main entrance to the estate, I paused to read a bulletin board directive declaring that any Engineer Corps truck driver found guilty of violating the Army code of the road would be immediately transferred to the Infantry—presumably, the ultimate punishment, sort of like being banished to Ile du Diable, the French penal colony on Devil's Island.

I finally found out what I had joined: the Corps of Engineers. That solved part of the mystery, but why engineers? I didn't know how to build anything. In fact, I wasn't the least bit accomplished with my hands or mechanically inclined. Only later were we told that we were at Bentworth Hall for three weeks of intensive, specialized training and that when it was completed, we would be returned to our outfits.

A rather affable major in a clean, well-tailored uniform seated us in what had once been the mansion's main ballroom and welcomed us warmly as his newest proteges. "Was dinner OK?" he asked with a big grin. He knew full well that it had been, but he was obviously searching for an opening line to preface his talk to us. He said we were to be taught the fine art of mine and booby trap detection and removal. Now the suspense was over and we finally knew what our futures held in store. Somehow, because of the way the major presented his plans, our new careers in the Army seemed more exciting than foreboding, especially if that level of food quality was maintained.

He told us we would be molded into demolitions specialists, one of the most vital assignments in the combat Army. But he stressed that the extreme danger of this delicate work required that it be an all-volunteer unit. We were offered the opportunity to back out then and there if we wanted to. At that point no one did.

"Here you don't make mistakes. Just one. That's all," the major intoned. Then he laid all his cards on the table saying that Germany's most brilliant scientific minds had spent years developing the most sophisticated, advanced mine and boobytrap systems of any nation in the world.

"These scientists have developed explosive devices that defy detection and disarmament. If you men are smarter than all of these scientific minds, you may, and I repeat may, live through this war to tell about it." Delving deeper into his subject, the major told us we would be formed into a 12-man special unit doing the "dirty work" for the whole 333rd Regiment. "You'll be troubleshooters," he added. "Do you want out yet? If so, this is your last chance." One man, who from his appearance was the oldest member of the squad, stood up, walked out of the room and started packing his gear for his return to his former company.

I began wondering why I had defied the ageless army advice not to volunteer for anything. Perhaps, in this instance, discretion would have been the better part of valor. As I learned some months later, the mine squad dropout had returned to L Company, but had "cracked" after a few days of fighting and had been sent, suffering from combat fatigue, to a rear area for treatment and rehabilitation. When our special anti-mine unit carried out its first actual combat mission into German-held territory, far in front of our most forward infantry lines, he probably never would have been able to withstand the stealth, the gut-wrenching fear and the hair-trigger pressures we felt while trying not to blow ourselves up. At least he was one of those who lived to return Stateside at war's end, I assume.

The next morning, we started on a tremendously intense, 14-hour-a-day training schedule, every day for three weeks. Booby traps were planted under our mattresses, behind the cast iron doors of our barracks' potbellied stoves, under our chairs or plates in the mess hall, beneath toilet seats and even in our duffle bags. The engineer school cadre continued to pound the all-important message of constant awareness into us by planting insidious traps everywhere imaginable.

The startling explosions of dynamite percussion caps whenever we made a false move served as constant reminders that our shield of vigilance was still not impenetrable. One night, a barracks door was blown off its hinges by a loud but harmless rigged boobytrap when the squad returned to its quarters. The man who carelessly opened the door without first checking it didn't regain his composure for a couple days.

As the training continued, we became so apprehensive, even paranoid, about booby traps that many of us were almost afraid to move lest we explode another planted "instructor's lesson." Gradually, we came to understand what the instructors were trying to drill into us: never accept anything at face value and never ever let your guard down. To do so would be to die, they assured us over and over again.

Army regulation manuals were discarded. The byword was improvise, for in booby trap detection and deactivation there was very little teamwork. More often it was every man for himself, almost commando style. There were no rules during the three-week school except to stay alive at all costs. It was strictly the students against the instructors—and they were good, extremely good.

An acre of land had been cleared behind the mansion and developed into German mine fields, which day after day became our classroom. The first objective was to clear out all antipersonnel mines—S-mines; Bouncing Bettys; the R.M.I.43s; the E.Z.44s; the Holzmine (wooden box) with its 11 pounds of explosive; the Schu mine, known in German manuals as the 43N; and the 20-pound Riegel anti-tank mine. Each deadly device, one after another, became part of our lives.

The instructors repeatedly reminded us the mines we were learning on were live, not dummies, for, as they reasoned, live mines brought home the message more succinctly.

It wasn't until after the course had been completed that we were shown that the mines with which we had been working had been fitted with blasting caps that, if detonated, would surely have scared the hell out of us but would not have caused much physical injury.

The last week of the course was devoted to the infamous anti-tank Tellermine the Germans had used so effectively against British and American tanks in the North African and Italian campaigns. During the coming months, under actual battle conditions, we would be called upon to remove—usually with a rope—literally hundreds of them buried under roads and snow to clear paths for our advancing tanks and infantrymen in Germany and Belgium.

During the work-intensive days, we became adept at handling dynamite, nitrostarch, plastic explosives, primer cord, nitroglycerin, blasting caps and bangalore torpedoes to blast through barbed wire defenses. Our eventual return to our companies came without fanfare but from that point on, I felt segregated from the rest of L Company, sort of a specially trained elite GI with a skill not shared by the others. My somewhat detached status afforded me more leisure time free from routine infantry training and made passes to nearby Andover more easily attainable. In one sense, my time was my own until I was needed. I enjoyed this above-average status in the company for I was no longer considered part of the ordinary foot ranks. I quietly basked in the pleasure of being considered special.

Andover was mostly a one-street town lined by stucco houses, stores and pubs. The English version of a drug store was where one bought tobacco and fish and chips. The first time I tried to buy something, the girl behind the counter, seeing my puzzlement at the English coins in the palm of my hand, smilingly reached over and took the proper amount from me. A Canadian naval officer queued up behind me, started laughing and offered to help. He explained that he too had had some difficulty when he arrived in England. The British coinage system, even though it uses the decimal system, befuddled me as long as I remained in Britain.

On one occasion while walking along the main street of Alton, I met a comely English girl named Emily. After exchanged smiles, we talked awhile and she took me home to meet her parents. They proved to be typically reserved. I made my excuses to leave as soon as it was polite to do so for I had been uncomfortable with them throughout the evening. With nothing else to do in the small town and incapable of fathoming Emily's clipped-word accent, we sat through the same movie, "Ali Baba and the 40 Thieves," five nights in a row. I had always been led to believe America and Britain spoke a common language but I was finding out they speak English and we speak American, two distinctly different tongues.

Back at the camp, I spent most of my leisure time reviewing over and over in my mind German defensive strategies and tactics. I tried to get into the German mind, to think as he would think, to remember everything I had been taught. I knew that my life would someday depend on it. Experience is the best teacher, we had been told, and I tried to gain that little extra edge by fathoming German logic.

Booby trap effectiveness is limited only by the cunningness of whomever plants it. It was a deadly game, a perfect example of the hunter and the hunted. I forced myself to remember this always, at least until I got into actual combat where everything was promptly forgotten and then quickly relearned all over again in different form.

My recreation time in the special demolitions squad was spent umpiring baseball games, mailing part of my $50-a-month pay allotment home, reading the steady batches of letters from my folks, emptying my first Christmas box into my stomach, locating musical groups with which to jam and listening to British radio news. I soon tired of the BBC's slanted perspectives and analysis for it invariably reported British troops forging ahead on all fronts, valiantly winning the war almost single-handedly, while American forces in support loafed their way across the continent. Two short months later, I would find out that just the opposite was true.

As an illustration of how obedient, perhaps even subservient, the GIs of that era were, it never dawned on me while mailing part of my pay back home as savings that I was being called upon to fight and possibly die for $1.66 a day. The government surely knew how to extract a bargain from its young citizens.

Whenever writing home I kept my letters cheerful, upbeat, informative and opinionated. I wonder now in retrospect whether I ever actually fooled anyone on the home front with my letters. In mail received from home, I was told that my sister June's husband, H. Whitney "Whit" Parmenter, was stationed in northern England with the Air Corps. On one occasion I daringly contacted him by phone posing as "Colonel Blunt." He, for military security reasons, could not divulge his exact location during my call. Resourceful to the end, I tried to enlist the assistance of the local Red Cross unit in effecting a reunion with him in London, halfway between our two camps, but they ignored my request.

Imagine my surprise when, the next morning, I received a letter through British mail from Parmenter detailing his exact location, train connections and full instructions on how and where to meet him near his air base. Armed with this information, I obtained a 48-hour pass from my company commander without much problem.

The train trip from Andover to Hanley, Staffordshire, where Parmenter was stationed, should have taken no more than six hours. Instead, it took 15 hours of missed train connections and a series of arrivals at wrong destinations. How could I, new to the country, have known that in England there are so many towns with the same names on different rivers or in different counties? If I missed any part of the entire British island during my attempt to reach Staffordshire air base, to this day I still don't know where it was. Unwittingly, I had taken a grand tour of all England.

When I finally arrived at Stoke-On-Trent in the midlands and located the local Red Cross Recreation Center where we had arranged to meet, I relaxed in a huge leather lounge chair to read a newspaper while waiting for him to arrive. A thrown rolled-up magazine suddenly tore the paper from my grasp. Parmenter had arrived in typically unceremonious manner and never had anyone looked so good to me. We swapped all the latest news from home and abroad and then bedded down for the night in double-decker bunks, 20 men to a room, at the Red Cross club. It seemed like only moments later he was shaking me awake. It was 0530. "Hurry up. We're late. I can't miss the train back to the base," he urged. Irreverently dubbed "The Shack Up Special" by the flyboys stationed nearby, the train had us back to his Air Corps field in plenty of time.

When Parmenter announced proudly, "Hey fellas, this is my brother-in-law. He's in the Infantry," the red carpet was rolled out for me. It seems that most of these airmen were meeting their first bona fide live combat infantryman. During my short stay there, I absentmindedly neglected to tell them I hadn't yet received my first baptism of fire. I was enjoying all the attention.

I presented my military ration card at the base PX but clerks there would have none of it. They filled a huge cardboard box with every luxury in stock from cartons of cigarettes and boxes of candy bars to cans of fresh pineapple juice and even fistfuls of pipe cleaners. Where back at my base we had so little, here in the glamor branch of the military they had such excesses they could afford to literally give it away unrationed.

The next pleasant surprise came when we turned in for the night in beds with sheets, soft pillows and clean blankets. I envied my brother-in-law's creature comforts and later teased him about them, even drawing a cartoon about the differences between the two branches of service. To top it all off, I watched in awe as a master sergeant swept the Quonset hut floor one day. It was his turn to do so, I was told, something unheard of in the Infantry, to be sure.

Parmenter was able to wangle a pass to visit my unit in Andover overnight and on the way back by train, we stopped over in London to sightsee for a few hours. We checked into a YMCA near Charing Cross station and started walking the streets with no particular destination in mind.

If I had been seeking the war all those months, I finally found it in Britain's capital in the form of the blitz. This time, it wasn't Heinkel and Stuka bombers raining death and destruction from overhead, but rather the unnerving randomness of German V-2 rockets and V-1 "Buzz Bombs" descending randomly on the city. Most of London proper had already been flattened; only the shells of most buildings were left standing. Walking the streets as visiting sightseers was largely impossible because of mountains of burning rubble. Firefighters valiantly tried to stem the desolation. Thousands of Londoners were huddled in subways or in the cellars of shattered and bombed-out buildings. The war was no longer far away for me. It was there and it was then.

But life went on, almost routinely, it seemed. The indomitable spirit of the British shone through as I had never seen in people before. They actually sang and joked about the bombings. It was almost as if the songs and comedy would make all the misery go away. But the soul-searing hurt was there; I just didn't know how to recognize it. Forty years later, on a vacation to England, I attended a play in London, "Underneath the Arches," depicting the blitz era. I watched as the audience vigorously sang some of the show tunes along in chorus with the performers, all the while with tears streaming down the cheeks of the older patrons in the theater.

With thundering roars and concussions that could be felt in the gut for miles, the rockets fell all around us in London. The war I thought I wanted had suddenly come to me uninvited. Near misses rattled the YMCA building and shook our double-decker bunks violently as we lay with eyes tightly closed making believe we were unafraid or asleep. Parmenter said nothing but I knew he was sorry he had suggested the stopover on our way back to Andover. During the bombardment, we didn't bother to seek refuge in the bomb shelters, for getting some sleep was deemed more important. But there would be no sleep that night.

In all, I would estimate at least two dozen rocket bombs fell on the city before daybreak. Two-tone sirened police cars, fire apparatuses and ambulances wailed uninterruptedly in the darkness. I lay awake almost until morning, staring at the ceiling deep in my private thoughts about this destruction-filled world where I now found myself, so vastly different from the carefree life I had recently left behind in the States.

In the morning, we stopped in at a small Greek restaurant off Piccadilly Circus for a breakfast steak. Neither of us mentioned the events of the night before. As I looked around, everything seemed to be business as usual with the people of London. I wondered if I could remain as casual if it were my home being systematically torn apart day after day. The steak, sliced wafer thin, was so leathery it was almost unpalatable, but those were hard times in England and you said thank you for whatever you got. I tried to enjoy it.

To kill time waiting for the train to Andover, Parmenter and I lounged about Piccadilly Circus watching the people and talking about the war. Within minutes an American MP, complete with white helmet liner and twirling night stick, rousted us along, thinking we were there for the prostitutes. Despite being surrounded by walls of flames consuming whole city blocks before our eyes and telling the

MP that whores were furthermost from our minds and that we were family reuniting for the first time in more than a year, he still nudged us along.

Back at Andover, Parmenter, for the first time in his life, experienced how "the other half" lived. I scrounged up a straw mattress for him to sleep on the floor and I fed him some of our greasy mess kitchen chow. I also taught him how to wash his borrowed mess kit out afterward in a rubbish barrel filled with floating garbage and grease-covered hot water. I'm sure he was duly impressed for he didn't offer once to transfer out of the Air Corps and into the Infantry.

In the morning, he was gone again, back to his world and I to mine. I would not see him again until we were both civilians about a year and a half later. It was a sad parting; the brief visit was the only personal link we both had had with home.

As I settled into my routine back at Andover, I became aware right away of a noticeable increase in the level of activity about the camp. I was confident it wouldn't be long now and I would have the war I foolishly seemed to want so badly. The "lone wolf" status of our mine-removal squad soon allowed me to wangle another 48-hour pass to London, only this time alone. With all the last-minute preparations going on around me at the Andover staging area, I knew it would probably be the last time I would see the city before my odyssey resumed.

As the train pulled into Victoria Station, I was overwhelmed by the magnificence of what remained of the British capital and also by the devastation facing me wherever I went. I hired a hansom cab to give me a tour of as many attractions as could be reached by ground transportation, but there were only a few streets the driver could navigate. Although the cab was inexpensive, I switched after a while to one of the few double-decker buses still operating on the rubble-clogged streets. Everything in England, from food to gasoline, and from metals to silk and rubber, went to the war effort.

Later, during my brief furlough, I ventured into London's underground "tubes" to explore more of the city. Thousands of men, women and babies, homeless refugees from the ravages of German bombings, filled every subway station platform, lying on beds of blankets and surrounded by bags and boxes of family possessions. The crying of frightened, bewildered children filled every tube stop. Commuters, mostly paying them scant heed, picked their way around the unfortunate tribes of homeless nomads now relegated like moles to subterranean living. While the multitudes lived in squalor amidst their meager collections of salvaged possessions, the rest of the city carried on with a "stiff upper lip."

I sauntered across Waterloo Bridge spanning the Thames River and after walking down several long flights of stairs deep into the earth, I got on a Northern Line tube at Waterloo Station. I rode for 20 minutes and got off, figuring that I must be somewhere in the outskirts of London. Then came the staggering climb back up the almost endless flights of stairs to street level where I found I was back where I had started from: at Waterloo Station near the south bank of the Thames and only a short hop from the Elephant and Castle section of South London. Annoyed that I had wasted 20 minutes of my precious leave time and a whole shilling of my $50-a-month Army pay, I tried again but with the same result. After the third try, I gave up and walked back to London's Victoria Enbankment and the Strand theater district. No wonder the British were a half century behind the times, I thought. Their subways didn't go anywhere, just in circles.

Back at the Strand, the evening was still young so I went to a movie, "The Seven Nooses," a dismal English attempt at a murder mystery. I had almost dozed off when a Piccadilly whore who had apparently wandered a half mile off her turf in search of business snuggled down next to me and started fondling me. Still a virgin, I failed to respond properly. She soon tired of my lack of reaction to her amorous advances and, giving me a dirty look, stalked out of the theater, probably to seek out an older and more willing customer.

I was fortunate the next morning to be able to watch the changing of the guard at Buckingham Palace, one of the most impressive ceremonial traditions in the free world. The guards, all over six feet tall and decked out in crimson colonial splendor, the mounted horse company, the musically meticulous Queen's military band, were more impressive than anything I had ever seen in my young life.

Forty-eight-hour passes expire quickly when one is having fun and almost before I knew it, it was time to return to Andover. As the train pulled away from Victoria Station and brought me back to Hampshire County, I had the gut feeling it would be the last time I would see London.

Back in camp, the preparations for our cross-Channel hop were now in the final stages and we were advised to stay close to the company area. Hearing this, I hightailed it to the nearest PX one afternoon to stock up on as many goody items as I was allowed to buy. While waiting in one of the many long lines stretching from each counter, an 82nd Airborne paratrooper who had just returned from the fighting in France offered to sell me (for $35) a .32 caliber German Mauser semiautomatic pistol he had liberated during the Normandy campaign. It was a classic weapon and I carried it for many months before selling it for $75 to a rear-echelon trophy hunter.

During this monotonous period in which we held our breath on almost constant alert in Andover, a brawl at a local pub became the big news of the day. A group of about 35 GIs from the 84th decided to mix it up with about a dozen 82nd Airborne paratroopers fresh from having thoroughly whipped one of Adolf Hitler's crack SS divisions in France. Even though the paratroopers were outnumbered almost three-to-one, it was no contest for them.

Some of the Railsplitters wound up hospitalized, the others thrown battered and bruised onto the street. The paratroopers, as the story went, brushed off their uniforms and returned to the serious business of drinking their 3.2 English bitters.

It wasn't long afterward that orders came down restricting us to base with absolutely no contact allowed with the outside world. At midnight, two nights later, we were awakened suddenly and told to prepare to ship out. Bundling up against the night drizzle, we were herded onto the army's favorite transport conveyance—the six-by-six troop carrier truck—and jostled through the darkness to Andover and then by train to Southampton, Britain's largest seaport on the English Channel. Along the way, with blackout curtains drawn tightly, the car reeked of sweat, whiskey and cigarette smoke. The odors were overpowering and I had a hard time time holding back waves of nausea.

Like other train trips we had been forced to endure, men were crammed into compartments while others sprawled in the aisles and hung from baggage racks. Duffle bags and other gear, thrown haphazardly in the aisles, kept us trapped in our seats, if in fact, we had been lucky enough to get a seat in the first place. Men were on top of each other and the clatter of the wheels on the tracks was drowned out by the swearing and grumbling of the troops.

Eventually, we were poured out into another of England's pea-soup fog banks, this one even chillier and more uncomfortable than the ones we'd left behind. When my eyes adjusted to the night, I could make out a few remnants of bombed-out buildings standing like solitary fingers pointing upwards.

I had never been afraid of the dark before but on this night, surrounded by these ghost-like structures and a mob of nameless GIs scuffling through this cobblestone graveyard, I became a little rattled, wishing that dawn would come to wipe away the foreboding darkness. When we were eventually shunted into the sheltered confines of a huge shrapnel-pocked steel warehouse on the waterfront, I started to feel more protected and soon settled down.

Adjacent to the warehouse, I could make out a four-story pile of coal and as far as the eye could see in the murky darkness, there was no light or sound. It was eerie. And once again, the waterfront dampness and a cold wind blowing through the open-ended warehouse started me shivering uncontrollably. As I stood there waiting for some ship or boat to ferry me to France, I wondered if I would ever be warm again.

With the drizzly gray light of dawn, I could faintly make out the forms of gigantic ships berthed all around us. As the eye could penetrate in the mist, there were ships of all sizes and shapes but even with the coming of daylight there was still no sound on the waterfront. We washed down our K-ration breakfasts with chemically treated cold water from our canteens, a truly auspicious way to start our day. With that chore completed, we milled about for another hour grousing about how long it was taking the Army to get a lousy boat to take us 26 miles across the English Channel.

At 0800, we loaded onto an LST (Landing Ship Tank) and immediately forged ourselves a small space on the open deck, closed in only by heavy steel sides. Each of us became territorial as others tried to cram into our already staked-out areas. There was considerably more snarling and swearing and shoving as tempers became short.

A stiff wind blowing in off the surging gray channel swells that embraced the LST chilled us even more. After the first mile or so of being rocked up and down, most of us resigned ourselves to sweating it out, for the trip could only last so long. The LST crew offered to sell us warm chocolate carbonated tonic. Instantly, upon consuming some, the seasickness returned and men tried to push their way to the sides to throw up. The crew considered it all a big joke; they knew what the tonic would do to men being tossed from side to side by the heavy seas.

Fighting off the nausea, thoughts on a wide variety of subjects tumbled through my mind. Had I paid close enough attention in mine detecting school? Where was my bass drum my dad had shipped over to me? Where was the LST going and what would it be like in France? How would I respond to combat and would I measure up? Would I come home alive after this was over? What was it again the major had said to look out for in German Teller mines? Where would a Butterfly mine most likely be found? Should I tell my folks when I encountered combat? To the last question, I decided to delay telling them as long as I could get away with it by postmarking all my letters, no matter where I was, as if I was still safe in England to relieve some of their anxiety.

Men started peeking over the gunwhale of the pitching and rolling LST. "There it is," one man yelled. Everyone scrambled to their feet to get a first glimpse of France. From the newsreels we had all seen of the D-Day invasion back in June, we instantly recognized the low, sloping hills and the massive, ugly pillboxes lining Omaha Beach. We were following in the footsteps of thousands of valiant men before us and our path into combat now beckoned. At last I could finally become a hero.

By 0900, we were close enough to make out all the details of the epic battle that had transpired there five months earlier. It was November 2, 1944, D plus 146.

An overturned, burned out half-track, an apparent pillbox victim, lay partially underwater on the beach. Underwater German concrete anti-tank barriers snaked their way along the beach at water's edge. Twisted 75mm antitank cannons and rusted-out jeeps littered the beach. Gaping shell craters had still not been filled in by the tides.

LCIs (Landing Craft Infantry) were everywhere, most of them with ragged holes torn in their sides from the artillery shells that sank them and their troops before they even reached the beach. Now, as we watched, they were still being rolled from side to side by the surf. Ammunition crates, sandbagged machine gun emplacements, rolls of barbed wire—all the signs of what once had been.

As we scanned the beach and the hill beyond it, the entire boat fell silent. The ghosts of hundreds of men who died here still lingered on. Only the deep throaty rumble of the LST engine split the silence. The scene was finally hitting home for indeed, this had been one of the major battles of all history. I could not help but wonder again whether I could honorably carry out my duty under such horrifying circumstances.

"Hit the landing net," a loud voice barked out and over the side we went, clawing, slipping and falling. An LCI took us to within 50 feet of the sandy high water mark where we jumped off the sloping ramp into chest-deep water, half paddling, half wading, half drowning, spitting and gagging out mouthfuls of ice cold sea water, stumbling, bobbing up for air but eventually getting a foothold on the beach. At long last, we were on the continent.

On an adjoining beach a quarter mile to our left, the Quartermaster Corps had stacked up thousands of tons of ammunition and supplies destined for the combat troops at the front. Magazine and newspaper pictures of German pillboxes failed to portray the awesome massiveness of each bunker. The gigantic long-range cannons, blown askew, pointed to the sky waiting for the Allied aircraft that would no longer be coming. The pillbox facings still revealed the scorching they had taken from American flamethrowers.

One pillbox we made our way past was an entire hill in itself, at least 200 feet across and cleverly concealed until one was actually upon it. The only telltale signs that it had been a strongpoint were small weapon slits and observation apertures. Trees had even been planted atop the soil-covered fortifications. The camouflage was near perfect.

As we laboriously worked our way to the top of the hills flanking the beach, we encountered narrow paths carved into the hillsides and lined on both sides by white ribbons flapping in the winds that still blew briskly in off the ocean. "Achtung Minen," crude, bullet-punctured signs explained. With the cautiousness that comes only with knowing and understanding mines, I passed through. I had seen such signs before back at the Andover mine school.

Deep inside a shallow gulley, we were given a break to rest and to eat another K-ration. As I slouched in the trench and gazed back across the Channel toward jolly old England, I sipped on lemon-flavored water in my canteen to quench a deep thirst that had been building all the way from Southampton. I knew that in a few minutes the break would be over and it would be time to push inland where the fighting was and where we could join the war. It was only a few day's march away, I knew, but oddly enough, I felt no appreciable fear. No apprehension, just resignation. I was there to fight the German and now I was about to start doing it.

He was waiting for me.

3

No Turning Back

Looking much like a rag-tag mob surging its way across the debris-strewn landscape, we climbed over the gun emplacements, grunting as we dragged our barracks bags along behind us under the hot French sun. The mob scene eventually defined itself into two endless strings of men weaving across the desolate Normandy countryside on the most grueling, exhausting, spirit-shattering march that I would ever undertake in my life.

It was a forced march inland on which I collapsed into ditches beside the muddy road, was left behind by my company, and where I learned to endure the pain of sloshing along in combat boots soaked with my own blood from blisters as big as silver dollars. No matter how hard I fought it, no matter how determined I was not to show it or to cave in to physical exhaustion, tears flowed down my dirt-smeared cheeks.

Finally, the human spirit, stretched to its limit, gives up. I have no idea how many miles the columns had walked inland when I suddenly veered involuntarily out of the column and fell face first with a thud into a ditch, dropping my pack, duffle bag, rifle and helmet. No one even glanced in my direction. I don't know how long I was unconscious but when I opened my eyes, the line of staggering GIs, stretching as far before me and behind me as I could see, was still moving.

Fearful of punishment for being perceived as a slacker, I clumsily snapped up my gear and tottered forward again on feet that sent searing pain throughout my wracked body. I wondered how much more I could take but there was a determination, fueled by fear of the consequences and even retaliation from the brass, that drove me on.

Mercifully, as I trudged step after step in semi-conscious fashion, I eventually noticed the column had stopped and everyone was "taking five" beside the road. But I couldn't, for I had no conception of how many miles ahead my outfit had covered while I lay passed out in the ditch. With head hung down against my chest I forced myself to trudge on. My brain turned itself off and instinct took over. Each step was a small victory. You're getting closer, I told myself. Keep it going; Take another step and another and another. Show 'em. Show 'em what a Blunt is made of. Don't let your father down. Make him proud. Take still another step.

"Hey, look who's coming," some smart ass mimicked. I looked up and saw familiar faces. I had caught up to LOVE Company.

As I dropped my dufflebag with the overwhelming relief of having made it back successfully, a voice barked out, "Fall in. Let's hit it."

Moaning and groaning, the sea of OD-colored uniforms milled about trying to re-establish what might be called a military marching column. "Route step, march," the voice screamed again and we started hesitantly forward. The rest I needed so badly was not to be. A deepening sense of despair overwhelmed me.

Off to the left, in a depression below road level, I watched a group of about 30 men dressed in gray-green uniforms shoveling dirt and repairing a road through a French apple orchard. Through exhausted eyes, I paid scant attention to the workers or the nearby rifle-carrying GI's until the realization suddenly hit me. In a mental double-take, I glanced back over my shoulder, blurting out to myself, "Hey, those were German prisoners. I just saw my first real Wehrmacht soldiers." Somehow, they didn't seem like what I had envisioned the past month in England, and they surely didn't look at all like the grotesque posters with which we had been brainwashed during basic training. A few of them had looked up in our direction with sullen, even snarling expressions but still it had not dawned on me who they were. As I said, the exhaustion of the march had dulled my senses, even my ability to observe, but not the excruciating pain throbbing in my feet.

Mile after mile my downcast eyes stared blindly at the muddy road in front of me. Occasionally, I lifted my eyes and glanced at the countryside. The column was in the hedgerow country where some of the greatest German resistance had been encountered during the battle to break out from the American beachhead five months earlier.

These almost impenetrable natural barriers had thwarted the U.S. breakthrough and been one of the most perplexing adversaries to be overcome by our advancing troops. Through them, GIs had crawled and fought for every inch of ground, only to find another hedgerow a few hundred feet further on. Tanks became enmeshed in them and were easy targets for German armor and anti-tank guns. Flame-throwing "Crocodile" tanks and Shermans with flailing chains, and eventually some with specially built, V-shaped plow blades, had to be used to slice their way through. Signs of these agonizing battles—mostly burned and shattered American tanks—were everywhere. It was obvious, even to our uninitiated eyes, that the Germans had had a field day here.

Devastation was on every side. The road, the pastures and orchards were pocked with artillery craters. Scarcely a tree remained standing, most having been splintered and shattered by the violent battles that had embroiled the Normandy farm region during the summer. Horse carcasses rotting and smelling under the sun, burned-out German tanks lying grotesquely on their sides, blasted into twisted junk by violent force. Suddenly I realized that each of these tanks had been the coffins of at least four men. Though yet to hear my first shot fired, the scene was nevertheless somber.

We passed through a small town, now reduced to eye-level mounds of rubble. A bullet-riddled metal sign lying partially buried in the street read "Caen." It meant nothing to me. I had never heard of it. As we filed by, I became aware there was no sound, no sign of life anywhere. All that remained was total destruction. Each mile, the true face of war was being gradually implanted into my mind. Each kilometer was another lesson in life as the maturing of a boy continued.

The formation of straggling GIs was given a five-minute break every hour, just long enough for some to drag on butts, sip lukewarm water from canteens or munch on whatever they had in their packs or pockets. Most just tried to catch their collective breaths but the breaks were nowhere near long enough for the marchers to recuperate their strength, even slightly.

Some hours further down the road, we entered another village with only a few masonry walls still standing—again, in stark testimony to the violence of past battles there. What the Allied bombing had started, the artillery barrages, the tanks and the infantry had completed This was the death and elimination of a once-proud town and its people. I continued to see war in its purest form.

Still further along the battle-strewn dirt roads we came across our first French farmers toiling in their partially barren orchards. We waved at them and were answered with curses and a hail of rocks and rotted apples. What the hell was the matter with these ingrates? Didn't they know we were the liberators? As they shook their fists and waved their pitchforks or shovels threateningly at us, the French-speaking GIs in the column explained that they were calling us "filthy, American murderers."

They screamed they wanted the Germans back and they spat on the ground in our direction. Their verbal abuse continued until they were out of earshot behind us. These simple farmers blamed us for the Allied bombings of their homes and the destruction of their orchards and towns. Their provincial view of the war was limited to its direct effect on them. They had, I realized, little concept of what Germany had done to their country, of the many thousands of French who had been cruelly torn from their families and worked to death in German munitions factories or starved to death in concentration camps.

I am also sure these farmers were also unaware of the German rape of their women and of the retaliatory mass executions of innocent civilians as punishment for the heroic accomplishments of the Maquis, the French underground that, spurred on by fierce nationalism, had harassed the Germans at every turn. The Normandy farmers unjustly worshiped a false God, I thought, but who was to tell them otherwise? I could only hope that, in time, they eventually would realize the truth.

In a few isolated instances as we marched through the shattered French villages, we found grimy, gaunt children dressed in tattered clothing, crawling out of the rubble and tugging furiously at our uniforms, imploring, "Any gum bum? Any gum chum?" As we had experienced some weeks earlier in Glasgow and Edinburgh, any American response to the pathetic appeals instantaneously provoked a violent scramble of the biggest and the fastest. The scrawny, smaller tykes were left standing alone, sadly watching us as we departed on our arduous foot journey toward Paris.

I had little time or inclination to worry about the survival of the French citizenry, however. My own survival took precedence. Weighted down with duffle bag, full field pack, extra field rations, extra blankets, gas mask, nine-pound M-1 rifle, three bandoliers of rifle ammunition and miscellaneous combat gear issued to us when we embarked in England, my own well-being was my primary concern. I would remember this forced march as the most grueling, torturous experience of my young life.

In one respect, the suffering during the march inland from Omaha Beach was probably surpassed only by the weeks we later endured in the Battle of the Ardennes—the infamous Battle of the Bulge, Hitler's last ditch attempt to destroy the Allied front. There, beside the body-wracking marches from one town after another, we would be called upon to contend with smothering snow and the survival-threatening, excruciating cold.

As I plodded unsteadily through the French countryside, I became aware of a warm, sticky feeling around my shoulders. With my free hand, I lifted my field pack straps and and found smudgy, dark red-dish-brown stains on my filthy, mud-encrusted uniform. The word filthy is apropos, for we had not been given the opportunity to change uniforms since swimming ashore in the Channel after disembarking from England.

Besides hobbling on bleeding, blistered feet, my back and shoulders had now been rubbed raw and were oozing blood. People tend to see the infantryman, I feel, solely as a man walking along carrying a rifle prepared to do honorable combat, one-on-one with an enemy of our nation. Not so. He is perhaps more aptly pictured as an exhaust-ed, unshaven, miserable, dog-faced foot soldier who crawls face down on his belly in the mud and eats with his hands and whose chief recre-ation is reading newspaper headlines about the more glamorous branches of the service.

Once again, almost without warning, I began to feel lightheaded and dizzy. Everything around me darkened and I fainted in my tracks from pain and exhaustion. An endless column of foot soldiers stepped over or around me. As I sprawled on the dirt cart path, I remember hearing some shavetail lieutenant screaming at me, "Get up, you gaw-damn weakling. Fall back in or I'll court martial you. There's no place for babies in this man's army."

As I lapsed into unconsciousness, I just didn't care anymore. I had finally given up. At that moment, nothing, absolutely nothing mattered any more. When I finally reopened my eyes, a medic was bending over me. When he was satisfied I had partially regained some strength, he helped me to my feet and half carried me across a roadside ditch to a nearby abandoned German air strip. It was only a single steel mesh-covered runway that had been cleared from a patch of woods and now used, I presumed, by small artillery spotter planes. I rested, propped against a tree, while he worked on me. I tried to look around but my eyes, fogged by pain, recorded nothing. When the medic spoke, I was unable to respond coherently for none of my senses seemed to be functioning.

Eventually, after the medic bathed my bleeding feet with fistfuls of brown salve, I made it back to the column again to rejoin LOVE Company, which had already moved a mile down the road. As I wobbled and limped toward the company area, my platoon sergeant spotted me and came running. I stumbled into his outstretched arms. He grabbed my dufflebag and rifle and half carried me to where my squad was resting. I slumped to the ground and passed out again.

This time, I regained consciousness in a "meat wagon" (ambulance) with a different medic cutting my uniform shirt off me. "You're done walking," he assured me. I balked at this remark and demanded that I be returned to LOVE Company after he finished dressing my shoulder and back wounds with a different type of salve and some oversized thick bandage pads to cushion the abrasive effects of my pack straps.

"You're crazy, man. Ride," he urged.

"No," I insisted. I had something to prove, both to myself and that bastard lieutenant who had yelled at me. I was no baby. And no one was going to make me out to be one. I couldn't let the name Blunt be sullied by weakness in any form. After the corpsman patched me up as much as he could, I staggered back to the roadway and eventually found my company, many of whom were in as rough shape as I was.

I did not find out until much later that nearly a quarter of the GIs in the march inland had dropped out and were being trucked to our eventual destination. It was during this forced march across northern France that I started to form an opinion, one that would be reinforced many times later during combat: that the youngest (the teenagers) and the oldest (those approaching 38) were the first to cave in both physically and mentally under the rigors of soldiering. Judging by those unable to withstand the agonies of war, young men do not reach their prime strength until in their mid-20s and then lose it fast in their early 30s.

I could never face myself again, I felt, if I quit now. As nightfall came on, the line adopted the trunk-to-tail routine often seen with elephants in circus processions. I placed my hand on the shoulder of the man in front of me and the GI behind did the same to me. We let our chins drop against our chests and, hard as it may be to believe, we catnapped as we trudged along.

When the march finally ended many hours later, I was still on my feet. That was all that mattered to me, for I had challenged adversity and won. The column that started at Omaha Beach at 0900 that morning and had finally halted about midnight, 15 hours later, had covered an estimated 50 miles. Considering the fact that I weighed 135 pounds at the time and had lugged nearly 100 pounds of gear that far, I can't fully explain my dogged determination.

"Fall out and dig in," a voice called out from the darkness. Without question, we obeyed. The actual fighting was many miles ahead of us but there was still the constant threat of Luftwaffe strafings. Marching columns were some of their favorite targets, we were told. I flopped over backwards in my tracks, pack still strapped to my back, and collapsed on an earthen mound. In my condition there was no way I could muster the strength to dig in against an enemy who I knew was almost a whole country away from us.

Instantly, I was asleep. When daylight arrived, I was still flat on my back with my field pack underneath me propping me up. When I opened my eyes, I found I had slept not on a mound, but on a four-foot high pile of apples. I squirmed out of my pack and tried to eat a K-ration but when my stomach refused to accept it, I threw it away, saving only the cigarettes for future bartering.

We were told we would remain at that location for at least two days. Now somewhat rested, we dug in. In another classic example of Army reasoning, I was made a company runner responsible for carrying messages from one unit to another. Run? I could just barely limp, and company brass knew it. Perhaps there was a sardonic humor involved that escaped me.

With the temporary assignment requiring only that I be available at the beck and call of the company commander, I had free time to explore and bring up to date the daily diary I had been keeping since being inducted. When the last entry was completed, I set out to reconnoiter France. Not far from our temporary camp site, I came across a drab, mostly undamaged mud and clay farmhouse with a low-hanging thatched roof. It had been built in a square configuration around a courtyard featuring the largest manure pile I had ever seen. Several fat white geese strutted menacingly around the courtyard. It was the typical European farmhouse, similar to those I would see later in Holland, Belgium and Germany.

I was cordially invited inside by a smiling, elderly French couple and their daughter. Trying to be polite, I sipped some cider that they had hospitably broken out for I knew that to decline their hospitality would be to insult them. But it was no use; the cider tasted like urine, and after a single sip I respectfully declined any more.

We sat in the dirt-floor kitchen and tried to converse by candlelight as best we could, considering the language barrier. As we talked, I realized their first impressions of America and Americans was probably me. Consequently, I was on my "smilingliest" best behavior.

As I casually glanced around the kitchen, I saw there was no plumbing nor amenities, just a table, chairs, bare walls and a wall crucifix, not even a picture. I had never been in such a barren home and I felt a slight twinge of sympathy for these obviously warm, hospitable people from whom the war had stripped practically every possession. But even though devoid of any trappings, the room radiated hominess. A further shock came when I inquired about answering nature's call. I was directed to the next room where one relieved one's self over a slit trench dug in the dirt floor. It was designed and excavated narrow enough so the women of the family—or possible female visitors— could also squat comfortably and go.

The family explained that they grew apples and cultivated vegetables and were considered by nearby villagers to be quite well-to-do. Electricity and telephones were luxuries not generally enjoyed by most Norman farmers. The old man proudly showed off his prized possessions: his solitary sleepy-eyed ox and a primitive, but extremely sturdy, wooden-wheeled cart. He boasted, mostly by sign language and arm gestures, that the cart's five-foot diameter and solid wooden wheels made it the strongest vehicle in the whole area. He beamed every time he talked about it. I made sure he saw me looking on admiringly as I ran my hand over the wheel.

During another free period from company duty, I walked to the nearby town of Neuville, a quaint village of about 30 houses that had been pretty much by-passed by the fighting. The village boasted two cafes, a small, characteristically ornate Catholic church, a blacksmith shop and a store. A cluster of clay and cobblestone homes was split down the middle by a narrow, winding central street. One could walk through the village in a matter of minutes and then be greeted by more expanses of nearly flat farm land.

In one of the cafes, I found several obnoxiously drunk GIs who had rediscovered liquor. With their raucous voices and menacing rifles, they were holding the cafe proprietor and his family in hostage-like terror. What I had tried to accomplish the evening before by promoting French-American good will, these slobs were undoing in the village in minutes.

As a group of townspeople watched disgustedly, I managed to convince these "good will ambassadors" to take their bottles back to the bivouac area and party there. They staggered out as the townspeople smiled and waved gratefully to me, but not until they insisted that I take a gift bottle of calvados, a variation of local applejack, with me. I smiled and accepted it. I could always give it away or swap it for chocolate bars as I had been doing all along with my weekly cigarette allotments.

LOVE Company's first sergeant called me to the tent that served as a CP (command post). "You're being transferred, Blunt, to Anti-Tank Company. Report right away. Here are your orders," he growled, barely looking up at me. It was a general rule in the Army that the higher sergeants got in rank, the more distance they usually put between themselves and their men. This one was a prime example of that principle.

Ironically, after surviving Europe's answer to the Bataan Death March, I was now assigned to a company that traveled in trucks, not on foot. It was maddening to realize that because of the Army's red tape network, I had both feet almost completely covered with painful blisters and scabs and the same on my back and shoulders. All this excruciating pain could have been avoided if only some nincompoop, rear echelon clerk had done his job more efficiently. But moments later, I stopped feeling sorry for myself when I realized how many hundreds of miles remained before us on the route to Berlin, our ultimate goal, or so we were told. With renewed vigor, I quickly climbed on the truck that would take me to my new assignment.

Actually, the transfer from LOVE Company to Anti-Tank Company simply meant moving from one apple orchard to another, from one pup tent cluster to another, from being fed in one mess tent to a different one and saluting and having to contend with a new batch of officers. Maybe the mess sergeant in the new company would be better than the one I was leaving behind. He proved to be.

For the first, and only, time in my Army career the transfer to Anti-Tank Company made sense. The mine-detection and removal squad's job was more closely akin to combating tanks rather than foot soldiers. Again, time would prove that old Army manual false in the months to come. I was told the company would remain in its bivouac area another day and that my time was my own, so I took off again to explore the countryside.

I walked to another small village nearby, apparently too small even to have a name. At least I could find none posted anywhere. A horde of more than a dozen barefoot kids, ranging in age from about five to 15, mobbed me from every direction. As if rehearsed, they desperately clutched at me yelling in my ear in concert,"Any gum bum? Any gum bum?" over and over almost hysterically. Some GI with a warped sense of humor had apparently taught them this phrase as a joke. He was probably still somewhere in front of us, for I would hear the same high-pitched cry all over western Europe as the 84th gradually worked its way eastward toward the front.

As always, I accommodated as many as I could but, again, I seldom had enough confectionery gifts to go around. It was always frustrating to walk away leaving hungry, disappointed children wanting, their soulful eyes following my every move and desperately watching for any hint of food. Every time it happened to me in each village through which I passed, I reflected on how much of life's necessities and luxuries I had and how little these war-victim urchins had.

As I walked into the village, the expressions on the faces of the townspeople were anything but welcoming. Their eyes were suspicious, their faces sullen and silent. There was no expression of gratitude for the American conquering heroes. Apparently, other GIs had preceded us there. I wondered why the American soldiers had left such a negative impression. After all, before we jumped off from England we had been thoroughly briefed on how to behave in France. I even had my French etiquette book still in my pocket. Then it made sense to me: the only Americans they had seen were of the combat variety blasting their way with tanks and artillery across their tranquil farmlands without thought of consequence. At that time, there had been no opportunities or desires to foster Franco-American diplomacy. I was being judged by people who had previously cowered helplessly as their village had been devastated by our front-line troops.

When I returned to my new company area from my visit to the nearby village, I was caught up in a flurry of activity. Tents had been struck and men and equipment were being loaded onto a convoy of "six-bys." They were about to leave without me. My first opportunity to actually ride into combat and I had almost screwed up by goofing off in some French village. I scrambled to assemble what gear I could find and legged it for a slowly departing tailgate of a truck.

As the truck lurched along the crater-pocked roadway a few kilometers later, I looked out the rear and recognized the men of LOVE Company miserably slogging their way forward ankle-deep in mud, heads bowed in resignation. I had to resist the temptation to wave to them but, in fact, I didn't miss them at all. Furthermore, I didn't even want to look back at those who once had been my buddies.

As if conditions were not difficult enough, a pelting downpour started to drench us as we sat hunched over dejectedly in the uncovered truck. With the miserable rain and with the truck hitting, I swear, every shell hole in the road and throwing us back and forth and from side to side all over the back end, I was wondering if it was so wonderful after all, riding instead of walking.

The answer was tipped in favor of marching when we repeatedly had to tumble off the truck, which almost constantly became mired in the mud, and push it out. The rear wheels, whining and spinning wildly in search of the grip of solid ground and traction, flung half of the mud of France in our faces every time we grunted and shoved. As slipping and sliding pushers did comical pratfalls, arms flailing, into the mud, others fell on top of them. What had started out as comic-relief laughter soon turned to some of the raunchiest swearing I had ever heard—even for the Army. And, I might mention, the scene was repeated over and over as we bumped our way along toward Paris. LOVE Company, I imagined, was probably bivouacked somewhere nice and cozy waiting for the rain to cease.

At dawn, the convoy rolled into a large city with paved streets. Shouting at the first French civilian we saw, we learned we were in the Paris suburb of Versailles, one of France's showpieces. The convoy stopped to give us a few minutes to stretch our legs after the long, rain-soaked night on the road. We found ourselves in a broad square before a mammoth white building, the Versailles Palace, where the World War I armistice had been signed in November 1918. For a moment, I thought there was something symbolic in our stopping there but my blistered feet and shoulders were still too painful to allow me to think clearly. I turned my attention to opening a can of cold K-ration hash without slicing off a finger in the process.

As the convoy saddled up again after a few minutes, a shady-looking character with a pencil-thin mustache slithered up to me and rasped, "Feelthy peektures. One pack butts." One GI wanted to shoot him. Another threw a leg over the tailgate truck and kicked the filth merchant away from us. I learned later from other such roadside salesmen in Holland that pornographic snapshots and playing cards had been extremely popular with the occupying German troops. Frankly, at age 19, I found these pictures and those who distributed them disgusting.

Wheeling out of the city, we passed a road sign: "Paris, 15 km." How far we had come in such a short time from Andover, England. The riding-versus-marching issue finally was settled once and for all. Riding, I decided, was better, even in the mud and rain.

Soon afterward, someone shouted, "There it is, Paris!" Our necks craned out the back of the truck to see one of the crown jewels of Europe, but actually, Paris as seen from the tailgate of a smelly, jouncing Army truck was nothing to relish or write home about. We were offered only a glance at it for we were to be billeted in the outskirts, far removed from the city's much-touted beauty, charm and culture. I would eventually see it all, but not this time around. I had to pay my dues first.

Army life is not without its humor. As we drove through Paris, it appeared to those of us bumping around in the back of the truck that the scenery looked familiar, over and over again. "Boy, this city always looks the same," one GI grumbled. "At least the buildings do."

We started paying attention and suddenly it dawned on us we had been going around and around through the same broad square for about 20 minutes. The convoy was lost. Finally, some enterprising officer in the Jeep spearheading the troop movement apparently figured out how to read a map or, probably at the suggestion of his enlisted man driver, asked directions from one of the many MPs directing traffic at the intersections. Soon we were on our way again in a direction where the scenery changed constantly.

We rode until dark while trying to convince our stomachs to accept and digest cold, greasy pork and beans C-rations. At about 11 P.M., the truck lurched to a halt for the night and I jumped out the back end into a pouring rain. When I finally stopped sinking in the mud, I was up over my ankles and unable to extricate myself from the holdfast muck. As I had learned early in my military career, there are always options—in this case, the mud or the rain. I opted for the mud and crawled under the truck before the others thought of it. At least I would be protected from the downpour.

With my field pack and helmet holding my face just above the smothering mud level, my exhaustion brought sleep on quickly. The rest of my body was buried practically out of sight. The ridiculousness of our situation didn't phase me for we had not slept for two days and nights. First things first. To quote John S. Mosby's *War Reminiscences of 1887*, "No human being knows how sweet sleep is but a soldier."

Several hours later, I awakened to daylight and a strange sensation. The rain had stopped but the truck undercarriage was no longer protecting me. The vehicle had moved during the night. Why I was not crushed I will never understand; surely the driver could not have realized I was asleep underneath.

As I struggled to free myself from the mud, I gazed around at a scene of absolute physical misery. Some of the other men had tried to dig foxholes and had dozed off in man-sized swimming pools of rainwater. Others had tried to pitch their Army-issue pup tents and had wound up wrapped in the things. All of them had been flooded out. To get through the night, they had built a huge, smoky bonfire with foraged wet wood and were huddled around it trying to dry out, or at least bask in the warmth of the flames. To hell with blackout regulations. Survival and comfort came first.

C-rations were issued and we unsuccessfully tried to heat them by holding them near the fire. Finally, we were reduced to eating them cold and slimy. My stomach was learning it had no alternative but to accept whatever it got, no matter how bad it was. I fared better than the others; my breakfast that day consisted of candy bars I had received in an early Christmas package from home five days earlier in England. I ate most of them on the sly for there were some things you just don't share with anyone.

After breakfast, I tried to orient myself geographically. We were bivouacked on a large, flat plain stretching as far as the eye could see. Surveying the mud and the flatness of the terrain, I wondered whimsically when the tide would come in. In the distance rose an odd geographic configuration, a nearly straight-sided mountain crowned with a medieval walled city. Its ancient, stately appearance displayed a beauty that was in stark relief to the massive destruction that had been filling our eyes the past week. It was almost as if this exquisite creation of long-dead warriors was reaching up to the heavens for Divine approval.

As several of us approached it, the sheer vertical cliffs offered no readily available means of climbing to or entering the city. Eventually, we found a flight of winding stairs carved out of the stone cliff and we began our exploratory climb. There were no handrails. A misstep would have meant a fall of several hundred feet to the plain below.

A leg muscle-knotting 30 minutes later, we walked through the massive, turreted Port d'Ardon, the arched gateway to the city. Overwhelming the city was the twin-towered La Cathedrale, the most impressive edifice I had seen since arriving on the continent. It truly rivaled Notre Dame Cathedral in Paris. During my visit, I was told the cathedral was the oldest in all Europe and dated back to pre-Medieval times. Its hand-chiseled exterior and exquisitely delicate interior were breathtaking, even to someone who was generally ignorant of religious architecture.

The town was made up of the typical winding European cobblestone streets lined with connecting masonry buildings that framed the streets. Steeply slanted slate roofs gave the city a formidable appearance. There was a dark, time-worn drabness about the buildings, even in broad daylight, that reflected the centuries-old heritage.

The city, untouched by the passing war because it held no defensive or strategic significance, offered the lushness of tree-lined cobblestone streets bordered by block-long strings of attached two-story buildings. What a reassuring sight after so many miles of shell-splintered matchsticks we had observed all the way from the now-distant Omaha Beach. Many three-story gray masonry buildings clung precariously to the sides of the cliff. They had been there for centuries and I was sure they would remain so, at least as long as our visit lasted.

Across the broad square from the cathedral was a cafe ruled by a redheaded, buxom, 60-ish barmaid. With flourishing arms and a jovial face she bade me enter. In any other setting, any other line of work, she would not have appeared so appropriate. She was the perfect example of a boisterous Hollywood version of a French barmaid.

All the tables were occupied by French civilians, most of whom seemed cordial as I entered. Again, these people had not been directly victimized by the war so they had no real reason to have built up strong emotions, either for the Germans or for us. If there was animosity, it was well concealed. Hospitality abounded. A small sip of red wine to the cheers of the cafe patrons and I was on my way again. Before I left, however, I asked the crowd, "Parle vous Anglaise?" ("Do you speak English?")

"Oui," the barmaid answered with an enthusiastic laugh at my pronunciation.

"Quelle jour est il?," ("What day is it?") I asked hesitatingly.

"November 6," she answered in a delightful French accent.

"What city is this?" I asked, gaining confidence with each inquiry.

"Laon," she answered, also apparently feeling more assured of her English proficiency.

With a smile, a wave and a polite "Merci," I threw a few francs (two cents each) of Army-issued occupation money on the bar and bounded out the door. I could hear the laughter behind me as I walked away along the main street seeking out my next adventure.

About a block away, I spotted a long line of GIs waiting to enter one of the town's buildings. In the midst of the line was an Army chaplain. I was hungry, and figuring it was a restaurant or some other attraction, I fell in at the end of the line. No one talked much, just waited patiently for their turn to enter.

After a lengthy wait—I was impatient in lines even then—I was finally ushered inside by a scantily-clad, full-figured woman about 40. "Bon jour, madam," I greeted her pleasantly, still flush from my successes with the French language in the barroom and still not realizing the accuracy of my greeting. Only then did it dawn on me that this was indeed an attraction but not what I expected. While the GIs handed the madam fistfuls of francs, naked girls could be seen flitting from room to room in the corridors trying to equate supply with demand. I finally realized it was a whorehouse. Without hesitating to gawk, I beat an embarrassed retreat, wondering what the hell the chaplain was doing there—blessing the girls?

A few doors away, I came across a bakery emanating the scrumptious aromas of bakeries everywhere in the world. I had no trouble exchanging a pack of cigarettes—I always carried candy or cigarettes as trade bait with me wherever I went in Europe—for a fresh loaf of hot bread. There was no other pastry available in the shop, only long loaves of hard-crusted, delicious fresh-from-the-oven French bread.

Hiding the bread under my field jacket and looking furtively around, I walked quickly away from any other GIs I could see and sat on a curb, by myself, to devour the whole loaf. Nothing since has tasted better to me than that simple loaf of hot bread made of whatever ingredients were available in wartime.

Adjacent to the "house of horizontal refreshment" I found a barber shop. For another pack of cigarettes, the barber, an old man, sheared and shaved me and even cleaned my uniform. Pumping my hand vigorously, the old man felt, I am sure, that he had gotten the better part of the transaction. But for the first time in a very long time, I walked out of his shop feeling like a human being again.

I left my buddies to their individual pleasures in Laon and made my way carefully back down the steps to the plain below. The Anti-Tank Company bivouac was practically deserted, so I crawled into the back of a truck and sacked out on top of a pile of barracks bags. An army on the move quickly learns to grab sleep wherever and whenever it can. There was always precious little of it.

Early that evening, orders came to move out again and the bone-jarring ride continued. All convoy movements were made at night and under blackout conditions. The Luftwaffe was still evident, we were told, for with each mile of eastward travel, we were closing in on the actual fighting. We rode all night and then, with a more apparent air of urgency, defied the obvious danger and also traveled all that day. The landscape gradually changed from flat plains and gently sloping hills to more rugged terrain. We encountered steep hills and deep, narrow valleys. Another element was also being added to the scenery: the season's first snowfall.

Highways along the route were lined with civilians throwing flowers and bottles of wine at us while girls and young women blew kisses. In return, we threw gum, candy, food and whatever else we had back at them. I can testify from experience that when bottles of wine or cognac are thrown at GIs, they suddenly become as adept catchers as major league ball players. I never saw them drop a single thrown bottle.

Since the people of this region had not been free of German occupation long, their joy at seeing the reinforcing American liberators was overwhelming—a far cry from what we had experienced days earlier. I had heard that the people of Flanders were demonstratively emotional and now I was convinced. However, I felt guilty accepting all this adoration for I had not really done anything to deserve it—except being born in America. It was not until we heard the roadside reception committees shouting "Viva le America. Viva le Belgique" that I realized we had crossed from France into Belgium.

The carnage of war suddenly enveloped us again. Burned-out German tanks, horse-drawn artillery pieces, wrecked German and American trucks, rotted horse carcasses and shattered, overturned wagons filled the ditches on both sides where they had been bulldozed out of the way. Again, practically every building had been flattened and the strewn wreckage of those soldiers who had gone before us littered the roadsides.

But there was a new twist to the landscape: dozens upon dozens of small, crude wooden crosses made of sticks or small tree branches and crowned with helmets appeared in the ditches. Many had small bouquets of flowers on them. These, I learned, were American GIs, buried hastily where they fell. And the Belgian people were being true to the soldiers' memories. These were the first actual American graves I had seen. The war was now very near, I knew, and as we crawled past the roadside graves, the whole truck fell somber and silent, staring at the ditches.

The war had been through this region only days earlier and many of the smashed vehicles from both armies were still smouldering and giving off the stench of death. The graves with no flowers, we soon figured out, were those of Germans. When the convoy stopped for a 10-minute "piss call," I inspected some of the graves more closely. They were crudely constructed by grateful Belgians, mostly from scrap wood and bound together with twine or wire. None were marked with any identification whatsoever, not even dog tags. What I was looking at was the crude internment of scores of unknown soldiers. There could no longer be only one such tomb at Arlington Cemetery, but hundreds, probably thousands by now, throughout the European and Pacific Theaters.

I gazed at the snow-covered simple offerings of wild flowers scattered on each grave, probably picked from nearby fields by children. It was such a paltry offering, but a gesture of such significance and gratitude. Tears came to my eyes. Was this to be my future? The deepest sadness I had ever felt washed over me and as a bitter wind from the east buffeted the column, I prayed silently for these men. They were all strangers to me but comrades nonetheless.

I also prayed for the German dead; I had not yet learned to hate. As I stood there silently, I had no way of predicting the future, a future that would have me returning to Belgium within five weeks under some of the most terrifying conditions of the war.

I climbed back on the truck, wondering whether some German family would ever revere my memory if my battlefield grave were on their soil. The convoy had only started up when it suddenly slammed to a halt again. "Hit the dirt," men screamed. Instinctively, we dove overboard and into nearby ditches. Already, the inborn sense of preservation was starting to take over. A constant roar, similar to that of a large diesel truck, could be heard. The rumbling roar grew louder and louder, then abruptly stopped.

Looking up, I spotted an ugly, cigar-shaped plane with a piggyback rocket compartment and short, stubby wings. It was only about 300 feet directly over our heads and had already started its awkward tailspin spiral toward earth. It hit the ground and exploded with a concussive force a half mile away that shook the earth beneath us.

It was a German "buzz bomb." I had heard them in London but I had never seen one. The realization hit me I had finally arrived at the war. It was no longer something "out there somewhere." It was the first frightening sound of war I had heard—the first shot fired.

That "buzz bomb," I reasoned, with a one-ton explosive load, a range of 100 miles and fuel for a 20-minute flight had been aimed to reap death and destruction in London but had malfunctioned along the way and fallen near our convoy. Once we had brushed ourselves off and climbed back on the trucks, the convoy roared relentlessly toward the front, first north through the small town of Mons and then due east to Namur before paralleling the Meuse River all the way to Liege, near the junction of the Belgian-Dutch-German borders.

Liege was devastated, having been plastered by German Stuka dive bombers years before during the German invasion of the Low Countries, and then recently made a target of Hitler's "Vengeance" weapons, the V-1 and V-2. It was a story of quiet, innocent cities caught in the struggle between major nations at war. The devastation was far worse than anything I had seen in London and equal to what I had witnessed passing through the small villages of northern France. Here, not one building had been left standing intact.

The convoy didn't slow at all in its rush toward Germany for we obviously had a date with destiny farther east. There had been no cheering crowds in these cities greeting the American liberators, for these Belgians had suffered too much and perhaps saw in our arrival more destruction to come. There was only the silent staring eyes of people in utter despair who were now merely existing from day to day hoping and waiting for the war to end. It was the hopelessness of people whose nerves had been shocked almost beyond human endurance. The war was, for all practical purposes, out of their hands but it had left on them a mark that would take generations to erase.

I began to wonder where and when in hell we were going to arrive at our destination. The hours cramped in the back of troop carrier trucks had now evolved into days and the emotional strain of anticipation was starting to wear on all of us. The convoy had surely traveled several hundred miles nonstop and still we had not arrived at our destination.

By midnight, the truck column pulled into a war-ravaged village and we were ordered to unload. As we tumbled out of the trucks onto another of Europe's inevitable mud-carpeted streets, a bitter wind blistered our faces. While slogging around looking for a place to hunker down for the night, I wondered if the mud in which we were now practically living would ever end.

"Hey, Cap'n. Where the hell are we?" I yelled out at Captain (John C.) Bowen, AT Company commander. "At the end of the line, Holland," he barked out.

What the hell happened to Belgium? I thought to myself.

Even our full-length GI wool overcoats couldn't protect us from the wind whipping down the street. With the wind, a total blackout in effect and the artillery-shattered town closing in around us, I wasn't sure I was going to like this place.

As it turned out, it was the last time I would be offered a few days of orderly existence, if living in mud and snow and eating cold field rations can be called that. Even though I sensed it at the time, it was also the final respite I would enjoy from the terrors of combat. As one of the uninitiated, I couldn't fully appreciate how easy I had had it until then. The war I sought was just around the corner. I could hear it in the distance now and I could smell it. It wouldn't be long.

4

Land of Tulips

The first thing that entered my mind when I arrived in Holland was how similar it looked to everyplace else I had been in Europe. The mud was the same color, as gooey and deep as in England, France and Belgium. The houses were all constructed of stone, brick or masonry as they had been in the other countries. And the people were dressed just as shabbily as the Scotch, British, French and Belgians. The debilitating effects of the war had permeated many cultures.

Somehow, I had anticipated that conditions would be different in Holland, a country famous for its picturesque cleanliness and charm. But even Holland's once-lush grass fields and orchards had been chewed-up into oceans of ooze and debris by the violence of men and their war machines. Rather than empathizing with the Dutch people and perhaps even sharing some of their sorrow, I felt only disappointment that my expectations had not been met. The first night, our platoon bivouacked in an apple orchard and I tried to pitch my pup tent during a sleet storm but was thwarted by the mud, the wind and the cold. When I awakened in the morning, I found the wind had blown the tent down on top of me but it mattered little for I was too exhausted to care much about anything, much less a tattered GI pup tent whose pegs wouldn't hold firm in the soft Dutch earth.

As I remained in my sleeping bag a few extra minutes trying to collect my thoughts, a deafening roar split the air right outside my tent. I bolted to my feet as best I could with the sleeping bag zipper jammed tight and the tent tangled around me. While I hopped around hopelessly enmeshed, arms and feet flailing in every direction trying to extricate myself, I finally rid myself of the tent and bag.

Then I stared in disbelief at a Sherman tank from the 2nd Armored Division that had moved into the area during the night and parked right beside my tent. At 0600, the driver had decided to test his engine's rpm with ear-shattering acceleration. I looked around to find half the platoon laughing heartily at my startled reaction. I took some good-natured derision about the incident but then the ridicule died down. It appeared I was starting to get jumpy.

That morning, several small campfires were built as men tried to thaw out and heat their field rations. Half-warmed C-rations on a cold, empty stomach is the point where a soldier hits rock bottom. The ultimate punishment. After only a mouthful or two, I started to gag and, as I would do so many other times during my combat career, threw the food away uneaten. Once again, the chocolate bars, crackers and fruit cocktail from home would have to serve as survival rations.

Finally rebelling against being subjugated to the elements in such a primitive fashion, I started foraging for something to ease the discomfort and to fight back at the mud in which we were walking, eating and now even sleeping. In a nearby barn I found armfuls of hay that I confiscated from a farmer. He would not need it, I reasoned; the Germans had left him no cattle or other livestock. As I walked back to the company area through the network of smudgy little campfires the men were using to keep warm, I planned to stuff enough straw into my swayback pup tent to keep me off the ground. It required nearly a half dozen trips back and forth to the barn before I succeeded in my plan. I repitched my tent, this time correctly in daylight, and crammed it full of hay. It kept me soft and dry and my bleak outlook on life started to improve.

The date was November 11, 1944—Armistice Day back home. Celebrations would be going on in the States, I knew, but there would be none in Holland this day. As if to mock the occasion, it started to snow heavily, the first really big snowfall of the winter. As unwelcome as it was, by adding still more discomfort to our living conditions, at least the snow covered the ugliness of the mud and, after a few hours, offered a pristine appearance to the orchard.

As a temporary escape from my surroundings, I grabbed a few

minutes free time in my pup tent to write home and to compile more diary notes about what I considered adventures. Almost reluctantly, I decided it was time to tell my parents the truth about where I was. We had been told we would be in combat in a few days and I knew that perhaps then it would be too late. I couldn't shield them any longer from worry for I was certain they had already read newspaper accounts of where the 84th was and what it was doing. But the question was: how to do it gently?

I took the coward's way out, writing to my father at the bank where he worked and letting him break the news to my mother. At last, the charade was over and, as I wrote the letter, I felt greatly relieved at finally telling the truth.

About mid-day, a young girl wandered into our campsite and I struck up a conversation with her in German, the language closest to Dutch. She seemed pleased to have someone to talk to. She said the town nearby was Heerlen, then matter-of-factly asked me if I wanted to "ficken" or just "kuszen." It took a few moments for my brain to click into gear and realize what she was asking. When the question gradually sunk in, I was flabbergasted at her aggressiveness, but also a little flattered. No girl had ever come right out and asked me that before.

After a while I asked her, "Wie alt sind Sie?" ("How old are you?") "Zwolf" ("Twelve"), she whispered passionately. .

I shoved her out of the tent. I wasn't too young or virginal to know that to continue was morally wrong. After the initial shock wore off, I was greatly relieved that nothing had been consummated. That surely would not have been the correct avenue to make my family proud of me.

Later one of the townspeople told me that my little 12-year-old friend was a slut who had been the sleeping partner for a whole company of occupying German soldiers. As a result, she had been branded a collaborator by the townspeople and banished from Heerlen and the surrounding towns. She had dared to return from her exile to our campsite when desperate to find food. War, I was finding out little by little, was a series of events that shocked one's sensitivities.

After a few days, the rest of the Army caught up to us and we received hot mess kit chow again. When finished eating, the field soldier dumped any unfinished portions of food into a swill barrel and then dunked and sloshed his mess kit a few times in a barrel of soapy hot water to wash it off. I did this one day, but when I walked away for some unknown reason I turned around and looked back. Several small Dutch children, all severely undernourished, had darted for the garbage pail and were frantically scraping handfuls of garbage up and gorging them down their mouths. Then they scraped the sides of the pail with small spoons trying to get every last remaining scrap of food. As fast as they had appeared, they were gone again, bolting away through the apple trees.

I would seldom see any sight more pathetic. During the ensuing days we stayed in Heerlen, the platoon took to beckoning to these children whenever they reappeared and offering them mess kits full of hot food. As long as we were there, we were determined not to let these babies scrape garbage barrels again to stay alive.

Late one afternoon, two small Dutch girls about eight and ten wandered into our company area. With their blue eyes, blond hair and wooden shoes, they were everything my grammar school geography books had described about Dutch children. They told me I was the first American soldier with whom they had been able to talk, and when we found a common language—a mixture of Dutch and German—they invited me to their home.

I accepted. I was exhausted and needed some diversion. It was time, in my mind, to put the rigors of war on hold for a while. After a charming evening of conversation with the Dutch family, I was invited to remain there for the night. Again, taking the dangerous chance of being considered AWOL, or worse still being left behind if there was an unscheduled troop movement, I accepted and was settled into an antique bed complete with eiderdown pillows, comforter and mattress. Lying on a down mattress is like floating in suspension. You sink into the mattress and it seems to have no bottom. I had not slept so well since leaving my parent's home 14 months earlier.

From the company field kitchen, I "liberated" some sugar, flour, butter and coffee and, with my weekly ration of cigarettes, was able to supply my newly adopted family with items they had not seen during the four-year German occupation. With the food I brought, the Dutch family prepared a meal I could share with them one evening; they even scraped up a small piece of meat that they cut into five small pieces, one piece for each of us. I was afraid to ask what it was. From a secret hiding place appeared the inevitable bottle of wine.

With curtains tightly drawn, we ate by candlelight. Electrical power, destroyed by the retreating Germans, had not yet been restored. With a battery-operated radio, we were able to pick up a Maastricht station. The news commentator announced that the Americans were advancing on all fronts—their bombers were leveling many German cities and Deutschland was "kaput." The news set off a round of excitement at the table as we then polished off our "banquet of celebration."

The word "kaput" was new to me. I had not run across it in my study of the German language and it was not in the German dictionary. The Dutch family explained it had many meanings, such as "broken," "destroyed," "ripped," "torn," "smashed" and even "dead." I promptly added it to my vocabulary, and still use it today.

The Maastricht news announcer was, however, premature in predicting that Germany, as a result of American bombings, was kaput. Hitler had a big surprise waiting for us less than a month in the future—a surprise that cost America and Germany tens of thousands of their young men. And that surprise would cause the outcome of the entire war to hang in the balance for nearly six weeks.

As remembrances of our brief friendship, the Dutch family and I exchanged currency from our respective countries. The Dutch Gulden was worth 40 cents American money, a better rate than the Belgian franc, which was worth only two and a half American cents.

From this Heerlen family, I learned a lot about the Dutch people, their neatness, their quiet demeanor, their use of cognac to keep their feet warm, and the custom of wearing wooden shoes that had gone back centuries. I learned about their wartime economy and food shortages, whereby rationed butter cost them the equivalent of $26 for a quarter pound every two weeks—and even then for children only.

I was told of the Germans' scorched earth policy, hastily executed when the occupying forces withdrew before the Allied onslaught. The Germans burned every building and barn they could. They fired phosphorus shells and grenades into the orchards to burn the soil and make it useless for planting in the future. They slaughtered horses, cows, sheep, chicken, cats, dogs, geese, anything that could be eaten. They crushed apple trees with tanks and ground apple crops to pulp with vehicles. Farmers were forced at gunpoint to shake apples from their trees so that the fruit could be sprayed with acids. Mattresses and blankets were slashed with knives and bayonets and the down contents cast to the winds.

In a premeditated, systematic plan to reduce a whole nation to starvation level, the Germans had even contaminated wells and poisoned vegetable and fruit crops. They plundered everything they could find, and as they marched or drove away, taunted the Dutch people with, "Now you will have something to remember us by."

These were the conditions in which we found and would soon leave Holland. While there, I managed to make numerous side trips—to Maastricht, where I actually found a movie house still in operation; to a coal mine in Nierbeek; to Geleen; to Warbach; and Terwinselen. Everywhere, Dutch hospitality abounded. As in Belgium, we were the liberators, the saviors, the conquering heroes who had driven the despised Germans out. In Nierbeek, I talked to Dutch coal miners and even on several occasions entered their fascinating world underground. I swapped cigarettes with them for handmade silver rings with initials scratched on them. I gave them to my folks and sister, and I kept one for myself. When my mother and father passed away many years later, I reclaimed their rings; they remain some of my wartime treasures.

At the mine, I made a wondrous discovery: a shower, where I was able to scrape off a layer of French mud, two coats of Belgian mud and a top layer of Dutch mud. How the miners laughed as I stood for more than an hour, dreamily letting the steamy, hot water peel away four coats of European grime. There was plenty of hot water; after all, it was a coal mine and it was my first shower since leaving England two weeks earlier.

In one of the towns, I was disturbed by posters tacked to utility poles warning young women they would have their heads shaved, be banished from the church and then be driven from the village if caught fraternizing with American soldiers. Despite their hospitality, I wondered whether we were really considered liberators by the newly freed Dutch people or merely another occupying force to be tolerated until we left.

Another feature of Holland was the huge, wooden-paddle windmills interspersed amongst what before the war had been acres of tulip beds. I especially enjoyed walking along the miles and miles of earthen dikes that held back the North Sea. On top of some of these dikes, entire villages of single-story homes stretched almost endlessly.

The Germans, apparently in one last vicious act of vengeance against the Dutch people, had blown away an entire section of one dike, flooding miles of lowland countryside with sea water, rendering it useless for years to come. Most of the picturesque windmills I saw had also taken a beating when the first American troops pushed the Germans eastward toward their homeland. Gaping shell holes were found on most of the mills, and the wind-powered paddles had also been badly shot up. I can only surmise that these windmills had been used as artillery observation posts by the Germans in attempted delaying actions while the main bodies of Wehrmacht troops were pulled back, and that the damage had been caused by advance units of the American Army eliminating them.

My travels about Holland ended abruptly when the company was restricted to the company area and told to be ready to move on a minute's notice. Orders came that night to break camp. Most of us thought, OK, this is the big one at last, but we had no idea where we would be committed to battle or precisely when. The Army was not the best forum for communications. But one thing was certain: this was it.

We loaded onto trucks under cover of darkness and moved slowly through the night on a road that seemed, if possible, to be even more shell-pocked and rougher than those in the rear area. Our truck tipped and groaned furiously as the driver tried, without headlights, to stay on the twisting roads.

In spite of all this, we could hear continuous muffled explosions. Peeking under the truck's tarpaulin roof, we saw distant flashes of light silhouetting nearby low-lying hills. Someone was sure catching hell that night, but who? Other than the buzz bombs, these were the first actual sounds of war we had heard and it made the soldiers being thrown around the back of our truck silent and meditative. From the expressions on everyone's faces you could read apprehension. No one spoke; the time for horsing around was past. Perhaps the artillery fire we were hearing and the flashes we were watching were from EASY Company, for rumor had it back in Holland that it had already been detached temporarily and committed to combat.

The convoy slowed to 10 miles an hour as the road worsened. Apparently the battle had passed through this area only hours before. The stench of smoke and fire was overpowering. As we jounced along, thrown from side to side by the shell craters, we wondered what the fighting there had been like and who had been victorious. It was so dark in the starless sky, I could see nothing, not even the other 11 GIs in the truck with me.

The artillery blasts grew louder until they were almost deafening. Finally, the convoy halted at what was to be our final destination: a battle-ravaged village with muddy streets and buildings leveled by shellfire. It was not until morning that I found a blue and white sign that had been crushed by countless tanks and trucks in the street. I picked it up and wiped the mud off. Despite the dented, twisted metal, I could make out most of the lettering: Marianburg.

I asked Captain Bowen where Marianburg was, in Holland or Germany? "It's right on the border," was the only answer I got and I knew better than to press the subject. Obviously, he didn't know either.

It was slightly before midnight when we were told to find whatever shelter we could for the night. I entered the closest bombed-out house and, finding a kitchen with a couch, grabbed it first and staked out my claim. A wood stove, we found, was still warm, a sign that the previous German occupants had fled a short time before. From the sounds drifting back through the blackened town, fighting was still raging just over a hill directly behind the house in which we were partially sheltered.

I was fortunate in claiming the couch because minutes later I was assigned to ammunition detail. A temporary ammo dump was about 200 yards from my billet and the trip back and forth should have taken only a few minutes to go there, pick up a case of ammo and return. Actually, it took more than an hour, an hour I desperately needed for sleep.

I slogged along a muddy street and up a slight incline to where sentries were guarding an ammo supply dump almost as large as the one we had observed near Omaha Beach. When I told one of the guards what I had been sent for, he pointed to a sergeant dispensing crates of ammunition to a group of soldiers who were then walking away with them on their shoulders.

Just as I handed the supply sergeant my requisition list, two German Me-109s came screaming out of the night and swooped down with ear-shattering suddenness only a few feet above our heads. A huge battery of floodlights switched on as antiaircraft "pow pow" guns from the 557th AA Battalion desperately tried to zero in on the fighters, but they had no chance for the planes disappeared again into the night as fast as they had appeared.

But one thing was certain: they now knew our location. The German fighters had not bothered to strafe our position because it had obviously only been a reconnaissance flight, but one that had drawn a lot of ack-ack fire. Between the nearby artillery barrages, the screaming whine of the German planes and the anti-aircraft guns firing aimlessly at the empty sky, I was at last listening to my first symphony of war. Machine gun emplacements on all sides sent up brilliant displays of thousands of tracer rounds criss-crossing and arcing through the night sky until they burned out.

As if this was all not bad enough, German artillery opened up now that the 109s had flushed us out and I found myself crouched beside several hundred tons of live ammo watching the pyrotechnic display. Incoming 88mm German shells screeched over my head. Someone behind us was getting it. Eighty-eights in the hands of well-trained German artillerymen were as accurate as rifles. My combat indoctrination came suddenly, but not at all as I had envisioned it.

It wasn't until the night quieted down again and my nerves were back under control that I realized what a holocaust it would have been if the Messerschmitts had strafed the ammo dump or the German artillery shells had scored a direct hit. It would have, I am sure, obliterated what little remained of Marianburg and all of us with it.

When the all-clear sounded, the supply sergeant loaded me down with a vest of 81mm mortar shells and as many bandoleers of M-1 rifle ammo clips as a rifle squad would need for a day's fighting. But the walk back to my company area proved not to be that easy, for the load I carried mired me into the muddy street up to my ankles. The more I struggled, the more stuck I became and as I tried to pull each foot out of the mud, the other became more firmly gripped by the muck. All this with 70 pounds of ammo on my back. The return trip to my company that should have taken 10 minutes took more than half an hour.

We were instructed not to get too comfortable for we would be pulling out in a couple hours. But first things first—it was well after midnight and we had not yet eaten. One of the squad members rekindled the stove and I placed a can of C-ration pork and beans on it. Then I stretched out on the couch and, drugged by fatigue, lapsed into sleep.

Sometime later, we were all awakened by a sharp explosion in the kitchen. Instinctively, we hit the floor. I felt sharp pain, a severe burning sensation on my arms and back. I had been hit. I felt my face and my hand came away with warm, wet flesh. "Medic, medic," I cried out. I knew I had been wounded and from the amount of pain, I knew it had to be bad. For an instant, the angry thought flashed through my mind that I had been wounded before I had even gotten into combat. I felt my face and my hand came away with what appeared to be more blood. Reddish, brown stains covered the upper part of my uniform.

The others in the room rushed to my assistance, one of them lighting a candle to see how bad I had been hit. They lifted me gently onto the couch and by now, some flashlights had been found. "It don't look to me like blood," one of the men grumbled.

It wasn't. Only then did we recognize what covered my head and upper body. The can of pork and beans, left unattended on the hot stove, had expanded and exploded, showering me with its contents.

Surprisingly, no one laughed. They were obviously all sharing the same apprehension I was. There was nothing funny about one man's jumpiness in the face of combat. I didn't sleep the rest of the time we were in Marianburg for my head was a jumble of confusing thoughts about home, the German planes, the ack-ack, the artillery, and about what was to happen in a few hours.

5

The Jump Off

"Off your cocks and grab your socks. This is it, the big one you've all been waiting for," yelled a faceless silhouette behind a bright flashlight.

Being awakened so abruptly, a sudden wave of nausea washed over me. It wasn't fear as much as the culmination of physical exhaustion and a lack of proper food since coming ashore on the French coast 17 days earlier. The accumulated loss of sleep and the cold, greasy C-rations were ganging up on my stomach. And the stomach was now starting to fight back. As I collected my gear by candlelight and staggered out the doorway, the platoon sergeant said, "Blunt, you're on temporary assignment to BAKER Company for this operation. Move out."

BAKER Company, some units of which were still milling around on a nearby street, was already probing its way forward when I arrived. I was joining 200 strangers without the slightest idea what I was supposed to do or even who to report to. In cases like this, the wisest course of action in the Army is to shut up, tag along and wait for an order. The Army is not noted for telling its soldiers very much, and when it does, it's usually gibberish or nonsensical.

I fell in at the tail end of the nearest column and started following in the tracks of the dark forms shuffling along in front of me. The silence was eerie, broken only by the occasional clanking of rifles slung against steel helmets and the uneven squishing patter of thousands of footsteps on the muddy street.

The nausea got worse as the ruins of the town slowly fell behind us and the column became enveloped in a black void. There weren't even any stars in the sky to offer some bearing or perspective of where we were. Just a blackness that was so total it was difficult to distinguish the GI walking only a few feet in front of me. I struggled as best I could to keep up with the pace set by someone up front. To lag behind, even a few feet, would be to lose sight of the column completely.

After all these months of preparation, the fear of the unknown was finally hitting me and I recognized it for what it was. I didn't feel the least bit ashamed of myself for this emotion. The apprehension was building up too suddenly and was too great. My heart was pounding as I plodded into the unknown. I tried to subjugate my fear by forcing myself to think about home but it didn't help much. The instinctive feeling of impending death and the ink-like blackness were taking over my emotional being. I had never been afraid of the dark before, but on this night I was.

The column, in follow-the-leader fashion, silently veered off the road, possibly to avoid mines in the road, and started climbing a gently sloping hill to our right. Just as we reached the crest of the hill, we were suddenly, without any warning, bathed in daylight with grotesque, moving black shadows being cast every which way around us by gigantic floodlights.

"Jesus Christ," someone in front of me muttered. "What the hell's going' on? Every gawdamn Kraut in Germany can see us." But it was not the GI's privilege to question the wisdom of Army brass, just to obey it. In military terms, it was known as "blind obedience." Someone behind me muttered, "Yeah, don't ask why. Just do and die."

The rumor filtered down through the ranks that Brigadier General Alexander R. Bolling, commanding general of the 84th Division, had been given permission from Corps to use this highly unorthodox method of entering combat and, to this day, I still can't fathom the rationale behind the maneuver.

Around 0230 we crossed a long, flat open stretch of land, still basking in the glare of the floodlights, and eventually entered the town of Palenburg. The column was halfway through it before I realized it had once been a town. All that remained were a few jagged piles of masonry. The town had been literally flattened. As we climbed another sloping hill away from the brilliance of the floodlights, the darkness was reassuring; at least now we had some protection and wouldn't make such easy targets. I came across a GI asleep on the hillside and as I walked past him, I nudged him with my foot. "C'mon man. You can't sleep now," I said under my breath. Then I saw it: a bayoneted rifle with GI helmet on top stuck upside down in the ground beside the face-down sleeping form.

It took a few moments before it sunk in—I was looking at my first dead American. The patch on his jacket was a Railsplitter insignia. The war was now very close. This was no stranger; this was one of our own. I continued on, not looking back, but now having actually touched death, I was even less confident in my own virtuosity. Half a century has failed to erase the frightening picture of that first dead GI from my memory.

Through the night and the glare of the floodlights behind us, I sensed that I was passing the skeleton of what had once been someone's home. In my mind I damned the floodlights again, for now even though they were far behind us, they still cast us as perfect silhouettes against the terrain for the Germans we knew were waiting for us up ahead. As we continued across a sugar beet field on the far side of Palenburg, I was startled by a huge, black form that emerged out of the darkness before me. It was a smouldering American Sherman tank at the junction of two stone walls, and I had almost walked right into it. I would have to learn to rely in the future on smells as well as visual observation.

All the time we marched, the cadence of our footsteps played a duet with artillery shells swish-swooshing lazily over our heads. Much to our relief, it was all "outgoing mail" and after the first one passed overhead, we ignored them.

Climbing over a wall beside the burning tank, I fell on my face and when I landed, the ground felt different somehow. There was not the normal splattering sound usually heard when one plops down into European mud. I felt the earth with my hand and discovered I was lying on a well manicured lawn. Moving more cautiously forward, I eventually could make out the form of a large mansion, similar in appearance to those of the Civil War era seen in the American south.

The column halted and we were told to dig in. Before daylight, this once-magnificent estate had hundreds of GI foxholes punctuating its lawn like a colony of gophers. It was just another small price of war being paid by some anonymous German family. Eighty-one millimeter mortar emplacements dug in around us started thwopping away at the German forward positions. As we crouched in our holes, enduring the concussion of each explosion battering our bodies, watching and listening to the sounds of war, it was brought home to us that the enemy was only a few yards in front of us and waiting. As each explosion blinked a millisecond of light, I peered intently into the night trying to see him, but I could detect no one.

It was 0430, and we had been on the move about two hours before digging in. Strangely, the nervous fear had disappeared, replaced by elation, almost euphoria. I started to settle down, knowing that I had successfully gone into combat and nothing had happened to me.

I dozed off but a moment later a blast from a German shell nearby ripped my helmet off my head and sent it flying about 10 feet away. The parapets of dirt I had thrown around the rim of the hole while digging in had been blown in on top of me, leaving me even more exposed to the German artillery. The first shots and the first cannonades of my war had been fired. I learned afterwards from grizzly old regular Army non coms that an infantryman is considered a veteran if he survives his first day of combat.

German artillery was zeroed in on our position. The element of surprise, if there ever had been one, was gone. I proved, then and there, to myself and the world that a five-foot-nine-inch soldier could compress himself into a three-foot-deep foxhole. I did it, but I also learned fast to dig holes deeper next time, no matter how much work was involved, for the shell landing near me had shown me that deep holes were a matter of life or death.

A few minutes later, the shelling stopped and the ensuing silence was louder than any I had ever heard. All I could hear was the ringing in my ears and my thumping heart. It took only a few minutes to realize that German artillery barrages are nothing at all like the basic training 105mm shellings we had experienced back in Alabama.

After 20 minutes of figuratively holding my breath, the shelling started up again, only far worse this time. But, again to our relief, it was ours and we were battering them three rounds to their one. The shells exploding only a few yards in front of us pounded our position almost as badly as the German barrage had earlier.

I thought the American shelling had been retaliatory, but I was wrong. It proved to be the softening-up process before we attacked. A combat infantryman's knowledge and understanding of the war extends only as far as the foxholes on either side of his position, not into the map rooms at Battalion, Division or Army.

What a combat GI sees, he can attest to, and nothing more, for he is never privy to the overall picture. After a while, he doesn't even try to figure anything out, just exist and wait for the next order. The barrage continued for more than half an hour. Curled up in the fetal position with eyes tightly clamped shut in our holes, we were being knocked almost senseless by the concussion from each explosion. As each detonated, I was pitched violently from one side of my hole to the other, back and forth until, mercifully, they finally stopped. When I was satisfied the shelling was over, I peeked out of my hole and saw that dawn had broken.

The BAKER Company commander jumped out of his hole, yelling, "Let's go! Let's go! This is it. We have a city to take!"

I looked at my watch. It was 0600 on the dot, and we were "going over the top," just like in the movies. Men all around me were scrambling out of their foxholes and surging forward en masse. On November 19, 1944, the day I had awaited for so long, I met and fought the German on his own ground.

The ground attack started slowly, picking up momentum as we moved forward. When the city finally came into view, smoke filling the sky from one end of it to the other, we broke from a fast walk into a frantic sprint, darting jaggedly back and forth across a 200-yard-long sugar beet field. I galloped across a dirt road and catapulted myself blindly into a ditch, trying to escape from that exposed beet field as quickly as I could. But, I should have looked before I dove; the ditch was half-filled with water. I came up drenched, chilled and miserably uncomfortable.

I jumped up again and sprang across another field where I saw a BAKER Company rifleman lying face down on the ground. As I ran toward him, I yelled,"C'mon. Let's keep moving." Then I saw one of his legs had been blown off below the knee and the bloody foot stump was on the ground several feet away. He was still alive. Shuddering at the sight, I yelled, "I'll get you a medic," and kept running.

My heart jumped into my throat when it finally occurred to me I was running full tilt in a field infested with hundreds of wooden Schu mines. "Mines! Mines!" I screamed at the other GIs around me, but for the legless GI I had just passed, it was too late. I skidded to a stop and stared at the ground. Some were buried shallow, the rest just planted on the surface in no particular pattern.

The fear I had not felt back in Palenburg almost paralyzed me now. I stood frozen, afraid even to put my foot down. Slowly, I inched my way forward, putting as little weight as possible on each step. At that moment, I realized for the first time the insidious psychological effect mines have on a soldier. It struck home. I would take my chances with small arms fire or even artillery rather than these silent, deadly devices.

I was pushing my feet along the ground, not wanting to lift them, when an explosion about 100 feet to my left signaled another victim of the German minefield. This man didn't have to worry about being an amputee—both his legs and groin area had been blown away and he was dead before he hit the ground. I was instantly sickened when I shot a glance in his direction and saw his body still twitching on the ground, even in death. The sight of this second shattered body unnerved me. This was a rotten war, a stinking way to die.

The loud snap of a whip close to my head brought me back to reality fast. It took a few seconds for me to react; this was a new sound to me, a sound not described in Army training manuals. It was a sniper bullet, probably from somewhere in the city, now only a couple hundred yards away.

I threw myself on the ground, the mines be damned. The hidden German sniper fired again and dirt kicked up in my face, only inches away. I was his sole target and at that moment the war had become one-on-one and I knew he would never let up. I was completely out in the open, totally exposed with no place to hide and still had no idea where the shots were coming from.

Frantically, I started to crawl forward, rifle cradled in my arms. Every snake-like motion of my body meant I might be crawling over a mine but I had to make it to the comparative safety of a small ditch-like canal about 100 feet in front of me. The sniper fired again and again, each time the bullet peppering me with chunks of earth.

Finally, unable to take it any longer as each slug chewed up the ground around me, I jumped up and ran in a headlong dash for my life. No zigzag this time, just a mad burst of flailing legs. I made it to the canal and jumped in, wading furiously through three-foot-deep water and flopping against the far bank, out of sight of the sniper.

For several minutes I lay there panting and trying to quiet my galloping heartbeat, all the while furtively snatching glimpses of a quaint, water-powered mill beside a spillway about 100 feet away. This had to be where the sniper was concealed. The lack of sleep and food and the tension of the past few hours were apparently too much for me. As I crouched half-submerged in the canal water trying to regain my senses, nausea swept over me again and I started to gag.

From the sounds of intermittent firing, I knew the attack was still underway. Peering over the edge of the canal embankment, I saw men on both sides of me running toward the city. For a fleeting moment, I thought of remaining safely in the canal until the attack was over. No one would ever know the difference—the confusion surrounding me would shield my location and identity.

I watched dozens of GIs advancing on both sides of me past the canal and toward the city, and I was relieved that I was not alone. My eyes scanned every window of every building facing me for several long minutes and I saw no signs of life or movement from any of them. I watched for puffs of smoke signifying a machine gun or a sniper from a number of wooden sheds scattered randomly in some of the closest yards, but they all appeared empty.

Off to my left, American troops, their M-1s held across their chests, were running crouched low amongst the buildings without firing. When all the shooting finally tapered off and there still were no signs of German troops, I decided to try for a railroad trestle bridge, a clump of shattered trees and another canal directly in front of me. It seemed like a safe route and if I made it, I too would be inside the city.

I glanced to my right and saw ABLE Company working its way toward a row of pillboxes set slightly apart from the city. I made it to the bridge and swampy canal and started wading my way closer to the outlying buildings. I crawled up an embankment and out into the open again, pausing only a moment to look around before breaking into a run, this time firing my M-1 from the hip at an invisible enemy. When there was no return fire, I threw myself to the ground behind a low stone wall surrounding a backyard vegetable garden and emptied a clip at windows and doors about 50 feet away. Still receiving no response, I fired another clip as I sprinted to the closest building. I crashed through the back door and crouched in a hallway, again struggling for breath.

I had reached the city alive, but what was I supposed to do now? There was no one in sight anywhere. I got the sinking feeling I had been left behind somehow, totally isolated from the others. I cautiously inched myself deeper into the building and found myself in a demolished grocery and remnants store with shelves and merchandise scattered everywhere. Through a shattered window, I saw a slight movement in a doorway across the street. I drew a bead on it and paused. Lucky I did—it was another GI.

I yelled across to him, asking whether he could see anyone. I got my answer when a bullet ricocheted off a door casing near my head. "He's in your building on the second floor!" I screamed, cringing against a wall for protection. I heard three fast shots and moments later I spotted the GI waving an OK sign at me from a gaping hole on the second floor from which the sniper had been firing. He had eliminated the sniper and I felt safe in pouncing back out to the street.

I had broken one of the first rules of combat by giving away my position, and I had actually lived to tell about it. It had been lesson number one in combat and a mistake that I wouldn't repeat again. Every hour, I was learning the rules of survival.

I doubled back across the street and joined the other GI who had taken down the sniper. He was from BAKER Company and informed me it had taken his company two hours to fight its way to the center of the city. He also said that most of the city had been cleared except for a few diehard snipers here and there. To play it safe, we decided to check out some buildings on his side of the street. He went first while I lay in a doorway ready to give him covering fire.

As we leapfrogged our way down the debris-cluttered street, I spotted movement out of the corner of my eye. I whirled around and saw Sgt. Norman Betz, our squad leader and a retread from ITEM Company, sauntering down the street without a care in the world, accompanied by several other members of the mine removal squad from which I had been detached back in Marianburg.

He greeted me like a long-lost cousin and handed me a "vacuum cleaner" mine detector with the wisecrack, "Here Blunt, I'm tired of carrying this gawdamn thing for you." With that, he disappeared with the others down the main street past a grassy, triangular patch of trees at an intersection across from the *Geilenkirchen Beobachter* (*Geilenkirchen Observer*). After several buildings were searched and cleared of German stragglers, I signaled to the BAKER Company GI that I would check out a cellar near the square. As silently as combat boots allowed, I tiptoed down the cellar stairs and listened at a door where I could hear movement and muffled voices inside.

"Kommen Sie heraus mit hande hoch!" ("Come out with hands high!") I yelled at the top of my voice. Only then did I remember Sgt. Betz had swapped my rifle for the mine detector. The door opened a crack, a white handkerchief tied to a stick poked out, and behind it emerged a shabbily uniformed Wehrmacht soldier. I pointed the mine detector at him and asked him if he was alone. Looking terrified at the new "secret weapon" I held in my hand, he said there were others. When I reassured him they would not be shot, 21 more bedraggled, unshaven soldiers filed out. They had never seen an American mine detector and thought it was a weapon of some sort.

I stripped them of their knives, pistols and rifles and marched them down the main street with their hands folded over their heads. Seeing Sgt. Betz returning from his sightseeing tour of the city, I turned them over to him and reclaimed my rifle. At this, the prisoners finally realized they had been duped. Betz walked away, laughing. "Only you, Blunt, only you could pull this off."

The Germans told us they had been left behind to defend the city of Geilenkirchen at all costs while the main body of troops had pulled back. They had lost their will to fight, mostly because of hunger and the artillery barrage that preceded our attack. They were just glad to be alive and know that their war was finally over.

These frightened, half-starved Kriegsgefangener (war prisoners) didn't look at all like the images of vicious German soldiers with cruel, distorted faces displayed on posters back in basic training lectures. Facing them close up brought the war into sharper focus for me. I was dealing with men just like ourselves, only in different uniforms, speaking a different language and fighting for a different cause.

When everything finally quieted down and I could collect my thoughts, I realized my baptism of fire was behind me. I felt proud. I was finally able to sling my rifle over my shoulder instead of constantly keeping it pointed at the ready.

Geilenkirchen was a major rail and mining center with a population of about 20,000. It was also one of Hitler's bastions in his Siegfried Line defenses. In an attempt to bolster divisional pride, word was passed down from 84th headquarters that Geilenkirchen was one of the first and largest German cities—second only to Aachen—to be taken by American forces during the furious fighting to breach the Siegfried Line and push on to the Roer River.

The streets were filling up fast with men from ABLE and BAKER companies. With the city now secure, I went back into the cellar to sort over the arsenal of weapons I had stripped from my 22 prisoners before other GIs found them. There were enough rifles, grenades and machine guns in the cellar to hold off a battalion, had the prisoners wanted to. I claimed all the pistols, a German paratrooper trench knife and a Schmeisser "burp gun" before smashing all the other weapons against the walls. Then I checked out the rest of the cellar, to see just how German snipers operated.

The concrete cellar wall was an unbelievable eight feet thick, with four-foot square openings on the inside that tapered to about a foot square at the outer wall. The sniper merely positioned himself in these openings and had an excellent field of fire in practically all directions while being offered full protection from artillery.

One by one, I started searching other buildings for loot that would be useful to me. As I started down one of the streets, I heard a prolonged burst of machine gun and M-1 fire. I pressed against a wall and listened. When it stopped, I cautiously moved forward, my rifle up to my shoulder, not knowing what to expect for I had been told the city was cleared of Germans.

I snapped a quick glance around a corner and saw about 30 GIs guarding a group of German prisoners taken from the cellar of a bookstore. On the ground a dead American lieutenant and a German soldier were lying in a large pool of blood. I was told the Germans had surrendered under a white flag, and while being searched one had stepped from the back of the group and shot the lieutenant in the head with a concealed pistol.

The GIs had riddled him with gunfire. Looking closer, I estimated he had more than 100 bullet holes in him as each of the American soldiers had emptied their weapons into him. Now the GIs were staring at the Germans hoping someone else would make a move and give them an excuse to slaughter the whole lot. All remained frozen still, staring silently at the bloodied body of their former comrade.

I searched another building for loot and hit the jackpot. It had been a Gestapo headquarters and was filled with Nazi flags, pictures, whips and other torture devices. In a safe, I found numerous bundles of money which I threw out a window to the winds for there was nothing to buy in the city and the money was worthless to us. Perhaps if the civilian population ever returned to the city, the money might be of some use to them, but I didn't know how. I just knew it was fun to throw money away, even if it was only German Reichsmarks. I took several flags and destroyed everything else before I left. If I ever met any of our rear echelon troops, I figured to be in a good bargaining position with the flags.

I entered another building and stumbled over another German whose war was over. The building contained one of the plushest apartments I had ever seen but the war had passed through and not much of the elegance remained. Not being a particularly religious man, nonetheless I found something that day I still treasure. It was a small crucifix from Lourdes in France, a reminder of God. I shoved it in my uniform watch pocket and carried it through every battle. On many occasions, I pulled it out and looked at it for strength. I still have it today.

With the city now secure and with my anti-mine squad nowhere to be found, I decided to try out my newest trophy, the German Schmeisser "burp" gun—so called because its rapid fire, coming in short bursts, sounded like "bbbuuurrrppp."

I made my way to the canal I had forded earlier coming into the city and fired a few bursts into the water. I was enjoying myself when someone grabbed me by the shoulder and yanked me around. It was BAKER Company's commander who chewed me out for firing a German weapon near American troops. I didn't understand why he was so upset until he pointed out the possibility of some trigger-happy GI, hearing the sound of a German machine gun and thinking it was a Kraut, pumping me full of lead. Shocked at my own stupidity, I quickly threw the burp gun into the canal. After all, I was going to get all the target practice I needed in the coming months.

About this time, I heard "Hey, Blunt!" It was Sgt. Betz and the mine squad again. "C'mon. We've got a mission." I ducked into a nearby building, stashed my flags and weapons where no one could find them and rejoined the squad. We picked up our gear and started out on what we later called the "Betz Salient."

Our objective was to scout along a railroad track between Geilenkirchen and Suggerath, about two kilometers away, to assess the enemy strength in that area. We moved out slowly in squad formation—two men walking point, two others on the flanks for security and the rest bringing up the rear.

Betz and I took the point, running crouched low on either side of the tracks. About a half mile from Geilenkirchen, we came to a gate tender's shack. While I covered him, Betz crashed his way inside. It was vacant. Finding no German opposition, we stopped to rest and eat a K-ration. With my helmet as a pillow, I promptly dozed off on the rail tracks, warmed by the November sun. Thirty minutes later, Betz moved us forward again. We were soon joined by elements of ABLE and LOVE companies and it was good to see a few of my old buddies again.

In single-file formation, we moved toward Suggerath. A whip cracked again beside my head. The GI about six feet in front of me suddenly cried out, "Oh my God. I'm dead." By the time he pitched forward and slumped to the ground he had already been cast into the black abyss of eternity from which there is no return. As we threw ourselves prone on the ground, I saw only a small, bloody bullet hole in his back. He never made another sound after his initial exclamation. Before the shock of losing one of our squad had time to hit me, I wondered if he had cried out before he died or afterward.

When a medic finally ran up to attend to him, Betz moved the column forward again, each man solemnly glancing back at the corpse on the ground. The shot could only have come from a sniper in the gate tender shack that earlier had been checked out, now about 100 yards behind us. We doubled back and laid down withering rifle fire at the building. A white flag started waving from a window and the sniper surrendered. We surrounded him and then, in a spontaneous outburst of hatred, every man in the squad fired at once and then spat on the lifeless German. It was one for one. From many such instances later, I learned that snipers were seldom taken alive unless they were needed by G-2 for information.

When we returned to the field where our squad had suffered its first casualty, one of the other men was cradling his corpse in his arms as if to comfort it. He had been the dead man's friend back home, had been inducted with him, trained with him, shipped out with him and fought with him. And now his friend was dead after only two days of combat. The man sobbed like a baby. We pushed on silently, leaving him to his private grief. We knew that Graves Registration would be along soon and the two friends would be separated.

The anti-mine squad was now down to 11. Who would be next? I remembered that, shortly before, I had carelessly slept on the tracks a mere 75 feet from the sniper's position, a perfect target. The fates of war had decided that death, though walking close beside me, had instead chosen someone else.

As we came around a nearby barn, I found we were in another Schu mine field, only this time the mines had all been hastily thrown on the ground. Picking my way cautiously around them, in my concentration I was oblivious of small arms fire all around me. But I was startled back to reality by a machine-gun blast that splintered the barn wall above my head. The fire was coming from a monstrous pillbox just to our front. Men everywhere were hugging the earth and crawling to the rear. I sprinted about 30 feet and dove into a ditch where I could actually see the German machine gun barrels poking out of the pillbox. But I was still exposed and knew I had to move.

I zigzagged across a nearby road and threw myself into another ditch, where I hugged the ground as bullets kicked up dirt over my head. We were pinned down. Also in the ditch with me was an ABLE Company officer who was trying frantically by walkie-talkie to get a flamethrowing Crocodile tank to burn the box. A British-accented voice answered the urgent request with, "Send in more infantry. They can be replaced." The infantry was American, the tanks were British— another bitter incident of war that would remain with me for a long time. At the time, we were unaware that the 84th Division had been under temporary British command for more than a week.

The captain then called for artillery support and within seconds it was whistling overhead. After 10 minutes, the barrage ceased. Men around me charged directly into more murderous German machine-gun fire. Those who were not mowed down during these aborted charges were repeatedly forced to withdraw to whatever cover they could find. Eventually, they stopped trying and we all squirmed in the roadside ditch waiting to see what would happen next. The pillbox had effectively stalled our advance.

That day we learned that artillery is largely ineffective against underground pillboxes and the alternatives were to lie there and take it or retreat and work your way around, bypassing the fortification if possible. Most pillboxes could usually be taken, we found, with satchel charges by crawling from the rear and then throwing them through the gun apertures.

I started to dig in with my bare hands and then with my helmet. In a half hour, I had a hole deep enough to feel a little safer. Soon, I dozed off again but was awakened by a hideous roar.

Two British "Crocodiles" were flame-drenching the facing of the box for us while engineers crawled behind it with demolition charges. The charge was detonated and through the smoke, a single file of about a dozen Germans surrendered. The flames, they told us, had shut down their ventilation system and they had not been able to breathe. One of the GIs from the attacking force marched them back to Geilenkirchen.

As we advanced once again toward the sloping hills of Suggerath, we heard German anti-aircraft guns in the village. In a ball of fire, a P-51 Mustang fighter plummeted from the sky, trailing flames and black smoke, and slammed into the hill about a half mile in front of us. Even though we kept looking up hopefully, there was no sign the pilot had been able to bail out.

A stream of 57mm tracer shells cut into Suggerath as the wind picked up and it began to snow lightly. I passed another GI with his dogtags wrapped around his rifle stock and thought how peaceful he looked. Little by little I was beginning to accept death for what it was: a byproduct of war—some of them, some of us .

As I reached the top of the hill, shivering from the weather change, I was greeted by one of the prettiest sights I had seen so far. The town was aflame from one end to the other and I was momentarily entranced by the red glow illuminating the night sky and the buildings being consumed by flames. Beyond the village, the flames painted dancing shadows on a pine forest bordering a sloping snow-covered meadow. In all its savagery, the scene was quite beautiful, almost like a violent etching.

I wanted to get to the town as fast as I could to be warmed by the flames. In frontal formation, we drew no enemy fire as we moved in. As I walked down the central street of the inferno the flames felt good. The column halted and spread out, keeping a distance between us in case of a mortar barrage. A nearby GI informed me I had inadvertently filtered back into LOVE Company and he asked if I had anything to eat, saying that he had lost his rations and had not eaten at all that day. I broke out a D-ration hard chocolate candy bar I had in my field pack and gave it to him. In a ditch beside the road, I closed my eyes again, warmed by burning buildings all around me. It was 0200 and I had been awake, except for a few catnaps here and there, since leaving Holland the day before.

I think it was about an hour later when I woke up and found the other GI was still in the ditch with me, asleep. I looked around but could see no one else anywhere. I got the disturbing feeling the town had been abandoned. I shook the man beside me to whom I had given the ration and asked where everyone was, and then I saw the dented helmet and the bullet hole in it. My ditch companion was dead, meaning there was a sniper somewhere in the inferno surrounding us. I rolled him over and saw a bulge in his cheek. He had been eating my D-ration when his life had ended. His eyes were wide open in death. I had not even heard the shot nor had I heard him die. I hadn't even known his name. The sniper had apparently seen me and thought I was dead and not worth wasting a bullet on.

For a moment, I wondered whether I had made my unknown dead companion's last minutes on this earth happier with my D-ration.

6

The Siegfried Line

LOVE Company had pulled back during the night, leaving me alone in a Suggerath ditch with a dead man. They apparently had seen me asleep in the ditch and had assumed I was just another corpse to be picked up later. It took me a few minutes to collect my wits before deciding to go back and look for my old company. I wasn't even sure if they had pulled back or had pushed on farther. I decided to try backward. The known was always safer than the unknown. I walked back up the hill from which we had come some hours earlier.

I passed through an undefined line of foxholes and stumbled onto DOG Company. When I told them I was lost, they showed me where I could dig in but I was too exhausted and just stretched out in the snow to sleep.

"Hey, Blunt, c'mon over here. I've got room in my hole." It was Joe Everett, of Durant, Oklahoma, another member of the Anti-Mine Squad. When I had been temporarily assigned to BAKER Company back in Marianburg, Everett had been similarly sent to DOG Company for any mine-removal duties needed there.

During the trying times ahead, Everett and I shared many foxholes and tried to maintain our sanity by arguing constantly whether older or younger women were more desirable. Being only 19, I voted for older women. Everett, on the other hand, adamantly argued the virtues of young Indian girls on Saturday nights in Ardmore, Oklahoma. The reunion was warm. Since the jump-off had started two days earlier, I had mostly been alone, surrounded by strangers killing strangers.

With daylight, I could see Suggerath still smoldering before me and the ruins of Geilenkirchen in the distance behind me. About 600 yards to our right, another string of pillboxes looked like a row of unnatural humps in nature's landscape. No matter how cleverly disguised the German fortifications were, our eyes were already learning to spot them from a distance. The survival instinct was starting to build within us.

Silhouetted against the cold and cloudless blue sky, I could see groups of German soldiers walking back and forth between the pillboxes. I fired off an M-1 clip of harassing fire at them, perhaps out of spite or because it seemed the right thing to do at the time. They couldn't even hear me and just kept on going about their business, but I felt better having fired at them.

I broke open a can of C-rations and tried to eat it but the hash inside stuck in my throat. As I was spitting it out, "incoming mail" started pounding our position. Everett and I crouched against each other, crammed in the bottom of his hole, trying to crawl inside our helmets. The unmerciful beating we took was the worst shelling since the jump-off had begun. The Germans knew precisely where we were. The most terrifying aspect of an artillery bombardment is not that your mind goes blank, which it does, for all thoughts of home and family and the fear of dying are blown away when the first shell hits. Nothing remains. Nothing. You just cringe in mortal fear wondering whether the next shell will land on top of you. Sheer fear brings on a mental paralysis, a form of shock that blots out all senses or emotions.

A near-miss caved part of the hole down on top of us. I shall never forget the screeching whine of incoming "screaming meemies," that intensified until eardrums wanted to burst. After one such blast, I blacked out. When I came to, I was still in the hole and Everett had his arm protectively around me.

I could not focus my vision; everything looked fuzzy and gray. Even though not a word was said to me, I knew I had been crying. I could hear voices around me but I could not make them out. Joe shed some light on what had gone on after the shell had exploded outside our foxhole. The explosion had blown me up in the air and out of the foxhole and when the smoke settled, I had jumped up and started running around in circles shaking my fists in the air and screaming curses at the Germans. Everett said I was yelling, "Come and get me, you bastards. I'll kill you all!"

Everett, I was told, had jumped out of the hole amidst the bursting shells and tackled me. When I struggled with him, he hit me and dragged me back to the relative safety of our foxhole. From a nearby DOG Company foxhole, I heard, "There's another one cracking up." I lunged at the voice and started throwing punches. Everett pinned my arms back and sat on me until the shelling stopped.

Peering over the rim of our foxhole, we saw a group of American GIs running away from the distant pillboxes. In Army manuals, this was called a "strategic advance to the rear, but actually it was men running for their lives. The Germans had overrun their position and they were high-tailing for the safety of our hill. Within minutes, they were running through our positions and still heading west as fast as their legs would carry them.

When one of the DOG Company lieutenants panicked and yelled for us to join the retreating troops, Everett started pulling me down the hill. We ran toward the rear until we came to a culvert beneath the Geilenkirchen-Suggerath railroad track. We crawled through it to a gravel ditch on the far side where we found a medic bending over a GI whose elbow had been shattered by artillery fire.

I ran crouching along the ditch and skidded to a halt as I came face to face with two German soldiers who probably had been American prisoners and who were now both victims of their own artillery shelling. One had an arm and leg blown off and had apparently died moments before.

The other had been disemboweled and his mouth, nose and jaw had been blown away. How, I don't know, but he was still alive and as I stared at him, his eyes followed my every movement. With each breath, foamy blood drooled from his mouth onto what had once been his chest. Only a foot-wide gaping hole of bloody meat remaining of what had been his upper chest and his intestinal tract lay stretched out on the gravel like long twisted links of sausage. I could not take my eyes off this macabre scene.

Everett broke the spell when he returned to see why I hadn't kept up with him. The rout didn't end until DOG Company reached the outskirts of Geilenkirchen where it found reinforcements. During the confusion, my head had cleared—except for a blinding headache—and Everett and I, with a few minutes on our hands until the situation settled down, went loot hunting. We reentered Geilenkirchen proper.

In a priest's former home that was quite elaborate we found chinaware and table cloths on which to eat. We located the Anti-Tank Company kitchen and treated ourselves to our first hot food in nearly a week. DOG Company, if they wanted us, could wait—the opportunity for hot food came too seldom. Someone came over to me and said there was someone back at the priest's home looking for me.

A medic greeted me and informed me I was being sent to a field hospital back at Marianburg for mental evaluation because of the accident that had blown me from my foxhole. I protested, saying I wasn't crazy, but he shut me off. "You either come with me now or the MPs will take you back. Which will it be?" Saying good-bye to Everett with the flippant remark, "Hey Joe, keep the war going for me," I followed the medic to a Jeep marked with the Red Cross and climbed in. The trip took only a few minutes.

The hospital was a partially bombed-out building that had been scrubbed clean and was filled mostly with patients being treated for wounds serious enough to send them back to England or the States. I felt out of place; I hadn't been wounded, only subjected to a "close one." I was given a hot bath and a fresh change of uniform, both of which lessened the stigma of the trip to the rear. After a long soak, I shaved. The stillness of the field hospital was difficult to get accustomed to. I was put to bed and slept 19 straight hours from noon one day until 0700 the next.

After a breakfast of bacon, eggs and coffee on plates and eaten with utensils, a captain stopped by and told me I had an appointment at his office at 1000 so he could ask me some questions. I asked a wounded soldier in a bed beside mine who the captain was.

"A psychiatrist," he said.

I relished the breakfast I had been given and wondered whether I should string along for a while with what the Army thought was best for me. The doctor, a friendly sort, offered me a cigarette and had me sit down. He asked me to relate in detail what I had done since going into combat and what I thought of combat and the war in general. He kept nodding his head and taking notes.

Finally, unable to stand it any longer, I blurted: "I don't belong here. I haven't cracked up, have I?"

"No I don't think so but you have experienced a very severe shock to your nervous system," he replied. "Your answers have not all been completely rational but I think with a few days rest you will be just fine." When I was dismissed, I headed back to the hot food chow line.

After three days of these question-and-answer sessions, I was deemed cured and told I could return to my squad. That was fine with me; I was starting to get a little itchy by that time from the inactivity. A Jeep returned me to Geilenkirchen and dumped me off where I had been picked up. Fortunately, the Anti-Mine Squad was still there so I rejoined them. I found Everett had rejoined the squad after deserting DOG Company when it moved back on the line.

Interested in what I had been doing in Marianburg, the others envied my stories about the field hospital beds and good food. Soon after I bunked in again with Everett in his billet the Germans began shelling the city again and I found myself jumpy and cringing with every shell burst. It was a reaction I had not experienced before being subjected to the peaceful atmosphere of the hospital. I retreated into the cellar of the building, hoping the fear would go away once I reacclimated myself to combat conditions.

While my squad huddled in a room at the priest's house, a loud crash sent them all sprawling on the floor. When the dust settled, they found an artillery shell dud embedded in the floor near the doorway. It was another unexplained mystery of war. Had it detonated, it would have destroyed half of our squad.

In the cellar, I made a bed out of straw and tried to get comfortable. The two squad members who were closest to the sniper victim a few days earlier were unable to cope with their loss and they alienated themselves from the others. When they eventually became too terrified to venture out onto the street, squad members brought them their meals. Every time a shell exploded in the city, they cowered in a corner trembling.

When the company officers became aware of this, they transferred both back to Marianburg for rest and rehabilitation. Their assignment was to guard Anti-Tank Company equipment and barracks bags in a rear area. I was glad they would be doing their share in the war effort without being stripped of their honor and pride.

Battle fatigue hit men in many different ways. No one ridiculed battle fatigue victims. We all knew it could happen to anyone at any time, and we realized they needed sympathy and understanding. The mind and body could be tortured only so much before they sometimes snapped. Bodies usually healed in time but minds sometimes never did. Now the squad was down to nine men and our war was only five days old.

I spent much of my time looting houses and exploring. The people of the city must have been quite religious because every street intersection had Christ on the Cross statues mounted on posts. Practically every home was adorned with ornate wall crucifixes.

In one building, I found several Hitler Jugend (youth) snare drums that must have been used at political speeches and rallies. I had been carrying a pair of drum sticks in my pack all the way from the States so I had a ball for myself making enough racket to emulate World War III back at the squad billet. After having my picture taken with them I shoved one in my dufflebag to be taken home. I hoped that when my family back home saw the pictures they would think everything was a lark in Germany.

I was finding that it was amazing how much a barracks bag would hold. Mine now was filled mostly with war booty and very little actual Army gear. As I continued to "liberate" items from practically every building I came across, I found a toy-size spoon that would be handy for eating C-rations and shoved it into my uniform watch pocket with the crucifix. I still have it.

The next day, troop convoys started rolling through the city headed back toward Holland, away from the battle. Rumors were rife that we were being pushed back by the Germans and that soon Geilenkirchen would be overrun by their tanks. Orders came soon afterward to be ready to move out in 10 minutes. As we loaded onto a "six-by," I discounted the rumors, figuring the area had been cleared and our unit was now needed elsewhere for support.

We bounced along for some time when a non-com in the truck broke open a case of K-rations and flung them around at us. "Here. Now you guys can celebrate."

"Celebrate what?" someone asked.

"Didn't you know? It's Thanksgiving and this is your turkey dinner," he answered sarcastically.

Later, I read in the military newspaper *Stars & Stripes* that all European troops, especially those in the front lines, had been supplied with full turkey dinners and all the fixings. At least, this is what the Army wanted the people back home to believe, so in my next letter home, I described in great detail the dinner I had allegedly been given from nuts to cranberry sauce. I felt justified in telling my family this small lie for it served no purpose to tell them the truth.

When we arrived at our destination it was getting dark. We tumbled from the trucks and tried to find shelter from the cold. Finding a house with a section of the roof still intact, I cleared debris away from a corner in what had once been a kitchen and dropped my gear. Within minutes, I proved that even a pile of stone can make a good bed. Someone found a lantern and we were really quite cozy. We often felt that blackout conditions were fine for the rear echelon troops but comfort, something seldom achieved, was important up front.

Morning came much too soon, about six hours later. Curious as always, I went outside to explore and was met with the most gruesome sight I had yet seen. A building sign said the town was Prummern. I was told that the fiercest battle fought so far by the 84th had taken place there—by elements of the 334th Regiment against SS troops and Panzer Grenadiers.

Discarded rifles all had attached bayonets and American and German bodies lay scattered everywhere, usually side by side and some with knives still in their hands. An estimated 400 bodies littered a two-acre plot. Every house, room, street, alleyway, foxhole and shell crater contained at least one body, usually more.

The name Prummern would be remembered in 84th Division history; it had been written in blood. The grotesque sights there will be in my memory as long as I live.

I came upon a German corpse, slumped face forward in a foxhole with a Schmeisser machine gun pointed at four dead Americans who had obviously tried to rush his position. The German had a holstered pistol and trench knife attached to his ammo belt and I wanted them.

Fearing the corpse might be rigged with a boobytrap, I noosed a long piece of wire gently around his neck and crawled away a safe distance. I jerked at the wire repeatedly until the partially-decomposed head was severed from its body. Finally convinced the body was not boobytrapped to maim souvenir hunters, I crawled into the hole, picked up the stlll-helmeted head, studied it a moment and then threw it away.

Minutes later, I had my first Luger pistol and another Kraut trench knife. I took some blood-stained writing paper off the body and eventually wrote a letter home with it. I don't believe my parents ever knew what the brown stain on one of my letters was.

After claiming the pistol and knife, I tried to remove the German's sweater but the corpse was frozen too stiff to bend the arms.

Some of my squad members were gathered around a dung heap in a courtyard at our temporary billet. As they admired my Luger, a German 88 shell landed in the manure and detonated before we could even react. Though covered with manure and severely stunned by the explosion, not one of us suffered a scratch.

The Army had a saying: the Germans were so accurate with their 88s, they could put one in your hip pocket. It was also believed that with a muzzle velocity of 3,600 feet per second, you never heard the 88 that would hit you. When you heard the whistle, it was already too late, it was past you. The incident in the courtyard proved the saying. We had heard nothing before the explosion.

Word was passed around that hot chow, the first in several days, was available at the company field kitchen. As I walked back to my billet with a mess kit full of field slop, picking my way over dead bodies lying on the muddy street, I saw another GI carrying a mess kit coming toward me on his way to the kitchen.

Faintly in the distance, I heard the swish of a mortar round about to land. I instinctively dove for a doorway. The GI, apparently unaware, kept walking along. As I crouched watching, the shell landed in the street, a direct hit. The man disintegrated, leaving only patches and puddles of flesh and blood spattered in the mud. Graves registration would never find this one, not even his dogtags. Another unknown soldier. I sat and ate my food. I had not known hlm.

Afterwards, I tried to write home by heavily shaded lantern light but concussions from an artillery barrage blew out the lantern as the building shuddered convulsively, shrapnel ricocheting back and forth against what walls remained. When more of the roof collapsed, I retired to the cellar. After about 20 minutes, the shelling stopped.

I tried to make my way out of the cellar to make sure the barrage was not a prelude to a German counterattack but no matter how hard I pushed on the trap door at the head of the stairs, it wouldn't budge. I was trapped. Fortunately, a cellar window was just large enough to crawl through to the street. The concussions had completed the demolition of the house in which we had been temporarily sheltered.

I pulled two-hour guard duty one night, midnight to 0200, in an area overshadowed by a huge defense bunker. I walked alone watching spasmodic bursts of anti-aircraft fire illuminating the night sky. To escape a cold, drizzling rain, I wondered about entering the bunker for shelter and rest. But the thought of joining four dead, grenade-killed Germans inside in the dark deterred me. I stayed outside and walked my post, feeling totally alone.

Orders came to rejoin Anti-Tank Company for another territorial move. I was starting to accept the middle-of-the-night, nomadic lifestyle of the combat infantryman. It meant only more loss of sleep, more mud, less food, more cold, more work and worse living conditions. We pulled into another sea of mud in the town of Immendorf just before daybreak.

To understand the billeting procedure, I should first explain how German houses were usually disassembled by war. First, the doors and windows were blown out with bazookas and grenades to eliminate possible snipers. The roofs and floors usually burned their way into the cellar, with the remaining exterior walls collapsing outward onto yards and streets. All that normally remained of the houses after a battle were piles of rubble.

Soldiers seeking shelter either could clear debris away from a corner of the building and sleep against a wall, or they could try to get into a cellar and exist for a few hours by candlelight. Cellars were preferred because they offered shelter from the elements, but in the event of a lightning enemy counterattack, those living in cellars were most vulnerable for they could not evacuate the building as fast.

I used candlelight whenever possible for the effect it had on me, both psychologically and physically. Candles were wonderful for warming numbed hands and even feet, and they could partially dry out and warm up wet clothes. Candles could also warm up C-rations slightly but, most importantly, they offered a flickering flame of hope where often there was nothing but darkness and despair. Candles were excellent morale-builders. Candles had as many varied uses for the combat GI as his helmet, which was alternately used as a frying pan, shaving basin, toilet, pillow and even, sometimes, as head protection.

We were fortunate for in Immendorf I found a mostly intact billet consisting of three walls, a roof and cellar for my squad. I say fortunate, for according to Army plans, we were to spend a week there. As

Spartan as the living conditions were, it was a relief to be able to stay put in one location for more than a few minutes and figuratively catch our breaths.

The company kitchen was dispensing hot food with a new twist: pancakes and occasionally some bacon for breakfast. I quickly learned how to beg, steal or barter empty C-ration cans of pancake batter for butts, booze or candy with the company mess sergeant. This enabled me to make myself pancakes over an improvised portable stove as a midnight snack back at the billet. And, as luck would have it, the crowning touch was that my most recent Christmas package from home had contained a package of small maple sugar figures which I melted down and poured on my clandestine meals. Nothing ever tasted as good as those pancakes in the cold snows of the Roer River plains in early December 1944.

I don't remember whose idea it was, but about this time the mine-removal squad started meeting each night to read the Bible aloud. After each passage was read, squad members stopped and discussed it. We seemed to gain an inner strength, a peace of mind that pushed the war away for those few special minutes each night. The squad con-sisted of several Protestants, several Catholics and two Jews. None missed the nightly Scripture readings. Some even commented that per-haps our Bible studies might offer us some sort of special protection from above.

Immendorf was also the scene of one of my more grisly perfor-mances, one I am not particularly proud of. At a central crossroads in the town was one of its newly acquired landmarks, a burned out German "Panzerkampfwagon" (tank) with the burned remains of two dead soldiers propped upright inside. Both, either killed instantly or unable to escape, had been reduced to lumps of charred cinder when the tank had exploded and burned. Their heads were no more than two hunks of charcoal, their arms were burned off at the elbows, their legs at the knees.

Every day when I passed this landmark, I climbed inside and tried to kick the heads off what was left of the bodies. For a week, I kicked and jabbed at these two heads but they refused to separate from the torsos. Finally, in a fit of rage, I hacked them off with my bayonet.

Even in death, my uncontrollable hatred of the German forced me to vent it in barbaric ways. I felt compelled to mutilate and destroy. I was becoming inhuman and I wasn't even aware of the change in me.

One evening, I went into the courtyard to relieve myself. The night was clear, cold and silent. Suddenly, an anti-aircraft battery nearby opened up and I bolted through the pile of manure back to my billet. My buddies greeted me as if I were a skunk. The gun fire had unnerved me completely. Only then did I realize it was only some ack-ack firing at a marauding German observation plane. After everyone had a good laugh, I returned to the courtyard to watch the fireworks display quietly.

A platoon leader, a typical 90-day wonder, came by and asked for volunteers to accompany him on a reconnaissance patrol. Still not very wise to the ways of the Army, I volunteered. He said we would be reconnoitering in front of CHARLIE Company. I was to wear only a field jacket, wool cap and carry no weapons. We were to scout the area on an intelligence-gathering mission and not engage the enemy. If we were discovered, we were to try to escape rather than put up any resistance. Not too pleased about infiltrating unarmed behind German lines, I stuck a knife in my boot, a P-38 German pistol under my shirt and a D-ration chocolate bar in a jacket pocket. The lieutenant briefed me on the terrain we would cover and the password for the day. We would be back before dawn, he said.

We walked outside into a hard, cold rain. Ideal weather for such a mission, he claimed, for the Germans would not be expecting a patrol and perhaps, if we were lucky, German outpost sentries might even be seeking shelter somewhere from the elements. Often, our unorthodox methods of fighting caught the Germans off guard and I hoped this would be one of those times.

At the edge of town we started to crawl, and soon I was covered with mud, nature's own camouflage. I made my way through a break in a stone wall and over a hump in the ground. It was a German corpse. I recoiled, but after my heart stopped pounding and I settled down, I continued on. This was a filthy war. After a hundred yards or so, I was exhausted with mud down my back and thoroughly soaked by the rain when suddenly I heard a whispered challenge, "Orphan." "Annie," I responded quickly. It was a CHARLIE Company forward position. I told him I would be out in front of the lines for several hours and to pass the word along in case there were any trlgger-happy new replacements on the company line.

As I crawled, I instinctively felt before me for trip wires, mines or barbed wlre. I tried to orient myself with landmarks I had studied on the map at the briefing but I couldn't see anything. It dawned on me as I continued to crawl forward that I was lost, so I decided to abort the mission and crawl back to our lines. Every direction I probed seemed strange to me and I couldn't find any landmarks. Sensing a form before me, I hoped it was one of the buildings in Immendorf.

An American machine gun opened up in the distance but the echo distorted its direction. The form in front of me was a huge tree. I didn't remember any that large left standing back in Immendorf. I had been crawling deeper into German territory. I became aware of other forms and knew that I was in a wooded area where, I hoped, I could get some shelter from the rain. I crawled to the base of another tree before realizing the tree was a Kraut sentry towering above me only inches away, huddling from the weather.

Sizing up the situation quickly, I realized I couldn't go back and I couldn't move forward or around him without being discovered. There was only one alternative: to eliminate him silently. Slowly rising to my feet with P-38 in hand, I hit him as hard as I could at the base of his skull. He collapsed without a sound. Then I took my knife, rolled him over and drove it into his throat with a vicious twist. All I could hear in the rain was a soft gargling sound as I plunged the knife repeatedly up to the hilt into his chest. Stabbing him took all the strength I had in my arms.

I lay on the ground panting, my heart again pounding in fear. It was my first kill with a knife. I had been baptised with the sentry's blood all over my arm. I was near sheer panic, but had to find a way to get away from there as fast as I could.

"Wer ist da?" ("Who is there?"), a muted voice called out.

"Es ist nur mir" ("It is only me"), I answered in frightened desperation. "Ich muss pisse." ("I have to piss.")

"Sei ruhig," ("Be quiet"), the voice admonished.

In a rush, my breath came back for I had been holding it for what seemed like five minutes. My mind became twisted with terrified thoughts. Daylight was starting to come on and I remembered a dead GI I had seen who had been found by the Germans with a German pistol in his possession. They had rammed it down his throat and fired it, blowing the back of his neck off.

I didn't want to be captured with a P-38 but I hung onto it anyway. At least if I had to, I could give it a fight as long as the eight-round clip lasted. I knew my chances of making it back to my lines were slim and I forced myself to face my dilemma.

I crawled into a dried-up brook bed and waited, trying to figure a way out of my predicament. Bushes on both banks offered excellent cover that I hoped would buy me some time. Less than 150 feet away, I saw a German bivouac with men washing, shaving and cleaning their weapons. From their routine manner, it appeared they had not missed the sentry yet. I could see a tank, two 88mm guns, stockpiles of ammunition and supplies and a large group of soldiers digging in. They had slipped in during the night and apparently were planning to defend the area. This information was needed back in Immendorf, but I had no way to get there and no one to give it to.

By now it was daylight, and the early morning sun warmed me slightly and started drying my soaked uniform. About noon, I tried to break off pieces of my D-ration and soften them in my mouth without being seen but the brook bed was only about a foot deep.

As I watched the Germans, a commotion started and two of them came into the bivouac area carrying the dead sentry. I heard the word "Patrouille" (patrol). They were unaware the sentry's killer was still only a few feet away and, fortunately for me, they didn't bother to search.

At the sight of the dead sentry, a wave of nausea came over me. I quickly scratched out a hole in the gravel, placed my face in it and vomited up pieces of the D-ration I had been eating. They didn't hear me. I decided to wait until nightfall and again try to make it back to Immendorf.

At dusk, I chanced raising myself up—hopefully still hidden by the bushes—to search for Immendorf. As I did so, a rifle shot cracked near me. I slammed my face back into the gravel, angry that I had given my position away—but the shot was only a German soldier shooting at a rabbit for supper. With each call of nature, I could not move, not even roll over without being seen by the Germans, so each time I was forced to wet my pants, the price I was paying to stay alive.

I raised my head slightly, shooting quick glances around the countryside. Behind me to my left I could see rolls of defensive barbed wire, meaning the American lines had to be in that direction. I waited until it was pitch black and started crawling. My body ached all over from lying cramped in the ditch for so many hours. I crawled as far as I could on my stomach and then scrambled to a kneeling position. I wormed my way through the barbed wire and, thinking I was safe at last, stood up and started walking toward the town.

"Buck," a voice barked out.

I forgot, the password is changed every day. "Orphan Annie" was no longer the password of the day.

"Rogers," I gambled.

"Buck," the voice repeated, for the outpost had not heard my reply.

"Rogers," I yelled back. "I'm an American. I've been lost on patrol since yesterday. I don't know today's password. For Christ sakes, let me in."

"Buck," he yelled back for the third and last time before I knew he would start firing.

I dropped to the ground and yelled, "You dumb son-of-a-bitch, I'm an American."

"Advance and be recognized," the voice instructed.

I stood up and approached the outpost.

"What's your company?" he quizzed me.

"Anti-Tank."

"What's your company commander's name?"

"Captain John Bowen."

"Where ya from?"

"Worcester, Massachusetts."

'Where do the Red Sox play?"

"Fenway Park, Boston."

"OK. C'mon in," the sentry said, apparently satisfied.

"The password is 'Buckshot' not 'Buck Rogers,'" he told me.

I had guessed wrong, and had almost been shot because of it.

I had crawled back through DOG Company's line, about a quarter mile off course from where I had started the night before.

The lieutenant had returned without me, giving me up for dead or captured. When he saw me, he was excited to get any information I had. I felt good to have helped a little in the war effort, even though I knew the lieutenant would take full credit when the information was passed up to battalion.

Then I wolfed down some food and returned to my billet to change uniforms and sack out for a few hours, only to find all my gear missing. The squad, thinking I was dead, had divvied up all my possessions. Begrudgingly they returned everything, even my Christmas packages from home.

I was asked to show company officers on a map the coordinates of the German position. A few minutes later, the area was pounded by 105mm and 155mm howitzers. They must have hit the ammo supply, for we could see black smoke curling upward from the woods where the Germans were camped.

The boys in my squad made me some pancakes with bread, bacon and coffee and for a time treated me as someone special. It was an overwhelming relief to be back. Company command told me I had earned a pass back to Maastricht, Holland to rest from my ordeal. When I arrived there, after a short truck trip, I was given a shower, hot food, another fresh uniform and told my time was my own. I located a theater and treated myself to a movie. How strange it all seemed after the last few days. When I wrote home next, I casually mentioned I had been too busy to write.

Recreational passes have a strange way of being cut in half and rescinded. Almost as soon as I arrived in the Dutch city, I was ordered back to Immendorf. My reward for giving up half of my brief furlough was to pull guard duty at a forward position as soon as I arrived back.

As I tried to get comfortable in a foxhole that someone else had dug out of the frozen ground, my eyes strived to penetrate the night. Hearing a slight sound behind me, I whirled around and shoved my rifle right under the nose of General Bolling, 84th Division commander, who had crawled forward to check his troops. The star on his helmet didn't intimidate me, but the fact that I had almost shot him did.

He asked me how I felt, whether the food was good, how the officers were treating me and if I was homesick.

I answered, "Good," "Not too bad," "As well as can be expected," and "No," respectively to his questions. He patted me on the shoulder, smiled and disappeared again into the darkness.

I stared back into the night and, after about an hour, I noticed the sugar beets in the field before me were starting to move. I blinked and the movement stopped. Then as I stared at them some more, they started the movement all over again. I closed my eyes for a moment and when I opened them again, the beets were gone. Hallucinating had never happened to me before, and I felt silly. This was a malady usually experienced by green troops their first time on the line.

Almost motionless, I continued staring into the blackness. Suddenly, loud German cursing erupted right in front of me. Instinctively, I fired a whole M-1 clip at the voice, and other GIs along the line joined in. Gradually, the firing died out and it was quiet again.

In the morning, I found a dead Kraut about eight feet in front of my hole, his body riddled with bullets. While on patrol, he had stepped on a shovel and it had come up and hit him in the face, making him instinctively cry out in pain. The others with him had apparently managed to filter back into their own lines.

I took his Soldat Buch (soldier book) from him and kept his picture as a souvenir. Then I left him in peace. I collected many more such pictures in the following months and I still have them.

During a temporary lull in the fighting, I was called to the company CP and handed one of the all-too-familiar Army notification slips. Wondering what the brass had in store for me this time, I read that effective December 11, 1944 I had been awarded the Combat Infantryman Badge for "exemplary conduct in action against the enemy." It was the most coveted medal by fighting troops and I felt a sense of inner pride as I returned to my billet.

As I walked to chow one muddy day, I heard a tremendous explosion and saw a cloud of black smoke coming from a nearby field. A tank destroyer loaded with men had taken a shortcut through a hedgerow bordering the street and had run over a stack of discarded mines that had been cleared earlier from roadway traffic.

The sight stunned my eyes. The vehicle was burning furiously upside down and scattered around it were the remains of six dismembered GIs. The hedgerow was red with their blood, but the most sickening sight was a headless, armless, legless torso that had been thrown up in the air and was swinging to and fro, balanced on a temporary overhead telephone line. I turned away; I could take only so much gore.

Life in Immendorf was never quiet, for there were always the nuisance shellings by the Germans and occasional aerial strafings by Messerschmitt fighters. During one such episode, while reading the Bible one night, we all dove for the floor when we heard the roar of approaching planes. A .50-caliber bullet tore through the roof, shattering the shoulder of one squad member. He writhed in pain moaning on the floor until the medics evacuated him. The wound was severe enough to earn him a trip home and a discharge. The squad was now down to eight.

Rumors were rampant that German paratroopers in American uniforms were infiltrating the area, but nothing ever came of it.

On another night the stove in our billet, for some reason, blew up and ignited a wall. We grabbed our possessions and equipment and scrambled out of the building as what remained of it burned down. It didn't matter much to the squad because we had been told we were pulling out soon anyway. That proposed move, wherever it was to have been and for whatever purpose, was eliminated from General Bolling's plans in an instant by a turn of events with which we would soon be intensely aware.

The next evening, as I walked through the mud to the field kitchen for supper, frantic troop movements erupted all around me. The field kitchen was being hastily struck, officer and communications Jeeps were careening around company area streets every which way, men were clearing out their billets, drivers were heading for their trucks and tanks were jockeying for road positions trying to form a convoy.

"Moving out in 10 minutes," platoon sergeants started hollering. In what was undoubtedly the fastest troop movement we ever made during the whole war, we gathered up our gear and clambered onto a line of trucks and prepared for travel, again as always, to some unknown destination where we were needed. This one was no doubt something big, but we had no idea what. All we knew was we were on the move again with uncharacteristic urgency. When the trucks started rolling, I sensed from the winter sun disappearing through the trees on the horizon that we were headed south.

We knew other elements of the 84th had been able to overrun and occupy Lindern, Prummern, Linnich, Beeck, Wurm, Leiffarth, Mullendorf and Gereonsweiler, practically the whole area west of the Roer River. But the convoy didn't seem to be headed in that direction.

All we were told were bits and pieces of information indicating that 20 German divisions had broken through on a 60-mile front in the Ardennes Forest of Belgium three days earlier. And that if they succeeded in their push, the Allied forces could be thrown back to the English Channel. We were told that the 106th "Golden Lion" Division had been overrun with heavy losses during the German counteroffensive and its remnants had been pulled back 30 miles.

The pulverizing force of Field Marshal Karl von Rundstedt's spearhead had caused two of the division's regiments to practically no longer exist. The division had been so badly mauled, it had to be withdrawn from combat and reorganized. When the division regrouped, only 600 men remained to fight again. The others had been killed or captured. Battalions of new 75-ton King Tiger tanks were storming over the countryside pretty much at will, we were told.

It was Adolf Hitler's final desperate gamble to win the war—an all-out attack with every Panzer and infantry division he could muster. With this massive push through the defensively vulnerable Ardennes Forest, he had promised the German people his armies would be in Paris in three weeks.

The bulk of von Rundstedt's force was centered between Monschau and the northern tip of Luxemburg between Belgium and Germany. Our convoy commander eventually passed the word along that that's where we were going. None of us in the convoy truck were strategists but we all knew apprehensively that the 84th was about to participate in one of the most crucial battles of the European war.

The date was December 19, 1944 and it was obvious that minutes meant lives and hours possibly the battle. The convoy moved as rapidly as mud-slicked road conditions allowed. There were no rest breaks along the way, no delays of any kind. When men had to relieve themselves, they did it off the back end of the truck while trying to hang on at the same time. The scenery, with the last rays of daylight, told us we were back in Holland.

The convoy tempo never slackened as we chewed up kilometers steadily throughout the night. We all tried to huddle together as the cold in the back of the trucks worsened. Hours dragged on into more hours as Germany moved further behind us. Mostly, men sat silently contemplating what lay ahead for we had been told to keep noise to a minimum. Eventually, far into the night, the convoy slowed to a crawl as it continued to grind southward. Just before daylight, after 75 miles and about 10 hours on the road, the trucks stopped. In hushed tones, we were told to unload.

I wandered into the closest house I could see for shelter from the bitter cold. There I was greeted by a young, attractive dark-haired girl sitting in her kitchen by candlelight. She smiled a tired welcome and said, "Entre," a French word I had learned earlier. I asked her if she was "Francaise" and she answered, "Non. Belgique." We had arrived in the town of Haversin, she said. Like so many other villages and towns I had been in, I had never heard of it.

We were soon to learn what an important cog the 84th would become in the most crucial phase of the entire European campaign. The weeks to come would also prove to be perhaps the darkest interlude in the division's history, a time of untold suffering, staggering manpower losses and a period when the 84th's mettle would be tested. It would be a time of valor. A time of pain.

7

The Ardennes Salient

There was no fire in the house, but at least I was sheltered from the biting snow and cold mist. Using mostly sign language with the woman living there, I learned that the Germans, only hours before, had fought their way back into the area and were all around us. This news snapped me back to my senses fast. I took up a guard post outside with the jumpy feeling the enemy might appear at any moment out of the fog-enshrouded night.

It wasn't long before I heard in the distance the familiar sound of German tanks approaching the town. Moments later, a voice ran through the darkness yelling, "Load up! Everybody load up." We were hightailing it out without even a fight.

Haversin, we were told, was not considered militarily important enough to defend and the decision had been made to let the Germans have it uncontested.

Snow was falling quite heavily as the convoy lumbered along at a walking pace for two hours through what was fast becoming a zero-visibility blizzard. From the tailgate of the truck, I could see the convoy was inching its way along beside a fast-flowing river at the base of jagged mountains framing the winding road on both sides. Wind-driven snow squalls beat sharply against our eyes and soon visibility was restricted to only the two pinpoints of light peeking out at us from the blacked-out headlights of the convoy truck behind us.

The Germans, who were advancing almost unchallenged westward toward Liege and Brussels, had boasted they would be in Paris by New Year's. With the intensity Hitler's generals were pouring infantry and armored divisions into the the Ardennes Forest and the reports we were receiving of massive breakthroughs all along the front, the boast was becoming a more distinct possibility every hour.

As the truck column continued cautiously forward, my thoughts turned to the convoy truck drivers. They had been in unheated cabs for more than 14 hours, navigating with taped over headlights on narrow, unfamiliar, German-infested, slippery roads teetering inches away from sheer ravines. And all the while knowing that around the next bend in the road could be a German tank waiting for them. They were surely some of the unsung heroes of the whole campaign to beat back Hitler's troops. Our lives, and the success or failure of what had already become the bitter struggle for Belgium, truly rested in their hands.

About 0400, December 20th, the convoy halted again and we were told furtively in hushed tones to get out and bed down in a nearby barn. Having been without sleep for 23 hours, I didn't argue. I found a hayloft and before my head hit the hay, I was asleep.

I don't know how long it was, but I was awakened by a strange weight pushing down on my chest. Raising myself slightly, I found a chicken had roosted during the night near my chin. My sudden move startled it and it flew away with a scolding cackle. Hunger was welling up inside me for I had not eaten since the noon before and my candy supply from home had been depleted by the many missed meals prior to the desperate troop movement south away from the Siegfried Line.

At a farmhouse beside the barn, an elderly couple and their two grown daughters, with some sign language, offered me a complete breakfast of ham and eggs with fresh, cold milk, the first I had had since England. The family seemed oblivious to the impending danger and I couldn't tell whether they knew the Germans were coming back or just didn't care. I thanked the family the only way I knew, with a simple "Merci" and a pack of cigarettes.

They told me we were in the village of Heure.

At a platoon briefing, we were informed the Germans were believed to have the village surrounded and that an attack could come from any direction at any time. Our job, we were told, was to slow the German push to the sea at all costs any way we could. To guard against the possibility of a surprise Tiger tank assault, the mine-removal squad prepared several "daisy chains," ropes with anti-tank mines tied every two feet, at all strategic roads leading in and out of the village wide enough to accommodate Hitler's vaunted mechanized juggernauts.

As we did this, company officers were also planning contingency retreat routes if we were unable to repulse a full-scale German attack. Better to fall back and fight another day than to be captured and lost for the duration was the unwritten judgment. But these routes were to be used only as a last resort; our orders were to hold no matter what. If the Germans hit us in great strength, out chances were slim—we were few against many, and we knew it.

Those of us in the daisy chain detail took our position in ditches beside the roads and waited as the heavy snowfall tried to bury us. If the Tigers came, the chains would be pulled in front of the lead tank at the last possible moment. At the same time, another chain would be pulled behind the tank, boxing it in. If the mines didn't damage or destroy the tank, a bazooka team lurking nearby would try. The tactic then would be for the daisy chain teams to "shag ass" as fast as they could before the tank machine gunners could zero in on them.

Snow, nature's camouflage, blanketed the pine boughs we hastily cut to cover us as we huddled in the ditch. It provided us almost undetectable concealment. As we shivered in the blackness from cold, and perhaps fear, the sounds of small arms fire and the "harrruuummmpp" of artillery everywhere around us in the forest, we knew the wait wouldn't be long. The breath-holding agony stretched into hours as our eyes strained to penetrate the forest mist around us. But as the fearsome blackness gradually turned to the gray of dawn, the dreaded German tanks never materialized. Almost without notice, the cacophony of war had quieted down during our vigil and the forest was once again still.

Perhaps, as the American Army had concluded in Haversin, the Germans figured Heure wasn't strategically worth fighting for. Combat continued to offer isolated instances of unexplained fateful luck to both sides. The next night, we moved out again under cover of darkness as the snow persisted and the temperature dropped below zero, producing conditions we would have to contend with the whole time we were in Belgium. The column halted in a large city where we were dropped off in front of a school and told to get some sleep for we would probably need it later.

From a bronze plaque in the school corridor, I learned we were in Marche, Belgium. As I read the inscription, I had no way of knowing the significant role Marche would ultimately play in the outcome of the war in Europe.

No sooner had I closed my eyes, lying atop two tables pushed together in one of the classrooms, when I was told I had guard duty outside. After some customary Army bitching, I stumbled out to the street and ambled over to where I was told my guard post was.

But if I had to give up my sleep this way, at least I could try to make myself comfortable. To shelter myself from the falling snow, I stood under an arbor spanning a frozen brook and from there I could see in every direction, at least as far as the constantly falling snow allowed. I paced my post back and forth, just fast enough to keep from becoming frozen to the ground, all the while hoping the exertion would keep my circulation pumping to warm me. Dragging my feet from exhaustion, I shuffled past a door at the rear of the school building and decided to check it out. As I swung it open, a bright light blinded me. Being so used to blackout conditions, I instinctively slammed the door shut. A moment later, I laughed to myself—the blinding light had only been an electric light bulb in the school boiler room. I couldn't believe I had become unaccustomed to electric light in such a short time.

The boiler room was so toasty warm, I was seduced into goofing off for a few minutes. I pulled up a wooden crate, leaned back against a wall, took a half-frozen D-ration from my coat and started thinking about home. My eyelids drooped. Almost instantly, I was lulled to sleep.

Without warning, my eyes flew open as the sound of a burst of machine-gun fire rattled throughout my snug hideaway. My heart was racing—I couldn't tell where it had come from and I had left a whole platoon unguarded and unprotected. I jumped back outside and, crouching almost to the ice-slicked ground, crept around the building, M-1 at the hip, trying to adjust my eyes to the blackness while searching for the machine gunner. I found no one; everything appeared to be all quiet outside. Apparently, the firing I had heard had only been an echo. Needless to say, I didn't fall asleep again that night. I had involuntarily been reproached by a distant German machine gunner who had shown me he had more battle savvy than I did.

Day and night, the roads leading west from the town were clogged solid with refugees carrying their worldly possessions on their backs, in baby carriages or in wagons dragged through the snow, usually by the strongest family member. Despite our reassurances that American troops were there to stay and that the Germans would not reoccupy the city, the people were evacuating in droves. Having lived under German military domination and cruelty for four years, the people reflected no confidence in our ability to overwhelm their former oppressors. Their opinions were recited in the defeated, matter-of-fact tones of those who have endured too much for too long.

The cold silence of night was again broken by the familiar sound of German panzers. I ran from room to room, rousing the others in the platoon. GIs throughout the sector, also having heard the tanks, were taking hasty positions. Batteries of 57mm anti-tank guns—scant protection against the awesome Tiger—had been placed in strategic locations when we first arrived in the city. As bazooka teams raced to their predetermined positions at intersections, rifle squads tried to dig in to establish a firefight line to support them.

Orders, direct from General Bolling we were told, swept from foxhole to machine gun emplacement to artillery battery. Marche was to be as far as the Germans advanced toward Paris—the end of the line. We were ordered to blunt their forward progress and stop them there at all costs. As in the war movies, there would be no retreat. It was to be a fight-to-the-last-man affair.

I grabbed some explosive primer cord, several pounds of nitro-starch, my M-1 rifle and P-38 and several grenades before scratching, slipping and clawing my way up a steep, ice-encrusted hill behind the school. I figured the high ground was strategically the best place to be, even though there had been no orders issued or detailed battle plan given. It was, as so often the case in Belgium, every man for himself, each an army unto himself.

I joined a bazooka team already dug in at the crest of the hill where we could see in every direction. It was a perfect position with a commanding view of the main road as it snaked its way into the city from the east.

With only a few minutes to secure our position, the bazooka team ammo carrier and I also scouted an alternate position to which we could fall back and which could be used in the event we were overrun.

Then we waited, fidgeting in the snow nervously as the roar of tanks grew louder. In the distance, we could hear the intermittent chattering of slow-firing American machine guns answered by the belching sounds of German Schmeisser burp guns.

As the nerve-taut wait continued, our eyes gradually became accustomed to the first glimmer of daylight. We saw that our hill was cradled by rugged mountains on all sides and our position was in a deep ravine-like valley. The approaching tanks could enter the city only by a narrow, winding road below us and that factor, we knew, would weigh heavily in our favor. The monstrous German armament would be unable to maneuver, just come at us head-on.

The German offensive had already crushed its way 40 miles westward and the Allied front, which only days before had been steamrolling its way practically unimpeded eastward with devastating strength, was now punctured, bent, shaken. It was imperative that Hitler's forces be stopped at Marche for if they penetrated our position further, the entire Allied position would be jeopardized and in danger of collapse

German SS troops, heavily fortified by seasoned armored divisions, had attacked in full force for 12 days. It wouldn't be until January 3 that American and British forces could regroup, be reinforced and mount anything resembling a counteroffensive.

With daylight, the fog started to lift and word was passed along the line we would be facing elements of the 2nd and 116th Panzer Divisions—both with reputations as crack outfits in German Field Marshal Karl von Runstedt's arsenal. The 84th Infantry, we were told, was totally isolated and the impending battle would be, for the most part, bitter, personal and unsupported. If the uniform was gray, you shot at it, if it was brown you didn't. That was all we had to know. We were not offered the luxury of backup units; there were none. Cooks, mess sergeants, company clerks, truck drivers, supply personnel—everyone who could walk had been issued weapons and pressed into the line.

So weak were our defensive positions that, in many reported cases, for the first 10 days of the German offensive, American foxholes were spaced 50 yards apart as American divisions occupied positions with severely decimated forces. As a result, German patrols penetrated our lines pretty much at will.

Northeast of us, an entire division had reportedly been captured almost intact by the Germans during the first few days of the Nazis' explosion out of Germany. From the south we heard rumors that American troops and headquarters were fleeing hell-bent for the rear. Top divisional officers were calling the upcoming battle at Marche the potential turning point of the whole war in the European Theater of Operations.

Most of the American units in the Ardennes had been severely depleted by combat losses and by those who had been cut off and captured during the two-week-long confusion at the outset of the breakthrough. To survive the hit-and-run battles that were being fought over much of Belgium, American forces constantly changed positions and regrouped until some semblance of collective military reorganization was restored. It was during this stage of the campaign that the battle for Marche was unfolding.

The approaching tanks rumbling toward us through the snow-blanketed evergreen forests below were a prelude to some of the fiercest hand-to-hand combat we had experienced since jumping off from Marianburg four weeks before.

"Here they come," one of the bazookamen yelled as we counted more than a dozen tanks and half-tracked armored vehicles appearing around a curve in the road less than half a mile away. Thin threads of German infantry trudged along behind, properly spread out to minimize artillery losses.

At the same time, a squad of SS troops in frontal attack formation appeared through the snow drifts to our rear, firing as they came.

"They're behind us!" someone screamed. We had been outflanked. The German infantry was about to overrun our position on the crest of the hill. Caught by surprise, we opened up with a withering fire as the Germans broke ranks at a dead run toward our position. Their sheer numbers overpowered our position as both sides tangled with bayonets, knives, pistols and bare hands. If fear can overwhelm memory this was one of those moments. I know I fired and I also knew I couldn't use my grenades because both sides were intermixed. In less than a minute, the blur of violence was over and half of the Germans who came up the hill were scrambling back down, leaving six comrades behind along with three GIs sprawled grotesquely around our position. I must have picked a good group to fall in with. Physically and psychologically drained, we all fell to the ground, buried our faces in our arms and tried to lick our wounds and resume breathing again.

The woods around our position was littered with SS and American dead. We had held our position but there had been no winners, and the next action, if there was one, would be by graves registration.

Confident that the foot troops would not hit us again, at least not for awhile, we turned our attention to the tank column approaching the city below us. German troops stretched as far as we could see in the first gray light of morning. Anti-tank guns and bazooka teams were firing as fast as they could reload while support riflemen were cutting the Germans to pieces. But still they came, with almost unnerving determination. Half of the estimated 100 attacking infantrymen were outfitted in white camouflaged ski suits. These, we learned afterward while searching the dead for unit identifications, were SS troopers, the most bestial element of the German Army.

Not realizing how heavily defended Marche was, the panzers were not in battle formation, but were instead entering the city single file. As a result, they were sitting duck targets for our bazooka teams.

A German half-track at the rear of the column exploded in a blinding flash and black smoke started curling up through the forest. Belching orange flames could be seen through the towering pine trees. With the last vehicle knocked out and blocking any withdrawal route, the armored column could only move forward directly into the sights of our guns. Several of the standing tanks started arcing their turret 88s defiantly back and forth, seeking out those who had destroyed the armored vehicle.

The bazooka team on the hill beside me fired at the lead tank below us and its tread unraveled from its bogie wheels. Its menacing 88mm cannon pointed at us and fired. The shell slammed into the ground about 30 feet below us and the blast blew my helmet off, rolling it down the snow embankment. A helmeted kraut head appeared in the tank turret and pointed toward our position. We had been spotted. I fired several rapid shots at him and he slumped forward, jackknifed dead over the turret hatch rim.

He disappeared in a flash of flame and smoke a moment later when the bazooka team fired off another round, this one hitting the turret dead center and tearing a hole in it. Another German tankman tried to squeeze out of the hatch to escape, but he was cut down by rifle fire from below us. I crawled down the hill to within 20 feet of the disable tank and threw a grenade against the rear engine grillwork. At that moment, the tank exploded in a ball of fire, probably not as a result of my lobbed grenade. There were no survivors. My rushing the already burning and about to blow up tank with a fragmentation grenade was a totally irrational action, perhaps even irresponsible. I can only explain that I had grossly endangered myself due to the incoherent rage of battle. It had been my first direct involvement with a German tank, the most feared adversary faced by infantrymen in combat. A GI feels completely vulnerable against 50 tons of roaring armor spewing death in all directions from an arsenal of cannon and machine guns.

I crawled back up the hill only to face the biggest damn screaming, camouflaged SS trooper I would ever see running at me. Behind him were more SS troops, also yelling shrilly and almost on top of us. I fired my M-1 from the hip without even taking time to aim. Those who remained at the hilltop bazooka position were pouring rifle and pistol fire into the attacking German formation as fast as they could reload their weapons. The closest German trooper grabbed at his stomach and skidded face first toward me in the snow, his burp gun landing a few feet away. Since my M-1 was empty and there was no time to ram another clip home, I threw three quick fragmentation grenades blindly at the yelling Germans.

Then I ran, tumbling over and over down the hill behind the school. I landed in a heap near a line of GI foxholes. The bazooka team, unequipped to fight foot troops, had already hightailed it off the hill.

The snow was crimson with American and German blood. Most of the mechanized column had been destroyed and several dozen SS troopers had been cut down. The colors of the uniforms and the shape of the steel helmets, testified to the overwhelmingly lopsided losses: four wounded or dead Germans to each GI. Medics scrambled about tending to the American wounded. Here and there, clusters of GIs bent over their buddies offering whatever comfort or first aid they could while waiting for medics to get to them.

As they worked, I crouched in a ditch beside the road, fascinated, as exploding ammunition in one tank offered a violent pyrotechnic barrage. In one of the many paradoxes of war, I glanced behind one of the furiously burning armored vehicles and saw a GI tending to a wounded German.

Bone weary and sore all over, I climbed back up the hill to relieve the trooper who had charged at me of his Soldat Buch and pistol. I also "liberated" a small broach with three gold-colored stones which I later sent home to my mother. As far as I know, she never figured out how I had acquired it. Around me, other GIs were busy lifting souvenirs from German corpses.

After repeated tentative probing attempts to enter the city, the SS troops, fighting without the advantage of armored cover, finally pulled back and decided to bypass Marche in search of a weaker point in the American defenses. The 84th had held firm, withstood the best that von Rundstedt could throw against it, and was now lashing back with whatever resources and manpower remained.

Some weeks later, I read in *Stars & Stripes* that the 84th Division had keen credited with stopping Hitler's salient westward at Marche. Unable to advance further in that area, German commanders had split their forces, some circling north around us, the rest south in a pincer-like maneuver trying to outflank and entrap American forces. This made it possible for American troops to methodically dissect these weakened pincers and isolate much of the German strength into small pockets that, when eventually eliminated, produced thousands of prisoners and seriously weakened Hitler's military strength in Belgium.

It was about this time the 84th was awarded another badge of honor of sorts, one that inflated our exhausted egos and enhanced our divisional pride. Interrogated German prisoners revealed that we were referred to by German soldiers facing us as "The Hatchetmen"—no doubt because of our "Railsplitter" insignia—and "The Terror Division." I kind of liked that latter description because it made us sound fierce.

We were given a couple days to rest and regroup our forces, but we all knew our "break" would be short-lived. It would be only a matter of time until we would be needed elsewhere. The Germans were still in control of the campaign and occupied practically all of southern Belgium. The Battle of the Bulge was far from over. In fact, as far as we were concerned, it was just beginning.

Remarkably, considering the fierce struggle raging between the two immense armies around them, the Belgian people managed to adhere to their normal routine. Stores and markets remained open as shoppers walked the streets. I swapped another pack of cigarettes for a loaf of hot, fresh Belgian bread and a bottle of port wine, which I was told would warm my feet during those bitter Belgian nights.

The quality of the bread was poor but it was a vast improvement over C- or K-rations. As I had done back in Laon, France, I devoured the whole loaf by myself, only this time, I went back to the bakery and got another loaf for "Joe Loot" Everett.

In the midst of all the last-ditch combat defending the city of Marche, we were told by company officers of a pleasant Christmas surprise opportunity. For $10, we could wire flowers home for the holiday. As I learned afterward, the telegram and flowers had frightened my mother to tears; she thought they were notification of my death.

After reinforcement troops arrived to occupy Marche, we prepared to move out again. Meticulously trained German paratroopers, dressed in American uniforms and speaking perfect English, were infiltrating our lines all along the front to sabotage our efforts and assassinate our high-ranking officers They carried dogtags and IDs taken from prisoners or our battlefield dead. The German "Werewolf" plan, as troublesome as it was before we were able to get a handle on it, failed dismally because of American diligence and ingenuity once the plan was discovered. But it was, I must say, a strange feeling to be stopped and interrogated by our own MPs everywhere we went They often threw baseball questions at me and I sometimes had a difficult time verifying. I was an American but I wasn't much of a baseball fan.

The convoy hesitatingly explored its way along a planned route throughout the night. At dawn, we were informed the vehicles couldn't be risked any further in the daylight and we would have to hoof it the rest of the way to another undisclosed destination. After being sorely cramped and frozen numb on the wooden benches in the truck, it felt good to stretch our legs and try and get some circulation going again.

Under combat conditions, GIs could carry whatever gear they wanted. Accepting the fact there were only two kinds of combat infantrymen—the quick and the dead—I always traveled light for speed when conditions allowed. I usually carried a helmet, rifle, cartridge belt with first-aid kit, trench knife, canteen, pistol, two grenades and as many candy bars from home as I could cram into my pockets. Blankets, shovels, mess gear, extra ammo, field rations and raincoats could always be stripped off American dead as the need arose.

In severe winter weather, I added a sleeping bag, extra blankets, an overcoat, scarf, mittens, overshoes and as many pairs of dry socks as I could lay my hands on. Like most other GIs, I often took boots and especially overshoes off American dead. Combat is a time to be realistic; dead GIs no longer had need of clothing and gear. Conditions during the Bulge had reduced most of us to insensitive, unfeeling, basic survival instincts.

The convoy passed a road sign, "Hotton, 1 km." From a map, I found Hotton on the Ourthe river about six miles northeast of Marche. Small-arms fire and occasional exploding artillery shells could be heard and "outgoing mail" over our heads indicated the town had still not been taken. Another unfamiliar town, but having the distinction of being one I would never forget.

We crossed some railroad tracks and an arched concrete bridge spanning a narrow river that divided the town. Scarcely a building had been left intact. As we passed a burning Sherman tank, I reached up and grabbed a Thompson .45 caliber submachine gun from the dangling arm of a dead tanker. I carried it for several weeks before finally discarding it because of its weight and the unavailability of .45 caliber ammunition.

FOX Company had faced seven Mark V Panther tanks, a half-track and 20 German infantry in the small river community. Before it was over, four of the tanks had been destroyed and the infantry routed. The carnage of the struggle covered practically every street. There were body-draped, smouldering tanks, bullet-riddled overturned jeeps and wagons, horse carcasses, grotesque brown- and green-uniformed corpses covering streets and clogging doorways everywhere. Dozens of furiously burning buildings were devouring what remained of the town. The intensity of the fighting only hours before was total.

In the Army, certain matters come under the heading of first things first: a place to bed down and food to eat. I found a house that appeared to be more intact than the others and inside I found two dead Krauts. I dragged them out onto the muddy, snow-slicked street, relieving one of his helmet to eventually be mailed home as a souvenir.

GIs from the Graves Registration unit were busy throughout the town removing American dead. I counted four German and two American tanks destroyed.

Exhausted from the march, I sat down against a building along the river's edge and let the sun warm my face. Without warning, beset by depression and frustration, tears started to flow down my cheeks. I buried my head on my knees and quietly cried for my mother. Combat was a constant roller coaster of adrenaline-pumping highs and soul-searing depressions.

My thoughts poured one over another of how I had made an accounting of myself the past few weeks. I had slain Germans, helped destroy a tank, taken prisoners and gained vital military information. I admitted to myself that this all came about due to my penchant for getting lost at the right time and volunteering for details at the wrong time. To me, killing had almost become a thrilling sport—but I tried not to dwell on what that was doing to me as a human being. As an apparent mental defense mechanism, I had learned to cast such disagreeable thoughts out of my mind.

As I rested, I hoped the temporary lifting of the fog and the improvement in the nearly impossible weather would allow Allied planes to fly again. They had been grounded in England since the outset of the German breakthrough. The military advantage wouldn't be ours until our planes again ruled the skies.

Another close call in my military life was about to occur. A new replacement shavetail lieutenant, fresh from the States, wandered past me looking at the destruction around us and sniffed, "Hm. Fort Benning was worse than this." Enraged after what I had endured, and the losses we had sustained, I jumped up and lunged at him. A nearby GI tackled me before I could destroy myself by attacking this moronic officer. The lieutenant glared at me but let the near-incident pass without retaliation.

Through the grapevine, I heard later that Captain Bowen had heard about what had nearly transpired and had privately admonished the opinionated officer to keep his mouth shut until he found out what war was all about. I felt somewhat vindicated. The consequences of my actions could have been severe.

Exploring a wooded area at one end of the town, I discovered six German tanks lined up in a row, with no outward signs of damage. Crawling inside the first tank and fidgeting with the controls, I located the starter button but got no response from the motor. Through a freakish coincidence of war, the tanks had all run out of gas simultaneously as they reached the outer edge of town.

Had this not happened before they could reinforce the other seven attacking panzers, the outcome of the struggle for Hotton probably would have been different. Simple logistics. While the German was moving forward, his supply lines were being stretched beyond their limits while ours were being shortened as we fell backwards.

I joined a lieutenant from the Corps of Engineers and we planted TNT in each 88mm gun barrel, blowing them up and rendering them useless. It was fun and quite exciting as we then blew up the motors and turrets with additional charges. If the Germans ever retook the town—and that distinct threat existed every day we remained there—the six tanks would not be part of their reclaimed booty.

Realizing I had not eaten for some time, I left the demolition project and headed back to my billet to break open a K-ration. As I walked, I heard a muted wwhhuummpp overhead and looked up. A crippled B-17 Flying Fortress had exploded and six parachutes trailed down behind the lazily-disintegrating aircraft. I watched in silent fascination as parts of the plane plummeted to earth over my head. Almost hypnotized, I didn't know whether to run for safety or stand fast. The major bulk of the plane's fuselage landed about 200 yards away with an earth-trembling crash and started to burn. The tail section separated and fell swishing back and forth into woods thought to be occupied by the Germans, while a wing landed about a half-mile from the town.

Some of the chutes seemed to be coming down in American territory, close enough, it seemed, that we might be able to find them. I ran to the billet to enlist Joe Everett's help. Grabbing our rifles and some grenades, we were ready for Operation Rescue.

We legged it to a sawmill at the edge of town and then slowed down to a cautious walk, entering the woods using dead reckoning as an azimuth. Having no idea where the German lines were, we split up, walking about 50 feet apart through the dense forest to reduce the possibility of capture. I followed a narrow, cleared path leading up a hill while Everett crashed his way through the pines and plowed phys-ically through waist-deep snowdrifts.

We walked close to a mile up what might be considered a small mountain, crouching low, scrutinizing every tree, every bush for signs of movement. I followed a sharp turn into a gulley and paused as my sixth sense that had saved me so many times before warned me again. I froze against a tree and listened. I had a premonition of danger, that someone was out there. All I could hear was Everett, now almost 100 feet above me on the hill, bulling his way noisily through the under-brush.

I swung my rifle around at a voice that said softly from some bush-es, "Man, am I glad to see you." One of the aviators from the downed B-17 had spotted me first. I had sensed someone's presence but had not seen him wrapped in rolls of his parachute for warmth and cam-ouflage. He was a master sergeant radio man on the crippled Fortress and his face had been chewed up by the trees through which he had fallen. Fortunately, he had had enough presence of mind to crawl into the bushes to hide and wait.

I called to Everett, who by now had gotten far ahead of me, and he backtracked, all smiles. "Man, all the way down all I could think about was Kraut concentration camps," grinned the Air Corps sergeant lying in the snow. I dressed his wounds, gave him a candy bar and some water from my canteen. The chocolate bar seemed like an equitable way to repay the courtesies I had been shown at the air base back in England.

He told me his plane had been on a bombing raid over southern Germany when flak had made a sieve of the plane and had torn off two of its four engines. The fortress had been forced to fall back out of formation and, in doing so, had been at the mercy of swarms of German Messerschmitt 109s. When a third engine caught fire, the crew was ordered to bail out while the pilot and co-pilot remained at the controls, trying to reach American lines. Minutes later, the plane had exploded. This all happened at such an extreme altitude, I had not even heard the aerial dogfight before the bomber exploded.

After a short discussion, Everett took the sergeant back to Hotton while I continued to search for other Air Corps chutists who might have landed in the same vicinity.

Following the direction the sergeant had pointed me in, I worked my way deeper into the forest looking for other survivors. The snow drifts got deeper and the hills became steeper. Then I saw him. He was lying rolled up in his parachute in a small a clearing with a .45 caliber automatic in his hand.

I softly called to him but, without first looking, he answered by snapping off a shot at me. I dove into the snow, yelling "Take it easy you dumb, trigger-happy son-of-a-bitch. I'm an American. I've been searching for you."

After profuse apologies, he said he thought he had fallen behind German lines. I was fortunate the Air Corps had never taught its second lieutenant navigators how to handle weapons or shoot accurately. As I walked toward him, I could see he was in considerable pain. I checked him over and found he had a severe compound fracture of one ankle that was bleeding profusely. I gave him a shot of morphine from my first-aid kit and applied a make-shift splint from a small tree sapling and torn strips from his parachute. During all his painful ordeal, he didn't utter a sound of complaint.

The Germans, I knew, must have heard the pistol shot and I was eager to get back to the safety of the town. Half-lifting, half-carrying, I helped him hobble back down the mountainside. On the steep slopes I laid him on his back, grabbed him by the scruff of his neck and dragged him toboggan-style over the drifts. He still never uttered a pain-induced sound. The morphine had taken effect and my little "fly boy louie" was "morphed to the gills."

The physically taxing trip, about a mile but fortunately all downhill, took nearly two hours before we finally made it back to the warmth of the company aid station. Everett, who in the meantime had started back into the forest to look for me, met us at the outskirts of the town where we had stopped to rest. Seeing the lieutenant's bloody and broken leg, he ran ahead to get help from the company's medics. Within minutes, they arrived and carried the airman into town on a litter. When I arrived back at my billet, I sat and started to laugh.

"What's so funny?" Everett asked.

"Nothing," I answered. But then I explained.

The lieutenant I had rescued had been dressed in full uniform, complete with combat ribbons, 50-mission crushed officer's cap and shined brown oxfords. He could have been an advertisement for best dressed man of the year.

Then I looked around the room at my squad dressed in smelly, mud-covered, baggy uniforms that hadn't been changed in weeks, bloodshot eyes from lack of sleep, scraggly bearded faces creased by fear, exhaustion and hunger. "What were we walking advertisements for, death?" I said out loud. The question set off a round of laughter."

The Air Corps radio man, after being treated for his injuries, remained with us about two weeks to fight on the ground where he could actually see the enemy rather than impersonally bomb him from 30,000 feet. He took part in several skirmishes with German infantry, and during that time grew a beard and become just another "mud belly GI." Eventually, the Air Corps caught up with him and he was returned by the MPs to his squadron back in England for punishment. But what stories he would have to remember and tell.

Someone in the squad piped up, "Hey, guess what I found out today? Field Marshal (Bernard) Montgomery was billeted in this very room a couple weeks ago." I supposed that even the brass had to rough it once in awhile.

As we talked, the distant roar of a buzz bomb interrupted our conversation. I stood in the doorway watching it. With my youthful interest in aviation, I was fascinated by this new 25-foot-long Flash Gordon-type missile thundering overhead. Its stubby, 16-foot wingspan made it appear almost awkward, surely not aerodynamically correct. But, at the time, I knew nothing about jet propulsion. As far as I knew, the United States had not been able to develop anything like it as a potential weapon.

When its engine quit overhead, the silence was unnerving. "It's coming down here!" someone hollered. "It's falling short!"

As it tailspun to earth, we scrambled down a flight of cellar stairs. Nervously we counted the seconds ticking away until we heard the 2,000 pounds of explosives detonate and felt the earth shudder. The house shook violently and plaster cascaded onto us. We dusted ourselves off and ran upstairs to see where it had landed and how much damage it had done.

It had slammed into the earth about a half-mile away at an artillery battery, leaving a crater large enough to accommodate a small house. It had also ended the war violently and instantly for 18 American soldiers, we were told, and had destroyed three 105mm howitzers. Eighteen more telegrams would be sent to mothers or wives back in the States. The V-1 rockets, like land mines, were unpredictable and you grew to hate them more every time you saw them kill. Called "buzz bombs," "whizbangs," or "doodlebugs" by the British, many had been shot down by the Royal Air Force over the English Channel before they reached the island.

One day, walking along the street in Hotton, I was greeted by a recruit soldier I had trained as a cadreman at Fort McClellan. He had joined the 84th that day from a "repple depple," a replacement depot, and he said another of my trainees had also been assigned to KING Company. I promised to visit them when I had time.

The next day, I located the company on the other side of town. When I asked about the new replacement by name, no one had heard of him. I questioned the company first sergeant who said only, "So that's what his name was." For a moment, I didn't get the implication.

"He was killed last night by artillery," he told me simply. He hadn't even seen combat and, in fact, his name hadn't yet been entered on the company duty roster. I returned slowly back to my company area and sat under a tree, my head on my folded arms in a moment of quiet reflection. I became depressed from frustration at the total waste of war, especially for this man whose face I hadn't even remembered.

I pondered whether he had been given his pre-combat indoctrination by a combat-wise noncom to whom he would be assigned. If so, he was probably counseled not to fear dying but not to taunt death either. Replacements were instructed what to watch and listen for in a firefight and cautioned not to forge close friendships. They were usually told that the first day in combat was no worse than any other day, that eventually all become the same.

It is a truism in war: artillery fire respects no one. You age quickly into manhood when the first shots are fired.

8

The Battle of the Bulge

One thing about a combat infantryman is that he soon develops an intuition, a sixth sense, a talent for premonition. It had become evident even to the lowly GI huddled in the foxhole during the punishing December nights that the tide of battle had shifted. The Americans were no longer back on their heels and further German attacks would carry the mark of desperation. For two days, I had been uneasy about something I couldn't put my finger on—and time proved me right again. The lieutenant came to our quarters and told us the Germans were planning a massive tank assault in EASY Company's sector and we were needed to lay a defensive mine field of more than 1,000 anti-tank and anti-personnel mines in front of the company lines.

Biding our time, we waited for darkness for we knew the area where we would be working was under direct German surveillance. Forming a human chain at the rear of the supply truck delivering the explosives to us, we started sewing a systematic pattern of alternating anti-tank and anti-personnel mines. The plan was for one line of mines to cripple approaching tanks, we hoped, and the next line to slow down the accompanying German infantry, allowing EASY company bazooka teams, riflemen and machine gunners to take their toll.

As we planted each mine in position, we could actually hear German voices being telephoned by the calm, bitter cold night. Apparently, even in the well-disciplined German Army there were those who were careless about giving away their position with their chatter. This prompted us to be even more stealthy as, one by one, the mines were buried in the snow.

"Incoming," someone whispered under his breath. We hit the ground but there was no cover anywhere on the exposed, snow-covered field. As soon as I heard it, I knew it was the one with my name on it. My heart didn't even have time to stop before the 88 shell hit practically on top of me.

When I came to, members of the squad were bending over me and reassuring me I was alive. The shelling had stopped but I could not stand up for dizziness. I had been unconscious, they told me, for quite awhile and it was later determined at the aid station that I had suffered a concussion but no shrapnel wounds.

The shell, exploding only a few feet away from me, had thrown up a basketball-size chunk of frozen earth that had hit me on the head. My cheek had been gouged out and blood was running down my neck from a cut jaw. I was not wounded, only injured. There would be no Purple Heart this time. I was taken to a nearby ambulance where I rested until my head cleared somewhat. During the night, 1,147 mines were put down by the members of our squad. EASY Company would be able to rest easier that night.

From the ambulance, I could see anti-tank guns and bazooka teams digging in to offer deeper defense for the rifle company. Even in the silence of the night, I could also see reinforcement companies moving in silently under cover of darkness. I didn't really care which companies they were, for my head still hurt badly and my ears still gave off strange tingling sounds. But although still dazed and unsure of my reactions, I was reassured that when the Germans mounted their offensive and finally came at us, we'd have a big a surprise waiting for them.

By dawn, we were fully prepared and waiting, all eyes on the woods in front of EASY Company and all ears cocked for any telltale sounds that signified Germans. We could not move because, again, we knew we were being watched. By keeping low in our foxholes and by keeping the tank companies hidden in the woods to our rear, everything had to give off the appearance of an empty position. We broke open K-rations for breakfast and the waiting continued. Trapped in a foxhole, when a man had to defecate, he did it in his K-ration box and threw it over the side; when he had to urinate, he did it in a C-ration can or his helmet or in the bottom of his hole. Conditions were primitive and you learned quickly to improvise.

The morning wore on slowly and our necks, bent below the rims of our holes for hours, began to ache.

"Hey, Blunt," someone whispered from the next hole.

"What?" I whispered back.

"Merry Christmas."

Most of us hadn't even remembered what day it was. Under combat conditions, every day, week or month becomes the same. The days of the weeks or dates of the month had no particular significance to the foot soldier. Why bother keeping track of the date, for you had long since resigned yourself to the fact you were surely going to die that day anyway.

I removed a small, four-inch artificial Christmas tree from home out of my pack and stuck it in the snow at the lip of my foxhole. Also from my field pack, I took some newly-arrived candy bars, a can of C-ration pork and beans, a small can of fruit cocktail, some crackers and some peanut butter fudge my sister June had sent me. I passed some of my cache over to Everett in the next hole and we had a party.

I spent the next few hours staring at my little symbolic Christmas tree and thinking of home, but they were lonesome, melancholy thoughts. I wondered if the family had received my holiday flowers and telegram. As important as our mission in Europe may have been, crouched in a frozen foxhole in Belgium was no way for anyone to spend Christmas. I was having trouble reconciling the birth of Christ to all the killing around me.

The best Christmas present we were given, though, was to look up into an almost cloudless blue sky and see it filled with contrails from fighters and B-17 bombers so high we couldn't even hear them on their way to German cities. Showers of shiny tin foil (chaff), almost like Christmas tree tinsel, rained down from the bombers in an attempt to confuse German radar. The rain and fog back in England that had kept all aircraft except the Luftwaffe on the ground since the Bulge had erupted nine days earlier had finally lifted and now squadron after squadron of Allied aircraft were streaking east and southward over our heads. What a beautiful, morale-boosting sight it was.

We were also wished a Merry Christmas by the Germans, in the form of an artillery barrage. However, it stopped almost as fast as it started so we figured they were just sending over some greetings on this special holiday.

As the day wore on the anticipated attack never materialized, but still we were trapped in our foxholes because we knew it could come at any moment. As daylight faded into Christmas night, we heard a new sound in the sky—not a buzz bomb or a German fighter, but a whistling roar that made us all look up. A German plane was streaking across the sky faster than anything any of us had ever seen before. We watched the plane fly from one horizon to the other in a matter of seconds, almost like a bullet.

"What in the hell was that?" someone asked incredulously.

"It beats the hell out of me," another answered. "Must be another one of Hitler's secret weapons."

"How come we don't ever have any secret weapons?" the first voice asked.

Someone piped up saying they had read about some jet propulsion system the Germans had been working on, something like a rocket plane. "That must have been one of them," a voice from an adjoining foxhole reasoned. It was the first jet aircraft that I had ever seen. Still in the developmental stage, Germany's scientists had managed to get a prototype, the Messerschmitt 262, in the air and into limited service during the last five months of the war. But it came too late to turn the aerial tide in their favor.

That night, I huddled in my snow-lined foxhole wondering how my family back home was celebrating the holiday. I hoped that, unlike me, they were sitting down to a turkey dinner despite all the ration point restrictions and war shortages back there. Deep in my thoughts, I became aware of a high-pitched screaming noise that grew in intensity as it got closer. The screeching noise was coming straight at me. I curled into a ball, my tightly-folded arms pulling my helmet almost down to my shoulders, and cringed in the bottom of my hole. Just when I thought that I would be smothered by the sound, it suddenly stopped with a splintering crash and was replaced by overwhelming silence.

I knew that cold night air magnified sound but this had been something different. Hardly daring to breath, I listened for other disturbances or motions that would tell me what had caused the ear-piercing racket. Cautiously, I peered over the rim of my foxhole but nothing in the dark offered a clue. For several minutes, I remained motionless, M-1 gripped firmly in hand, ready for anything, still waiting for something to happen next. But all I could hear was the sound of my own heavy breathing and the rustle of the night winds in the pines around me.

When I couldn't stand the suspense any longer, I crawled out of my hole and bellied my way slowly through the snow drifts toward the last splintering sound I had heard before everything had gone silent. Having no idea what to expect, I shoved a grenade under my cartridge belt for extra protection.

The soft crunching of the snow under my belly was amplified by the cold, and I was sure anyone nearby could hear me. I crawled through ground cover evergreens for a couple hundred feet and then, deciding there was nothing out there that posed a threat to me, started to slither back to our lines. I was sure I must have at least reached the German outpost lines and I didn't want to celebrate my holiday there. But again, my usually good sense of direction failed me.

I crawled in a circle and tried to find the path I had plowed through the snow with my body which would lead me back to my foxhole. As my eyes tried to pierce the night, I faintly made out an image that was strangely out of place in the forest's natural setting. I paused, held my breath and stared at it. In the darkness, I could make out the shape of a strange, eight-foot, shiny silver-colored metal object shaped like a cigar—or maybe like a torpedo—protruding out of a snow drift at a 45 degree angle. I lay there listening to the object for several seconds and when I heard no sounds emanating from it, I figured it was a dud bomb of some sort.

Not knowing any better, I inched my way closer and closer until I could almost touch It. Only then could I read the letters stenciled big and clear on its side: "U.S. Air Corps."

How foolish I felt when it dawned on me the sound that had practically caused my heart to jump into my throat in my foxhole was nothing more than an empty aviation auxiliary belly tank jettisoned from a P-51 fighter returning to England after an extended flight protecting B-17s over Germany. Sheepishly, I realized this was not one of my finds I could brag about to the platoon.

On December 27, our problems in the field were compounded when it started to snow heavily again. If there was anything the American GIs in Belgium didn't need, it was more snow. But we could do nothing about it, just slouch shivering in our holes, throw anything we could find over our heads for protection from the elements and continue to endure.

About this time, we received some good news to offset the ferocities of the Belgian winter. Captured Germans were beginning to tell our G-4 interrogators that the 116th Panzer Division no longer existed as a viable fighting force. Months in combat, most recently against the 84th, had decimated it to where it was only a numerical designation or a thumbtack on a strategy map at the German high command. On the ground, the division was a shambles.

This news, coupled with Hitler's 2nd and 9th Panzer divisions being systematically destroyed by our forces every day, fueled our speculation, and deepest hopes, that the tide of battle was at last turning in our favor. But I am not sure whether any of us fully realized just how long the road before us still remained. The euphoria of achieving victory after victory against the German Army in a steady succession of Belgian cities, towns and villages was misleading and only gave us a false sense of hope. But our confidence was high, and that had to count for something.

From our positions inside our holes in the earth, even we could sense that the momentum had shifted and was now gradually becoming ours. As a result, Hitler's dream of walking again before the Eiffel Tower in Paris was only that: the fantasies and rants of a demented madman.

The German assault we had been waiting for never came and gradually we resigned ourselves to spending another night in our earthen homes. Throughout the night the temperatures continued to plummet. There was no way one could keep warm, even with a candle, for the illumination it would give off in a foxhole would reveal our position to the ever-present German eyes. It was also not advisable to stand and stretch or to exercise for the same reason. One thing you learned early on in the Bulge was not to stand up unnecessarily, making yourself a better target for some Kraut's Mauser rifle.

I tried to stamp my feet on the bottom of the hole but the pain was becoming too severe. It continued to snow heavily. All we could do was just sit there accepting it, waiting for it to blanket us. Perhaps the mantle of snow would bring some deceptive warmth with it. When my feet finally went numb, I was relieved to feel the pain subsiding. But I was also numbed by exhaustion and so didn't realize what was happening to me. Snow and sleet filtered down my back and froze on my cheeks. Soon, my feet were encased in snow and ice and I could no longer move them. And, more disturbingly, I just didn't care anymore.

As the temperature dropped well below zero, my whole body became numb and I gave in to the sheer fatigue that had been building up in me for days. I slept. Some time later, I was awakened by Joe Everett punching me and telling me to move or I would freeze to death. I tried to but couldn't, and I lapsed back to an unconscious sleep. The mind-numbing cold had finally conquered my instinct for survival. I just lay helplessly in the hole letting the cold take its toll.

Several hours later, Everett was hitting me about the body again. It was almost daylight and the snow hadn't slackened off at all. My face was frozen stiff and my eyebrows, cheeks and jaw were encrusted with ice. I could not turn my head for my snow-drenched overcoat collar was frozen stiff as a board. My glazed over eyes could see only 20 to 30 feet in front of my foxhole.

My feet were encased in a block of ice up to my ankles in the bottom of the hole. Everett pounded on my legs but there was absolutely no feeling or movement. He and another nearby GI chipped away at the ice with their bayonets, lifted me out of my hole and dragged me across the frozen ground. I tried to stand up but my legs repeatedly buckled under the weight of my body.

The two men continued to work on me. Eventually, supported under the armpits, I was able to stand up and hobble around slightly. By now the snow around our foxholes was more than two feet deep and extreme pain in my feet and legs started shooting throughout my body. I didn't fully comprehend what was wrong with me. All I knew was that I was frightened and I couldn't stand up without help.

I was carried to a meat wagon hidden in a clump of trees not far away, where I was given a mess kit of hot oatmeal and hot coffee and told to rest awhile to thaw out. When circulation returned to my legs, excruciating pain that had been dulled by the numbness gradually became almost unbearable.

The medics, seeing my discomfort, covered me with several more blankets to hasten the thawing process and turned up heaters in the patient compartment of the ambulance. After a medical conference, most of it held out of earshot, I was moved to a field hospital tent about a mile behind the lines to continue thawing out. A team of doctors examined and probed at my legs. Later, by chance, I overheard them discussing the probability of evacuating me to a rear area hospital where my badly-frozen legs could be amputated.

I was able to sit up enough to look down at my feet. The sight that greeted me was unnerving: both feet had been reduced to ugly, purplish-blue mutations with large blistering pieces of torn skin peeling off them. I stumbled off the cot I was lying on and started almost hysterically pleading with the doctors not to do this to me.

"I'm a musician, a drummer. I have to have my feet," I implored, now crying unashamedly. "Please, don't do this to me. Please."

"We can give your feet one more day but then the decision will he final," one doctor said impersonally, as he walked away to tend to other patients. I was given a pain killer and soon dropped off to sleep.

The next day, I was examined again and as I lay there almost terrified at what the doctor might say, I heard one doctor mutter to the other, "There is some improvement. Let's hold off awhile." The surge of overwhelming relief, the sudden realization that I would be spared from being footless the rest of my life, brought on an upheaval of emotions. Tears filled my eyes as I stared at the ceiling, reciting a prayer of thanks. Then I shut my eyes and allowed the tears to flow down my cheeks onto the pillow.

Three days later I was released, heavily bandaged, back to my unit. Frostbite and trench foot during the Battle of the Bulge disabled more GIs than the enemy did, I was told afterward, and men who sustained minor non-life threatening wounds often froze to death quickly if left unattended for more than a few minutes. Others froze when they became too exhausted or apathetic to keep moving.

Most of those living and fighting in foxholes during December 1944 and January 1945 in Belgium learned quickly that the only thing worse than not being able to sleep during the sub-zero nights was being able to; quite often those men never woke up.

These were truly some of the darkest days for us and for the division, the trying days when GIs urinated on their M-1 rifles each morning to free up ice-encrusted chambers; the trying times when it was not unusual to require five hours to dig a three-foot deep foxhole into the deeply frozen earth, and by that time you were usually on the move again. Laboriously scratching foxholes into the frozen earth was an almost constant and futile process.

Hot food, during the rare times when it was available, solidified in our mess kits before we could eat it, and water constantly froze in our canteens. It was later published in Allied military newspapers that the winter of 1944 was the worst on record in 40 years for snow and bitter cold. *Stars & Stripes* wrote of forty-below-zero temperatures recorded during the Bulge.

We experienced constant food and ammunition shortages, since supply lines could not be kept open in blizzards. Getting supplies through usually meant long, arduous trudging through waist-deep snow drifts with ammunition crates on mens' shoulders.

GIs were turned into human pack mules. Nothing mechanized, not even tanks, could move during these savage storms. In one sector, American dead were evacuated to the rear on captured sleds pulled by Belgian draft horses. For a month, we went without hot food.

To this day, whenever my feet are subjected to extreme cold, the pain returns, a constant reminder of what once was.

When I returned to my squad, Everett, as always, was waiting for me. Soon he was regaling me with more stories about his prewar life in Oklahoma. No one, but no one, can tell a story like an Oklahoman.

On January 3, the 84th mounted an attack in sleet and snow along with the 2nd Armored Division. Foot soldiers went where tanks and trucks couldn't. By nightfall, the Germans had been driven from Odeigne. The Allied counterattack to crush the Nazis had begun.

Back in my foxhole, I knew I could never survive another ordeal like the one after Christmas but my meandering, gloomy thoughts were cut short by the sound of approaching tanks.

The long-awaited German assault on our positions—now a counterattack against the advance of the 84th's other elements—was finally underway. But the snow whipping our faces blinded us, making it almost impossible to see from which direction. Our anti-tank guns opened up at targets their crews could not see, and spasmodic German infantry fire all along the line showed us they too were rendered sightless by the snow. They were probably firing merely to intimidate us as they felt their way along.

Even though we could not yet see them, a series of loud explosions in the swirling snow in front of our position told us that German forward tank units had entered the mine field we had put down days earlier. The swirling snow was whirling to our advantage—the tank crews were unable to spot the mines we had laid in their path.

Interspersed with the sound of battle were the eruptions of a different sound, German tanks being destroyed by their own exploding ammunition. The mines were doing their job far beyond our wildest hopes. Tank-mounted 88s continued to fire blindly through the squalling snow in our direction, in most cases, without an actual target in sight, just where they guessed we might be. Most of their bombardment was ineffective, falling off to our side. The hills echoed and re-echoed with the thunder of battle as I strained my eyes trying to see even a single German to shoot at, but I was blinded by the white avalanche falling from the sky.

A roar behind me spun me around in my hole, whereupon I glimpsed a Sherman tank from the 2nd Armored Division bearing down almost on top of me. Our own tanks couldn't see in front of them either. I curled up against the bottom of my foxhole as the tank rumbled by, searching for a German tank to engage. Being run over by a tank was no big deal; we had practiced this tactic many times back at Fort McClellan during basic training. The only problem then, and it surely wasn't one with the Bulge's rock-solid earth, was being covered by the dirt the tank treads squashed down on top of you during the passby.

After about 20 minutes, the Germans withdrew and I still had not fired a shot. But the standoff didn't last long—the Germans poured a heavy artillery barrage at us while they regrouped to hit us again behind the exploding shell fire. The snowstorm eventually let up somewhat and I was able to survey the battlefield.

I shall never forget the carnage of smashed and burning tanks littering the field. The main thrust had been about 200 yards off to my right where the 2nd Armored had taken a beating. There were at least a dozen destroyed tanks from both sides, with American losses outnumbering the German. For the first time, I had witnessed a major tank battle, or at least the sounds and results of one. There had apparently been only a few German troops trailing behind in support of the tanks and it appeared that the heavy snowfall and American resistance had reduced the ferocity of the infantry engagement between the two sides. A terrible price, however, had been paid by each tank battalion and the final outcome had still not been determined.

A company of Shermans, reduced in number by the initial battle, was regrouping behind trees to our rear even as reinforcements were arriving. I could see medics wandering about the battlefield checking the dead and attending to the wounded.

We waited nervously for the next onslaught.

"Hey Joe, say something funny so I can laugh," I called over to Everett's hole during the lull in the fighting.

"Did I ever tell you about the . . . " but he never finished his sentence—the German tanks were moving at us again with an even thinner line of infantry straggling along behind them.

This time we could see them but they were still beyond effective rifle range so we held our fire. The tanks were laying down a withering field of machine-gun fire as cover for their infantry and they were getting close enough for us to actually see the tank guns belching flame at us.

Almost holding our breaths, we waited for the lead tanks to enter our mine field so we could open up with everything we had. When the German tankers saw our Shermans now out in the open and maneuvering for position, they swung into a frontal line from one end of the battlefield to the other, about 200 yards.

This, I thought, would surely be a battle to the finish and, for all practical purposes, it was. The more maneuverable Shermans weaved and dodged, choosing their targets at will and sniped away as fast as their 76mm cannons could be reloaded.

As each German tank erupted in blames or was disabled, we picked off crew members attempting to escape and as each American Sherman was knocked out, we laid down intense covering fire for the GIs who were scrambling from their burning cans and dashing back to our lines. The smaller 76mm guns and light armor of our Sherman tanks were no match for the reinforced armor and 88mm cannon of the Panzers.

When the Mark Vs stopped to avoid our mine field, the German infantry picked up the momentum and started a running, frontal assault. Our rifle barrels became hot as we fired as fast as we could expend one clip and reload another. Our machine gun emplacements cut the Germans down like a scythe through wheat while riflemen lobbed fragmentation grenades at the Germans who had gotten past the machine-gun fire.

The Germans started to withdraw, firing as they went and turning only occasionally to hurl "potato masher" concussion grenades at us. Most of them fell short of our positions and exploded harmlessly, throwing up fountains of snow. Not anticipating such defensive strength and determination, the German commanders pulled back to probe for a weaker sector. We knew we had broken the back of their attack. The German fanaticism we had observed earlier during the Battle of the Bulge had waned considerably during the more recent fighting. By now, more often, if they were beaten back once, they resorted to less heavily defended avenues of approach. The Wehrmacht was no longer throwing itself blindly and ferociously into hails of American bullets as it had done weeks earlier on the Siegfried Line.

When we were confident the Germans wouldn't be back, Everett and I helped the medics search the Shermans for possible wounded. No survivors were found. These armored vehicles were aptly called "steel coffins" by the infantry. Beyond the mine field, we could see German medics also carrying away their wounded unmolested. Correctly, as has been the custom of armies throughout the ages, no one on either side fired a shot.

Beyond the mine field lay at least 50 SS and Wehrmacht panzer troops in the snow. It had been a senseless slaughter. The contrasting colors of black uniforms, white snow and red blood painted a ghoulish beauty on the landscape.

When the American lines were finally pulled back, I was taken by Jeep to Hotton; my feet were still too swollen and painful to walk. While someone in the squad lit a coal fire in a potbellied stove in our billet, I tried to pry off my overshoes but my feet and ankles had become so enlarged that I couldn't get the shoes off. Everett cut them off with his trench knife and then wrapped my feet in strips of drapery material soaked with canteen water.

Miraculously, my feet started to feel better. I snuck a candy bar out from under my sleeping bag where I had hidden it and the sweetness settled my upset stomach. I stretched out on the floor, plunked my head down on my overturned helmet and fell asleep.

No sooner had I closed my eyes when someone was yelling, "Fire! Fire!" From instinct, I jumped up. The room was illuminated by that red-orange glow that can only be produced by flames. Pungent, lung-constricting black smoke curled along the ceiling and cascaded down the walls around us. The coal stove had become overheated and had ignited a wall. Almost instantly, the heat was searing our throats. We grabbed our gear and fled barefoot across the street to another squad's billet where we watched our building burn to the ground. When there was nothing else to watch, we fell asleep again.

Precisely at 0600 every morning, the Germans sounded reveille for us, a single artillery shell exploding in the middle of the street nearby.

As I walked to chow one morning, I heard group laughter coming from the distance. Wandering in that general direction, I found our platoon sergeant dancing a burlesque routine in old-fashioned womens' clothing. Doing anything to keep our flagging morale high, he strutted around bumping and grinding like a stripper. The men were convulsed with laughter. It was good medicine for our somewhat sagging spirits.

Later that day, in a freak accident, a Jeep ran over the sergeant's foot, crushing it, and his dancing days on the Belgian stage were over. I never saw him again. Now the squad was down to seven and the war was still a long way from being over.

Orders came that we were to move again, this time to fill in as riflemen in a depleted company on the line until replacements could be brought in from France. I tried to beg off because of my feet but I was assured we would be traveling by truck and, besides, I could still fire an M-1. We carried only sleeping bags, rifles, and ammo, hoping the assignment would be temporary and that soon we would be back with our own outfit.

Dressing properly for the winter of '44 in Belgium was a study in improvisation. I wore several variations of layered clothing trying to stay warm: long-john underwear, woolen uniform pants and shirt, a sweater, field jacket, full-length wool overcoat, two pairs of gloves (American wool and German leather), wool cap, helmet, two pairs of wool socks, combat boots wrapped in torn-up woolen strips, and oversized galoshes. Then, if I was to be positioned in a foxhole, I wrapped as many blankets as I could around me cocoon-style.

For the temporary transfer to the rifle company, I bound my feet in more drapery material and pulled two pairs of oversize socks over the wrapping. I left my boots behind in favor of overshoes packed full of newspaper. Only then was I ready to go.

We arrived at the other company—I never learned which one, but it no longer mattered to me—and were told to dig in.

After 20 minutes of only being able to scratch the frozen surface, I hit upon an idea. I was still carrying a small quantity of nitro-starch with me since Marche. I wired it up, placed it in the hole I had started, warned those around me, and fired it. A second charge blew a hole below the frost line and the rest of my digging was comparatively easy.

Almost as soon as I finished digging, my eyes started to droop and I was fast falling asleep. I felt a hand on my shoulder and looked up to find the company commander bending over me. "I understand you're all out on your feet, but I suggest you stay awake if you can. The Krauts are all around us and very close," he said.

That's all it took. I was wide awake again and staring into the woods surrounding our position. Eventually, dawn came and with it came the fog that had plagued us since our arrival in Belgium. Out of the gray mist, the outline of a man emerged unexpectedly who threw a K-ration in my hole and then disappeared again as the mist closed back in around him. It was the company mess sergeant offering room service breakfast to the troops.

Somewhere in the fog shrouding the trees before me, a short burst of machine-gun fire shattered the morning stillness. Later, we heard that six Germans dressed as Americans had tried to pass through our lines, but when an alert sergeant had challenged them and their subsequent actions were not American, he had cut them down just as they went for their weapons.

That night, some of us were moved again to reinforce another company about a mile away; we had become, it seemed, a bastard squad without a home. At the new location, I found a barn with a hayloft and, having been awake for nearly 40 hours, I was finally able to catch a nap away from the surveillance of the company brass.

When Everett, that master Oklahoma scrounger, found a field kitchen with hot food, we hobbled there and filled up on bread, oatmeal and black coffee. With stomachs now full, the world looked a little brighter. The mess sergeant said he had been told we were in the town of Briscol.

On the way back to the barn, Everett and I heard the laughter of men whooping it up. A Belgian farmer was chasing a GI around in circles threatening him with a pitchfork. Then the farmer broke off the chase and came running into the barn where we were quartered. When he screamed and shook his fist at me, I let out a threatening bellow and fired a pistol shot into the wall over his head. With me chasing him, he stumbled back outside where other GIs took up the cue and started firing their weapons in the air. The farmer kept running first one way, then the other in fear and anger, then fell clumsily on his face in the snow. From the French-speaking GIs in the platoon, we learned that he blamed Americans using his barn as a billet for the damage the Krauts had done to it with artillery fire. I had more important things to worry about than one irate farmer and his dilapidated barn.

I ventured into a nearby bombed-out home, where I found a Victrola and a cracked French record. I placed it on the turntable and, pushing it around manually with my finger, could make out a scratchy French version of the "Woodpecker Song," a faint reminder of home.

Investigating several rifle shots in the village, I found that a a cow and some chickens had been shot. When I looked in on the GIs, they were already decapitating the chickens with their bayonets and skinning the cow. It appeared that at long last we were going to get some decent meat.

Smelling smoke, I turned and saw the barn on fire. Some GIs had decided that if the farmer hated us that much, they might as well give him a good reason. Everett and I barely managed to salvage our gear from the barn before it burned to the ground, much to the delight of the entire platoon. We never did get any steak from the cow, because right after breakfast we were told we were moving on foot to the nearby village of Manhay.

The steady slapping and crunching of feet in open-file formation on hard-packed snow brought us closer every minute to where we hoped opposition from the Germans would not be heavy.

As we neared the village, I looked into a ditch beside the road. The body of a naked woman in her early 20s lay face up, with terror permanently contorting her face. She had been slashed wide open from throat to crotch and her breasts had been hacked off. The woman's body was the centerpiece of drifted snow, dyed crimson with her blood. Beside her lay the crushed body of an infant boy about 18 months old, its head bashed unrecognizably. A nearby tree against which the baby apparently had been swung was covered with blood and patches of flesh.

The Germans had evacuated the town only moments before and had left this gruesome signpost for us. They should have known that each one of these grisly scenes only intensified our hatred for them and strengthened our resolve to fight.

I had not truly known why I was fighting in Europe until I began witnessing these atrocities. I wondered what kind of sadistic beasts could have done this. For what possible crime had the woman been subjected to this unspeakable punishment? Shaking my head in disbelief, I walked past the woman's body without even a backward glance.

Farther down the road, my wonderment was answered by a scene of sheer, total atrocity that I would see repeated in several towns ahead of us, and then again, months later, when the 84th liberated concentration camps across the Rhine River on the northern plains of Germany.

But I had not seen everything yet. In the village just ahead was a heavily damaged church and in a snow-drifted grave yard beside it were the frozen, snow-covered bodies of nearly two dozen elderly people, their hands tied over their heads. They had been lined up systematically and machine gunned, apparently in retaliation for some apparent crime against the Germans. We had already learned that it was German practice to retaliate against a village by executing inhabitants when a German soldier was murdered or German equipment sabotaged. In the center of town, an elderly man was sitting in the remains of what had once been his home. He cradled a lifeless, blood-covered infant in his arms. The despair in his eyes indicated a grandfather in shock. I crossed the street so as not to disturb him.

Later that day, Everett and I held a pistol competition in the church ruins, using smashed religious statues for targets. The idea was to see whether the Colt .45 or the 9mm German P-38 or Luger was the most accurate pistol. After firing clip after clip and reducing the statues to rubble, we agreed the German weapons were superior by a wide margin.

The most comfortable billet I could locate for us in Manhay was a grist mill containing a pile of grain that made a most comfortable bed. That night I lit a candle and caught up on my journal and correspondence home. In my letters, I soft pedaled the truth considerably as I related the events of the past week. Again, nothing was to be gained by detailing for my parents the unspeakable horrors I had experienced and endured. I wrote of peaceful walks in the woods and good food. My conscience didn't bother me for stretching the truth a little. I figured the end justified the means. In youthful patriotic pride, I also did quite a bit of opinionated flag-waving in my letters home. It would take many years after the war to smooth my memories and to mellow my intense fervor and stubborn beliefs.

In a recent letter, my mother had written that my father often stayed up until the middle of the night, if other commitments forced him to, to ensure I had a letter each day. With such devotion, there was nothing I couldn't endure. I now knew why we were fighting, and the cause, I felt, was just. I wrote for nearly an hour and then walked outside to stretch my legs, for the night was quiet and I was hungry.

I walked to the company kitchen where I got a K-ration and some hot coffee to wash it down. I must have been hungrier than I realized, for the cold cheese ration actually tasted good.

Because of the condition of my feet, I was excused from guard duty and was able to sack in back at the grist mill until about 0430 when I was awakened and told we were moving again. We were told only that the town was "hot" and to be ready for anything. Slowly, the truck convoy probed its way along another shell-cratered road lined by towering pines, their snow-covered boughs displaying a gentle serenity that was beautiful, but deadly, for they sheltered the German.

As so often before, we found out where we were only when we located a sign or asked a civilian. Grandmenil was another in a long list of names that meant nothing to me. All I knew was that the name sounded French, the country was Belgium and the Germans were waiting for us around the next bend in the road or in the next town.

9

The Tide Turns

The convoy stopped short of the town and we were told a recon patrol would be sent in to probe for Germans. We were already sharply aware the Krauts could be driven from a town and then stealthily reoccupy it again a few hours later. We had been going around in circles with the enemy like this every day since the massive German breakthrough in the Ardennes. Grandmenil would be no different.

Accurate military intelligence was at best sketchy, for the whereabouts of German troops—or our own, for that matter—was always in doubt. There were no front lines, no rear echelons, there were no company or battalion boundaries, no safe or unsafe sectors. The Germans were everywhere, and so were we.

It was not unusual for platoons to function independently from their companies, and it was almost customary for squads to be separated from their platoons during these most complicated and confusing early weeks of the Bulge. Furthermore, because of the fluid situation, inter-platoon communications were practically impossible. It could only be hoped that German commanders and their troops were as confused as we were.

The recon party consisted of a jeep for EASY Company's commander and his radio man, one for an infantry squad and one for us demolition specialists bringing up the rear. I loaded a mine detector onto our vehicle and, accompanied by a lieutenant observer, cautiously approached the town. At the brow of a shattered hill offering a commanding view of the village, we paused momentarily to make a final observation, but as we did so, the EASY Company command jeep impatiently motioned us forward to check for mines.

Before we could react, the captain's jeep at the front of the patrol exploded in a ball of smoke and fire. It had been blown onto its side and was burning furiously with its passengers scattered about on the ground. While the infantry squad rushed to their assistance, the officer in our mine detection jeep and I dove for a nearby ditch as several riflemen pounded away at an unseen target in the village. With binoculars, we located a monstrous Tiger tank cozily tucked between two bombed-out buildings about 200 feet away. We found out later it was one of the new, gigantic super tanks developed by Hitler toward the end of the war, another of his so-called Geheimnise Waffen (secret weapons).

In front of the tank position were two burning American half-tracks, their crews draped over the sides. The tank commander had been picking off American vehicles pretty much at will as they entered the village. They too had probably been part of a recon unit probing the town.

The tank turned its attention to the infantry squad with us who were laying down heavy rifle and machine gun fire in their direction. But .30-caliber bullets against a steel-enforced Tiger tank were almost as troublesome as fleas to an elephant. We were in exposed positions and unable to move forward or backward. The lieutenant motioned for me to follow him in a flanking attempt around one of the buildings shielding the Kraut tank, while our driver crawled forward to the riflemen and told them we needed diversionary fire. I reminded him I could not make a dash for the nearest building because of my swollen feet. The only other alternative was to crawl a circuitous 300-foot route over open fields using every defile we could find.

As we started to crawl forward, I wished for one of the white ski suits I had seen used by the German Sturmschutzen (storm troopers) back in Marche. All I had was the highly visible full-length brown wool army overcoat, which I was sure would make me stick out against the snow-covered field.

Fortunately, the tank crew seemed to be concentrating its machine gun fire on the riflemen; streams of bullets could be seen raking the roadside where they were positioned. We couldn't see any other fire coming from the buildings. If there were any German infantry guarding the tank our riflemen were making them keep their heads down.

Our only chance was to make it around one of the buildings concealing the tank and get behind it unseen before the tank crew diverted their fire in our direction. When we finally crawled to a point about 15 feet behind the tank, the deafening roar of the 88 pounding the hillside almost lifted us off the ground each time it fired.

Communicating by hand signals and eye language, we quietly swung ourselves on top of the tank. When the lieutenant pulled the tank's hatch cover partly open, we heard yelling inside and saw a pair of hands grab at the cover in a tug of war with the lieutenant. I pulled the pin on a fragmentation grenade and shoved it under the heavy, round hatch cover just as the lieutenant released his grip. I saw the grenade was wedged between the hatch cover and the hatch rim, keeping the cover from being slammed shut.

With only four seconds before detonation, I gave the grenade a hard sideways kick and it fell inside as the lieutenant and I dove headfirst off the tank and rolled behind one of the buildings. With the muffled explosion and the screams from inside, the hatch cover flew open and white smoke billowed out. We clambered back onto the tank and emptied our pistols down the turret hatch to finish the job. Then we waved forward the riflemen who were crouched in the ditches watching us. The command Jeep casualties had already been evacuated in our Jeep to a rear area aid station.

Infantry manuals says tanks can't be knocked out with a fragmentation grenade but now the book would have to be rewritten. For this exploit, I heard later the lieutenant was awarded the Bronze Star medal for his bravery. His citation hadn't mentioned me; the only award I received was the thanks of the infantrymen in the recon patrol after the fire fight was over. None of them had been killed or even injured.

With the lieutenant skulking around, it was impossible, and probably improper, to lift the Soldat Buchs from the dead tankers as my Tod Preisen (death trophies). It is apparently a strange quirk in some mens' personality that prompts them to collect trophies when an adversary has been vanquished. Hunters collect animal heads, fishermen mount prize catches, gunfighters of the old West notched pistol grips after each shoot out. I wasn't notching my M-1 stock but, instead, lifting Soldat Buchs from dead Germans I had faced down.

After checking out all the destroyed buildings for possible snipers or German stragglers, I found one house mostly intact. It became my first choice as a temporary billet. To inspect it closer, I lit a stubby candle I always carried with me. I recoiled slightly, startled when I discerned a pair of wide-open eyes staring at me. After slashing my M-1 toward the eyes, I found a terrified Belgian woman covered with a blanket and huddling in a corner, obviously very sick. I assured her we were Americans and told her I would get her some medical help when I could.

With no dry wood around with which to kindle a fire in the kitchen stove, I broke off chair legs and stripped off window ledges. Within minutes, I had the woman warm and smiling weakly. I opened a C-ration and placed it on the floor beside her.

"C'est le Guerre" ("That's war"), I said, admittedly a rather stupid remark but it was all I could think of to say at the moment in my extremely limited French. She just kept staring at me, probably afraid and, having just watched me burn pieces of her home, uncertain about what was to happen next.

When a French-speaking squad member arrived, the woman said she was an elementary grade school teacher who had been too ill to evacuate the town with the others when the Germans and Americans had faced each other in a seesaw battle there earlier. The Germans had not discovered her and, satisfied there were no Americans remaining in the village, had passed through quickly, leaving only one harassing tank behind to slow up our advance.

Once relaxed, she said she had not eaten for two days; the C-ration was a banquet for her.

By nightfall an infantry company was occupying Grandmenil and the threat of a German counterattack was past. But intense German artillery fire kept us pinned to floors and in cellars most of the time. When it subsided and shifted to LOVE Company's position in another sector, we ventured outside and saw our artillery already in place and returning the fire. The blasts from our 105mm howitzers illuminated the snowy forests, giving them a deadly, but beautifully serene, appearance.

Joe Everett and I pulled outpost guard duty together at one approach to the town. Trying to keep our spirits up, we were quietly laughing and joking about life in Oklahoma and Massachusetts when we heard a truck coming.

Joe crouched in a ditch to cover me while I stood in the road with rifle aimed at the cab to challenge the driver. The area was still infiltrated by German paratrooper saboteurs posing as Americans and everyone and everything that moved was being questioned. When I asked for the password, an obviously tired and cranky driver opened the canvas cab door and snarled, "It's none of your fuckin' business."

I waved him on. No self-respecting Kraut staring down the barrel of a loaded M-1 would respond that way. The guy could only be an American. When I told Everett what the driver thought the daily password was, he laughed so hard and loud I was sure every German in Belgium would hear him.

Our relief finally came, and the quarter-mile hike back to the billet was more like five miles as the pain in my feet swept through my body with each step. To lighten my load, Everett carried my rifle, and no matter how slowly I limped along, he stayed with me.

After drinking a breakfast of soupy, hot oatmeal and black coffee, I started to explore the town but was stopped short by another gruesome example of German savagery.

Outside the town's only church were the frozen, snow-covered bodies of 18 men, women and children, their hands bound behind their backs. As in Manhay, they had been lined up against the church wall and machine gunned. Their partially decomposed, blue, shriveled-up faces, distorted in agony, stared up at me as mute testimony of the horror that had taken place in the village before our arrival.

My mind went numb as I picked my way amongst the bodies. I could only stare at them for a few moments before shaking my head in shock and walking away.

In another section of the town, I found four frozen SS troopers in an open grave and, with rage welling up inside me, I jumped into the grave and smashed their heads with my rifle butt. But with the heads already frozen into blocks of ice, the blows caused no outward damage.

On a sloping hill overlooking the village, I found a mutilated German SS corpse beside a barbed wire fence separating two pastures. Someone had already hacked away at the body. I sat and stared at it for a while and then, totally without reason or provocation, sent the head skimming across the snow with a savage kick. The surge of pain that shot up my leg from my foot was worth it. I chased the head as it skidded over the ice-covered pasture and kicked it again and then again, playing soccer. During the whole episode, I felt nothing but macabre elation. Eventually tiring of the sport, with punishing stabs of pain growing sharper in my feet, I sat down beside the mutilated remains of the German and ate a K-ration.

It was in Grandmenil that I became part of the first actual murder by Americans I had witnessed while fighting. A Jeep with two German prisoners perched on the front fenders, their hands clasped behind their heads, came by as I was on my way to the field kitchen for breakfast. Seeing me limping, the driver stopped and offered me a lift.

As we bounced and swerved along the rutted, mud-slicked road, the driver nodded casually to his front seat passenger and, without a word, they each pulled out their Colt .45s and simultaneously fired single shots into the back of each prisoner's head. The impact of the slugs made the Germans jerk upright convulsively in spasms as chunks of flesh, bone and blood spewed from their skulls. The two lifeless forms slumped off the fenders, hitting the road bouncing and sliding in the mud into gutters along the road. I glanced back at them—the POWs' legs were still twitching. Other GIs walking in the area hardly glanced at the two dead Germans.

Still without a word being spoken, the GIs in the jeep holstered their side arms and soon we were at the field kitchen where the driver dropped me off. I thanked them for the lift.

Breakfast that morning, I remember, was pancakes instead of oatmeal for a change. I enjoyed them thoroughly. On my way back to my billet, I noticed the Krauts still lying face down on the road but someone had pushed them both off to the side so as not to impede traffic.

To many GIs, a German was a German no matter what uniform he wore, but to me there was a vast difference between Wehrmacht soldaten and SS storm troopers. One took prisoners, the other executed them and perpetrated unspeakable atrocities against defenseless civilians. There had been no acceptable reason to murder these two Wehrmacht soldiers who, like ourselves, were serving their country, right or wrong. I was torn, on the one hand, between my hatred for the Germans for their atrocities in Belgium and, on the other hand, what I considered the limits of human decency. What I had just been involved in after accepting a ride seemed to me to go beyond that limit. I was ambivalent about how I should feel about the episode, but

I was certain about one thing: I never could have committed such a brutal murder.

One of the thrills of mail call whenever it occurred, beside the flow of letters and food packages from home, was the arrival of *Down Beat,* the magazine that brought me up to date on all the music news back in the States. My father was able to get a copy put aside for him before they sold out each month at Walberg & Auge, Worcester's leading music store at the time. In the privacy of many bombed-out buildings in Europe and many cold, lonely foxholes, I read this magazine over and over again, practically memorizing it each month.

One mail call included a snapshot of a window display, complete with pictures and two captured Nazi flags at the bank where my father worked, telling of my first-day exploits at Geilenkirchen, taking prisoners. I smiled as I reflected on his fatherly pride.

Another diversion during the Bulge was listening to Axis Sally's propaganda programs whenever we could "liberate" a battery-operated radio. Her inside knowledge of our troop movements and personal names was uncanny and her attempts to lower our morale were hilarious. If only she had known she didn't have to do this, that Army field chow was already doing it for her.

Other favorite reading material of the soldiers fighting in Belgium were the propaganda leaflets dropped regularly on our positions by German "messenger" planes. My favorite, and one I saved for my souvenir collection, showed a handsome 4F civilian fondling a scantily clad wife back home in front of a mirror showing a skeleton (death) choking a soldier. I never saw any concrete evidence that these crudely drawn leaflets had any adverse effect on our troops. Usually they were considered excellent for starting fires to heat C-rations.

Stars & Stripes reported a rumor that Bronze Star medals were going to be issued in K-ration boxes so everyone in the rear echelons could be assured of one. I believed what I read, since I had recently received a letter from home stating that a relative, a lieutenant colonel, had awarded himself one in Paris for "meritorious service above and beyond the call of duty." Apparently, he had not yet heard of Purple Hearts being awarded for swivel chair ass blisters, or he would have given himself one of these also. After all, high ranking supply officers have to be able to strut around too.

Newspaper clippings sent from home, instead of filling my letters with interesting readable materials, often infuriated me, for the distortions of the truth as I was observing it firsthand were difficult for me to accept. One clipping lashed out at America's GIs for the high incidence of frozen feet during the Bulge campaign.

Another claimed the Luftwaffe was no longer a viable threat to our troops, while still another newspaper account claimed German casualties were five times those of American troops, which I perceived to be a deliberate lie. I stopped reading American newspaper clippings when one stated the American casualty rate in the Bulge was the lightest of any campaign in Europe so far. I couldn't figure out what war these clipping were referring to, surely not the one in which I was engaged.

We were being visited by the so-called, no-longer-existent German Luftwaffe every night and day, strafing, bombing and harassing us at least four times as often as we saw Allied planes in the air. During the fogged-in early days of the Bulge, American fighters and bombers were grounded for nine days in England. The Luftwaffe, however, managed to get into the air over our heads every one of those days.

As far as the casualty rates were concerned, I only knew that in the Siegfried Line fighting we struggled for each yard or mile, but in the Ardennes, we were clawing for every inch. And in doing so, I had observed the numbers of American dead in both battles and could offer eyewitness testimony that the newspapers were grossly distorting the truth.

One clipping claimed the Allies had already captured hundreds of thousands of prisoners and tremendous quantities of German equipment and supplies. But during the entire Ardennes Campaign by then, I had never seen more than a few prisoners taken at any one time. During the final stages of the Bulge, when remnants of some Kraut divisions had been encircled and cut off, thousands of prisoners were, to be sure, taken, but many thousands more had already been able to slip safely back to the Fatherland to face us again. I couldn't find where the clippings had mentioned that fact.

By the time the Germans had been cut off and encircled at Houffalize, only the stragglers and abandoned vehicles remained. And sometimes it looked like half the vehicles they were using in their rear areas were captured American Jeeps or trucks. As for the hordes of prisoners the papers claimed we were taking, we would meet most of those again in the Rhineland.

One nationally syndicated story criticized GIs for falling victim to trench foot and called them poor soldiers for not following clear-cut Army regulations about proper foot care.

Soldiers in combat, the article stated, should replace their wet socks every day with clean, dry ones. Also, a soldier should remove his boots at least once every hour and massage his feet for 10 minutes. Furthermore, a soldier should never put his feet in water if temperatures were going to drop below freezing. And lastly, he should wear overshoes with no holes in them and buckled at the top at all times.

The article forgot to mention that GIs should also take a break at 3:00 every afternoon for milk and cookies and brush after every meal.

It was apparent to me the gullible print media was being victimized by the Army propaganda machine and the American public was being sorely misinformed about the war effort. Often I wished the letters from home hadn't contained newspaper accounts that my parents thought would be of interest to me but instead only infuriated me.

A company runner came to our billet and informed us we were moving out again to relieve EASY Company on the line, but being unable to reveal our presence or intentions with a noisy truck convoy, we were forced to hoof it from 1600 to 2400 to a densely forested section that, for some unknown strategic reason, had to be defended.

Only stubbornness made it possible for me to complete this march on my pain-wracked feet. The stealth move on foot meant we were moving into this area secretly to surprise the Germans. We were told to dig in. This order brought hearty laughter from everyone for, at best, we could scoop out some of the two-foot deep snow and hope it was enough to protect us from artillery shrapnel.

Blunt luck was running true to form: I was told I had the first two-hour guard duty. Conditions had become so chaotic we no longer were even using daily passwords. "Shoot at anything that moves" was the order of the day. We were told that if it moved, it wasn't an American.

No sooner had I settled into my post than I was asleep. I have no idea how long I slept but suddenly, I heard the soft crunch of a step on snow and felt a hand on my shoulder. It was only my relief. I don't know if he realized I was asleep but if he did, he didn't say anything.

With great effort, I pushed my way back through the heavy snow that, in spite of the thick overhead evergreen cover, had blanketed the earth crotch-deep. About the only advantage of snow like this, most GIs knew, was that it made no sound when men moved through it. I weaved my way through the dense pines and then across a wide open fire break. Exhausted from the exertion, I stopped and flopped over backwards to catch my breath for a moment and to look up at the stars.

The night was still and throat-pinching cold. For a moment, it was as if I had been transported into another world, one where everything was peaceful and there was no death. I allowed my reminiscences to wander back to the happy times when I had camped as a Boy Scout in weather like this with my father. But after a few minutes, I snapped back to reality and realized there was no protective cover anywhere near me, so I pushed on to where I could find concealment from the enemy if needed.

When I arrived back where my squad was more or less dug in, all I could see were bodiless heads protruding from the snow drifts. Off to one side, a voice whispered, "Hey, Blunt. C'mon over here." It was Danny Driscole of Scranton, Pennsylvania, who had come overseas with me in LOVE Company and who, like myself, had volunteered for mine duty.

He had fashioned a pine bough lean-to over a two-man hole he had somehow been able to excavate. He had also made a soft bed out of more pine branches and had a shielded Sterno can burning for warmth. It was one of the happiest surprises of the entire winter campaign so far, for I unexpectedly had someplace to nestle in and, to some degree, escape the cold. Later we wrapped up in a shared blanket and fell asleep.

Come daylight, a building sign we could see in the distance told us we were near the town of Odeigne. When a search-and-seize patrol determined the town was abandoned, we moved cautiously into the nearest buildings to seek shelter. Soon word was received we would be there only a day and a night. But that was enough—the town, most of which had been reduced to rubble, would at least get us out of foxholes and the snow for a few hours.

Almost as soon as I started out on my normal reconnoitering of each new town we entered, I was confronted with another grisly sight:

more murdered civilians in the local church yard, an almost identical repeat of those in every village through which we had passed. These unspeakable atrocities seemed to be a ritual for German SS troops as they retreated from each village.

I tried to eat a can of cold, greasy C-ration pork and beans but the water in my canteen needed to wash it all down was frozen solid. I threw the can away and went hungry.

A bearded GI pushed his way into our lean-to and asked, "Anyone here know somebody named Blunt?"

"I'm Blunt," I answered. He motioned for me to follow him. As I tagged along behind, I asked him where we were going. He merely grumbled, "C'mon, Cap'n wants ya."

I knew I had met the company commander when my escort said to another bearded GI, "Here he is." The other GI wore no insignia whatsoever and his overall appearance was as bad as ours.

"You the one from the mine platoon who speaks German?"

"Yes sir. Some," I answered.

"Where did ya learn it?"

"High school and college back home."

"Ya understand it too?"

"Some," I said.

He told me one of his men had brought in a prisoner during the night and he wanted me to interrogate him. "Can ya do it?" he asked.

"I'll try," I said, nodding

To his company messenger slumped against the CP wall he grumped, "Get the gawdamned Kraut."

The black-uniformed German was SS and a picture of Hitler's perfect Aryan type with longish blonde hair, blue eyes, in his mid-20s and with a sullen, arrogant look about him. He stared at me and I stared right back at him. I had nothing to fear; I was armed and he wasn't. He was the first German to whom I had ever spoken directly.

I asked him his name and he told me. I took his Soldat Buch, verified the name and gave it to the company commander.

"I don't want to know his gawdamned name, I want to know how many fuckin' Krauts there are out there and if they have any armor," the captain almost screamed.

"Panzer Kampfwagon?" ("Tanks?") I inquired.

"Nein," he answered without blinking an eye.

"Wie viele Soldaten ist da?" ("How many soldiers are there?") I asked.

"Sechs und Sie sind hungrid," ("Six and they are hungry") he retorted, still glaring at me.

"Haben Sie Artillerie?" ("Do you have artillery?")

"Nein," he said, shaking his head.

I relayed all this to the captain who just grunted with each answer. The sum total of what we learned from the Aryan trooper was that there were no tanks or artillery, just six hungry soldiers who wanted to surrender.

"You believe the son of a bitch?" the company commander cursed.

I shrugged my shoulders. "As far as I'm concerned, they're all a bunch of lying bastards," I told him. He nodded in agreement.

As I walked out of the EASY Company CP, I heard him say out loud to no one in particular, "I'll have to take a chance, I suppose."

Back at the lean-to, I told the others why I had been called.

About an hour later, we heard a violent exchange of burpgun and M-1 fire. Moments later, a GI came crashing through the trees near us, gasping for breath. When he saw all our rifles pointing at him, he threw himself on the ground. He couldn't get the words out but when he finally calmed down, he told us he was a platoon sergeant who had taken a squad out to bring in the six hungry Germans the SS trooper had told me about.

They had been met by several tanks and what he described as a "fuckin' battalion" of infantry.

"We tried to fight but we didn't have a chance. Some guys didn't even get a shot off," he sobbed. They were massacred because the SS prisoner I interrogated had lied and we had been taken in.

After reporting back to the company commander, the sergeant returned and grabbed me by the arm snarling, "I'll show you what I do to gawddamned lying Kraut bastards." I had seldom ever seen such rage in a man's face before.

Furiously, we walked, almost ran, about a quarter mile to a POW enclosure where several hundred shabby, sullen-faced, defeated prisoners were sitting in the snow behind barbed wire fences. We told the guards who let us enter the compound that we were looking for one prisoner in particular.

We wandered through the prisoners until I spotted the SS soldier I had interrogated and I pointed him out. The sergeant stared at him for a moment and then smashed him in the face with the Thompson submachine gun he was carrying. Then he yanked him bodily up off the ground and mashed him again.

Blood spurted out from the German's nose and mouth and spattered all over his black uniform. The other prisoners, perhaps thinking their turn was next, started to murmur and grumble. They were getting uneasy.

"You better do this outside," I cautioned the sergeant. "The POWs are getting edgy." We were two against more than 200. From somewhere in the ranks, a German soldier cried out "Heil Hitler."

"Hell Hitler!" the now almost-hysterical sergeant screamed back before viciously bashing the SS trooper again.

"Tell them why this bastard is going to die," he continued screaming in rage.

As best I could in my limited German, I informed the large group of prisoners, many of whom were now on their feet and surrounding us, that the SS storm trooper had lied to us and 11 Americans had died as a result. The SS trooper was now unconscious on the ground, his face crushed beyond recognition and bleeding profusely from massive face and head injuries.

"Take a shot at him if you want," the sergeant offered. Remembering all the murdered civilians, the disemboweled woman and the dead babies, I kicked the prostrate SS trooper with all my might in the groin. He curled up in a ball on the ground writhing in pain. At this, the sergeant actually laughed for the first time.

We dragged the prisoner outside, rubbed snow on his face to revive him and then pulled him to his feet. "I want them to see this," the sergeant said, the rage still erupting from inside him.

The SS soldier never changed his expression of arrogance and he never said a word throughout the beating. "I'll show you, you son-of-a-bitch. Die, you bastard," the sergeant yelled and with that he emptied a whole clip of .45 caliber slugs into the German. Then, he casually slammed another 20-round clip into his Thompson and emptied that one too.

The German's body humped up and down and tumbled back and forth in the snow as 40 slugs slammed like sledgehammers into it. When the sergeant's Thompson was emptied for the second time, the

SS trooper's badly shredded and disfigured body twitched slightly as his last nerves finally died. Then there was just the multiple rivulets of blood forming a large crimson stain on the snow.

Only then did we turn, glare defiantly at the other prisoners in the pen, and walk away. As we did so, I glanced back at the other prisoners to make sure none were coming after us. To a man, they stood silently watching us, apparently aware that in war, this was an act of justifiable retaliation.

Back at the company area, I found the squad prepared to move out again but our packing was interrupted by a series of high-pitched, terrifying roars close by, a sound none of us had heard before. We could see flames streaking upwards from the tree tops about 100 feet away for several seconds and then as suddenly as the sound had started, It was silence again.

We looked at each other and wondered if Hitler was unleashing another of his secret weapons that he had promised the people of Germany would win the war for them. Several of us carefully worked our way through the trees, rifles and pistols at the ready, to investigate the racket and the fire.

In a clearing a few yards away, we found an American rocket launcher with a rack of about two dozen tubes on it mounted on a jeep. As each rocket was fired, those stacked above it in the rack dropped lower into place for firing. The entire battery was expended in a matter of several seconds. It was a most impressive sight that none of us had ever witnessed before. We waited until the launcher was reloaded and watched in awe as it was fired again with ear-shattering volume and velocity.

Back at Driscole's lean-to, we were told the move would be delayed. About midnight, the call came to fall back. We were all given crates of M-1 ammunition to carry. Each crate weighed about 65 pounds and it was all I could do to lift it onto my shoulder.

In single file we tried to plow through the snow but soon, hitting waist-deep drifts, we were forced to push our way bodily a few feet at a time. It was a silent move through the forest under a black, moonless sky—no cigarettes, no talking.

Every few steps I stumbled and fell for the load was just too heavy for my frozen feet to support. One GI, seeing my predicament, came over and swapped his carton of K-rations for my ammo crate but if the ration crate was lighter, I couldn't tell the difference.

I continued stumbling every few feet until a burly non-com came by and told me to leave the rations there and rejoin the column. In an hour, we had been able to cover about a mile to where a convoy of trucks was waiting for us. I was helped into one of them and I crowded into a corner. I had not felt this bad since the 50-mile march in from the French coastline. A sign told us we were pulling into the town of Opagne and when the column stopped, I dragged myself into the nearest shattered building and collapsed on the rubble-strewn floor.

In the morning, Joe Everett was tugging at my shoulder to wake me up. An early riser, he had already found a field kitchen with hot food. Breakfast in the field was always the same: black coffee, butterless dry bread and hot oatmeal. You learned fast not to complain about the food, for if you did, you got nothing and anything was better than C-rations, even Army slop.

Everett and I explored a bombed-out church in the town. As we entered the courtyard, we found about 30 more civilian bodies slumped against the church walls. As in the previous three towns, their hands had been tied behind them and they had been bowled over like tenpins. Their haunting, staring eyes and distorted faces mirrored their last moments of life while facing their executioners.

As we passed by the church, we glanced inside where a solitary GI, his head bowed reverently and with a Thompson submachine gun cradled across his knee, was praying before what had once been an altar. I can only presume he was praying for the souls of those he had seen piled up in death outside in the courtyard, or perhaps he prayed for his own. Quietly, we left him alone with his God.

As Everett and I walked back to our billet, we discussed the future of Europe, agreeing it would take decades to restore what once had been. The war was leaving countless millions of people in upwards of a dozen countries dead or homeless. The soil and many of the rivers had been poisoned and polluted, forests had been decimated, 80 percent of the homes, commercial buildings and industry had been destroyed. Bridges and railroads would have to be rebuilt, farming would be difficult for many years and entire networks of roads had been made practically impassable. It would indeed be a long rebuilding road back for the peoples of Europe.

Across from our billet, mine fields had been taped off and left intact, for to attempt to disarm or remove the mines while they were frozen to the ground was not feasible. If the mines were in the way of a strategic move, they were detonated by rifle fire or by a quarter pound of explosives; and if they were in the road, we tied ropes to them, crouched in ditches and yanked at them until they exploded. Slow and noisy, but safe. When we moved on, and we did almost constantly, we left most of the mines behind to become someone else's problem during the spring thaw.

Later in the day, to break up the monotony of waiting for the next move, I returned to the church to practice my pistol marksmanship, again using religious statues as targets. At the time, this practice didn't seem sacrilegious. After all, the church was only a building and it had already been destroyed. I wasn't yet aware of the meaning of symbolism.

The next morning, I awoke to find a strange woman bedded down beside me in the bombed-out building that served as a one nighter home for the squad. She had squeezed in between Everett and me during the night. We questioned her and found she was a school teacher who was hungry and frightened. The rationale behind her moving in with us, she said, was we would perhaps give her food (we did), close to us she would be protected from death (she wasn't), and if we got to know her, we wouldn't kill her (we didn't).

We fed her and the next day, she was gone again.

A company runner came by and told me Captain Bowen wanted me at the company CP. I reported in and was informed there was an opening available for me at the Officer Candidate School in Paris. My Army records, stating I had been chosen for OCS at Fort Benning while a cadreman at Fort McClellan six months earlier, had finally caught up with me.

The previous June, I had been deprived of a commission at Fort Benning because of a clerical foul-up. A corporal and I, after our transfer orders had already been cut, were found to be in excess of the quota allowed for that OCS cycle. Our rejection form said our acceptance would be kept on file until other transfer orders could be cut. Bowen said they had been reissued and I had been reaccepted

Having witnessed the high mortality rate of junior officers during the Battle of the Bulge, and having built up a healthy dislike for the brass, I declined the offer without reservation. Bowen tried to convince me of what a great opportunity I was passing up but my decision was firm.

By war's end, 19 junior officers in the regiment—practically all of them platoon leaders—had been killed. In LOVE Company that I had left behind when I transferred to Anti-Tank Company for mine duty, 32 of the 200 men in the company were killed during the six months the division was on the line—16 percent, or about one in every six. In Anti-Tank Company, only one man had been killed and no officers. I knew I had made the right decision back in England to volunteer to become an "anti-tanker."

My feet were showing no signs of improvement. When the pain got to the point that I could no longer walk and could, in fact, barely stand, I removed my overshoes and unwrapped the rags and newspaper from around my feet and ankles. The sight that greeted me was frightening. My feet had turned almost black and the skin was peeling much worse than before. I tried to massage my feet but even touching them brought on searing pain.

Taking one look at my feet, Everett advised, "You're a damn fool if you don't go to a hospital and have those taken care of."

I vetoed that advice immediately and loudly. I filled a compress full of snow and applied it to my swollen feet to reduce the swelling. There I left my overshoes off for a couple hours and warmed my bare feet near the stove before finding some oversized dry socks and putting them on.

One of the squad members suggested I try to wear combat boots again to support the feet better and restrict the swelling. We found a large pair of combat boots that had been taken earlier from a dead GI. With much effort, I got them on and tried to stand. A wild pain shot from my feet to my head but I was standing and I found I could walk better than I had been able to do since Christmas. I was foolishly confident I could lick this malady by myself.

At 0500 on January 6, we were told me were moving out again. The convoy stopped at a crossroads and we were ordered to dig in and defend it, if needed. From the attitudes of the company officers, this crossroads was apparently of extreme strategic value, for I was assigned to a machine gun team and I could see a network of other automatic weapon emplacements around me. We were told it was the main link between Houffalize and Laroche on the Ourthe River.

A short distance behind the intersection was a patch of woods. For some unknown reason, probably just youthful curiosity, I decided to check it out. Assured by the other machine gunners that I wasn't needed for awhile, I took off. I wasn't afraid of mines, for the Germans seldom placed mine fields in wooded areas. Several hundred feet into the woods, I spotted a bunker and another and still another. I had stumbled onto something big, I thought, but I was committed. It was too late and I had come too far to turn back for help.

Dodging furtively from tree to tree, I approached the first snow-covered bunker When I hit the entrance, I threw a grenade inside and flopped in the snow. After the explosion, I jumped inside. I felt foolish when I found all three emplacements were deserted I scoured them for souvenirs and was rewarded with a beautiful, hand-carved, staghorn knife with a four-inch blade.

Rather carelessly, I started plowing my way back through the snow to my machine gun position As I circled around a large pine tree, I came face to face with a Wehrmacht soldier. From instinct, I whipped my M-1 around and fired blindly while falling backwards. Without looking, I fired off another round, this one hitting him in the shoulder. Had I looked first, I wouldn't have fired; he had already thrown his rifle down and had his hands in the air in surrender. The bullet had knocked him down and as he lay in the snow, he raised up an arm, stammering in English, "Kamerad, I surrender." All the fight had gone out of him.

"Sind Sie allein?" ("Are you alone?") I asked.

Hearing my German, he started jabbering at me in his mother tongue so fast I couldn't understand him. I slowed him down and tried to figure out one sentence at a time.

When I showed regret for having shot him and wondered what to do with him, he said there were about 65 others hidden in the woods, all of whom also wanted to give themselves up. As I dressed his wound, he said their officers had been SS but they had abandoned their command when the Americans came close. These whipped Wehrmacht soldiers had not eaten in three days, he said, and they wanted to surrender to get hot American food. He also said they had also admitted to themselves for many weeks that Germany's war was lost.

He burst into tears when he finally realized I was not going to kill him, and immediately pulled out pictures of his wife and children. I assured him that he and the others wouldn't be killed; that unlike the SS, Americans didn't do this to their Kriegsgefangeners (POWs). He said they had been told by their officers that German prisoners would be machine gunned by Negro Americans.

Suddenly, without warning, he let out a yell, "Kommen Sie hier-her" ("Come here"). Wehrmacht soldiers poured out of the woods from every direction. I felt completely intimidated for they were all still armed and all around me. When I threw up my rifle, they all dropped theirs and, almost in unison, clamped their hands over their heads, but it took several minutes before my heart stopped thumping and I could regain my composure.

I sat the motley bunch of prisoners down, away from their weapons, and wondered what to do with them. I told them they would be fed as soon as they got to the POW camp, even though I had no idea where one was. Some said they had been in the army for only a few weeks, that they had been conscripted from their homes and sent into the front lines without any formal training.

My wounded prisoner said he was a 56-year-old "Unteroffizier" (master sergeant) and then he pointed to a young looking soldier In the group who he said was only 15.

Finally, I marched my ragtag German army back to the crossroads and sat them in a group until some brass showed up and told me where the POW enclosure was. When we arrived there, the Germans were being fed a supper of hot food. I told the POW camp commander my 65 prisoners had not eaten for three days and he promised me they would be given "double portions."

As I walked past the barbed wire fence, the "Unteroffizier" I had shot called out in halting English, "God Bless you, son."

These Wehrmacht "soldaten" were a far cry from the SS troops we had been facing all through Belgium, for these bedraggled soldiers were the beginning of the Volkssturm (people's assault force), a civilian array of children and the elderly that Hitler pressed desperately into service during the final months of the war.

As I walked back to the crossroads, I found it ironic the prisoners were getting hot chow that day and I was going back to cold C- and K-rations. The GIs back at the machine gun dugout started kidding me: "Hey, the war should be over next week with this guy around."

I took the kidding good-naturedly but inwardly I felt proud of myself. "That's 65 we don't have to shoot at any more," I kidded back. Later, a captain whom I didn't know came over and congratulated me on a job well done. I let him believe what he wanted to believe, for I neglected to say it had all been an accident that happened while I was goofing off instead of being in the machine gun emplacement where I was supposed to be.

I was told we were still in a section of Opagne—Odeigne, Opagne—they all sounded and looked the same to me. I sat in the snow, ate some crackers and candy from home and escaped from the horrors of war for a few minutes.

Nights in the foxholes were still bitter and lonely and daylight was always welcomed, for with it the loneliness usually disappeared. One particular dawn in early January broke bright and extremely sunny as I stared at the surrounding beauty of the Ardennes forests. After several hours, my head started to ache, my eyes became blurry and images started to shimmer. I thought my concussion was acting up, but soon afterward I was sightless.

I panicked and yelled for Joe Everett. He and several others, one of them a medic, came running. The medic put a hand on my head and told me not to worry, that it was only temporary snow blindness and that I would be OK in a day or two. He reassured me he had treated many such cases before. Then he placed an ice pack on my eyes and left. I kept taking it off every few minutes to see if my eyesight had returned but everything was black and I was scared, real scared. Only a short time before I had been terrified by the prospect of losing both my feet and now I feared I was going blind.

Several hours later, I could make out dim images and I relaxed a little. Full vision returned the next day.

A company lieutenant came by to personally inspect the condition of everyone's feet. Everett had, for my own good, he said, told company officers about me. The lieutenant, after seeing the ugly sight that had once been my feet, told me I would be evacuated immediately.

He had known about my feet since Christmas but in no way had offered to restrict or limit my duties. Now suddenly, he was making a big deal about being concerned for my welfare. Right away I refused and he countered by saying he could order me to the rear and that if I still refused, he would threaten me with court martial or even arrest.

I still refused, pointing out to him that the anti-mine squad was already down to only seven men. How much lower did he want it to go? We were the only ones around who had been trained to handle mines and booby traps. Finally he said pompously, "Fine. If you want your feet to rot off its OK with me." Then he waived all responsibility for what might happen to me medically for not seeking treatment. So much for his concern.

Two others on the squad also were found to have mild cases of trench foot and they were only too happy to go to the rear for treatment and perhaps a little rest and rehabilitation. Now, the squad was down to five. In what I considered punishment for refusing his evacuation order, the lieutenant ordered me and one other squad member to clear an area of mines at a proposed 155mm howitzer battery location. I grabbed my "vacuum cleaner" and headed out. We were taken by truck to the battery site where we swept about an acre of three-foot-deep snow before declaring it cleared. The "six-by" taking us back to the crossroads suddenly veered off the road and started plowing through the trees, the driver saying he knew a short cut.

Minutes later, the truck was stuck, the wheels spinning furiously and throwing snow and chunks of wood in every direction. We unloaded to try pushing it out as wooden boxes were being hurled past our heads and into the air behind us by the spinning wheels.

"Hold it!" I screamed. "Stop! Shut off the motor!"

"What are those things?" the driver asked.

I looked closer and then did a double take. They were German "holtz minen," wooden anti-tank, antipersonnel mines and they could be seen everywhere in the snow. We had already driven over dozens of them, and not one had exploded. In their haste, the Germans had neglected to remove a safety pin from the firing device needed to arm them. The troops that had thrown them there obviously had never handled such mines before.

Not wanting to be killed by some moronic truck driver taking short cuts, I removed my mine detector from the truck and hiked back to my company. I left the driver to get himself out of the mine field without my help. This episode, another of so many close brushes with death that happened to me during combat, made good telling back at Anti-Tank Company.

An officer came by and asked if anyone wanted to accompany him on a reconnoitering trip around the countryside. You guessed it. We grabbed a company Jeep and swung down the road toward Houffalize before branching off onto a narrow side road. As the snow on the path through the woods got deeper, the jeep started to labor. We were almost stuck and the lieutenant was struggling to back the vehicle back to the main road when firing erupted all around us.

We had stumbled into a hornet's nest of German troops and armor. Bullets were spattering everywhere. I could see about two squads of Krauts sprinting toward us from all sides. A tank also blew a round past us that exploded against a tree behind the Jeep. Burp gun slugs were throwing up snow geysers all around us as the lieutenant desperately swung the Jeep around so violently through the underbrush I was almost thrown out.

Deep ruts bounced us from side to side. Only when we hit the main road and screeched back toward the crossroad did we dare breathe again. After informing G-2 that a large buildup of Germans was deployed in the adjacent woods, the lieutenant looked at me and I looked back at him. We examined the Jeep and found nearly 30 shrapnel and bullet holes in the vehicle. From the expression in his eyes, he realized that I now knew he too was capable of stupidity. Officers did not like enlisted men to find out they were fallible.

At chow time that night, I couldn't eat; the jeep incident had frightened the appetite out of me. While I sat crunched down and hungry in the snow at the machine gun nest, I promised myself I would never again volunteer for anything, no matter what the reasons. I tossed and turned all that night.

Come morning, I stood up and, for some unexplained reason, my feet felt much better. I was able to hobble around with only a slight limp. I celebrated by eating a candy bar from home as I waited for the field kitchen to open up.

Roscoe C. ("Rockie") Blunt Jr. poses in his family's backyard in October 1943 after his induction into the Army.

Winners of the Expert Infantry Badge during Stateside training. Rockie Blunt, middle row, second from the right, at age 19, was the youngest soldier to win the award at that time.

The 84th Division "Railsplitters" saw their initial combat on the Dutch-German border after a grueling inland march from Normandy.

The rear entrance to a German pill-box on the Siegfried Line. These deadly fortifications were usually impossible to spot from the air or from a distance.

A minesweeping team heads into a village that has just been abandoned by the enemy. These men were the de facto spearheads of many an advance.

As a demolitions specialist, Rockie Blunt often found he had first dibs on loot. At left he poses with Hitler Youth drums he found in Geilenkirchen in November 1944.

Blunt maintained steady correspondence and a voluminous journal throughout the war. At left is an atypically short note to his mother written after he was allowed to sit in at a divisional band concert.

His correspondence with his father was highly detailed. "I can see now how a man changes greatly," he reflects at right, and then, "There is nobody in the world like an American Infantryman."

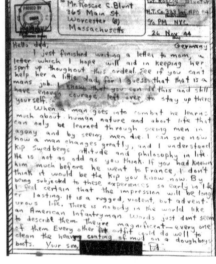

He often illustrated his letters with drawings based on the style of Bill Mauldin in *Stars & Stripes*. To his sister June, at left, he depicts the difference between a foot soldier and an airman.

In the propaganda war, the Germans won on style if not results. Above, an 84th Division flyer urges specific German units to surrender.

In the German flyer at right, an American homefront lothario seduces a soldier's wife while the soldier struggles with death in the mirror. (Leaflets courtesy of the Blunt collection.)

On December 16, 1944, the Germans broke through the American front in the Ardennes with a massive counter-offensive. Days later, the 84th Division raced into Belgium to try to stem the onslaught. The countenance of the infantryman at left reveals the grueling nature of the battle.

An American Sherman, above, struggles with the icy, forested terrain of the Ardennes. German armor, below, encountered more difficult opposition from the 84th Division than it had met during the initial stages of the offensive.

84th INFANTRY DIVISION
From Activation 15 Oct 42 to V-E Day 9 May 45

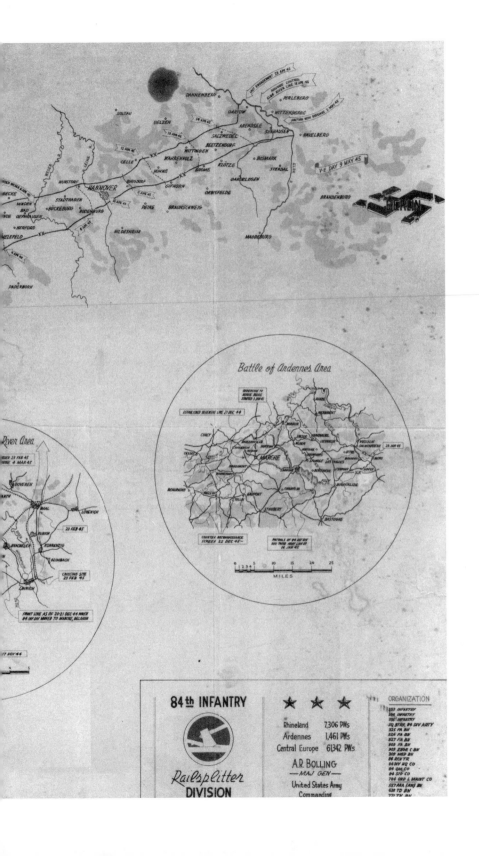

Scenes from the Battle of the Bulge. An American anti-tank gun, above, a tired infantryman, right, and an American casualty, below, who would later be retrieved by graves collection teams.

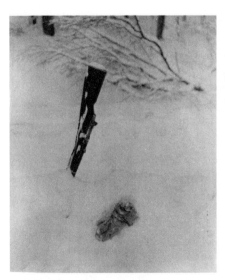

Medics tend to wounded U.S. soldiers during the Battle of the Bulge. In the freezing temperatures even minor wounds could prove fatal.

As the Americans counterattacked in the Ardennes they found that many Belgian civilians had been murdered by the retreating Germans.

Joseph Winston "Joe Loot" Everett hailed from Oklahoma.

Toward the end of the Ardennes campaign, Rockie Blunt enjoyed the hospitality of two Belgian girls. He was later surprised to find this picture had been printed in *Stars & Stripes* and even distributed back in the States.

In the half-light of morning, after the 84th Division had forced the Roer River, Blunt snapped this picture of a column of German prisoners carrying their dead and wounded.

Infantry, some with fixed bayonets, pause during street fighting in a German village.

An American assault boat that fell victim to enemy artillery during the crossing of the Roer.

The Americans had to fight their way step-by-step, building-by-building, through a succession of devastated towns.

Enemy opposition began to collapse as U.S. troops penetrated farther into Germany in the spring of 1945. After the fighting ended, Rockie Blunt's "bandsman" classification came through. He is pictured below at left with the Tophatters, the 84th Division band.

A German colonel arrives on the American-held, west side of the Elbe River, along with his "aide-de-camp."

In the final days of the war, thousands of Germans sought a means to cross the Elbe in order to surrender to the Anglo-Americans instead of to the Red Army.

Rockie Blunt, in a photo taken after the fighting had ended in May 1945.

A small portion of Blunt's souvenir collection. Throughout his service in Europe he kept a steady flow of packages going back to the States.

In 1996 Blunt was presented with the Bronze Star for valor. One of his sons, U.S. Navy Commander Richard Blunt, drove from his base in Texas to Massachusetts in order to personally present his father the award.

10

Smashing Hitler's Dream

After word came we were moving out again, we loaded onto a convoy of trucks concealed nearby in the woods. We were only a few minutes into the move when voices started yelling, "Hit the ditches, hit the ditches!" En masse, we dove overboard.

An Me-109 at treetop level was strafing the road, but he was upon us and gone again before most of us could react. One of the trucks in the convoy in front of us burst into flames. As I dug my face into the snow, the plane returned and made another pass over us. Before the pilot broke off, he had destroyed two trucks and killed two men, one of whom had apparently been slow getting off his truck.

As I climbed back onto mine, I thought again of the adage about combat GIs—the quick and the dead. This axiom, as true as it was, kept coming back to haunt us for we would see too many instances where as quick as a GI was, it was not enough. Fate and luck also played major parts in our game of survival.

The rest of the trip was uneventful and we arrived soon afterward in Grand Han, a small town left largely intact by the war. The civilian population was walking busily on the streets appearing, for the most part, totally unconcerned about the German-American conflict devastating the cities and towns all around them. They also seemed disinterested in our presence and I prayed I could find a little peace in this quaint, isolated Belgian village.

But there was to be no peace—in fact, no sleep, at least not for a while. During the Battle of the Bulge, shortages were constant—food, ammunition, gasoline, weapons, equipment, vehicles, but primarily men. It was not uncommon for GIs to be abruptly transferred from one outfit to another, from one duty to another, without orders or notice, often for a few days or even a few hours. Bodies were shuffled around to fill vacant slots in the table of organization, and usually the first available body would suffice. Because there were more foot soldiers than anyone else in evidence, they were chosen most often.

Apparently picked at random, I was told one day to report to graves registration for temporary duty. When I arrived at a building designated as a field mortuary, I was briefed on what I would be doing: picking up American dead in the field.

I didn't fully comprehend what was involved in the new assignment until after we had started. Another GI and I rode around the area in a three-quarter-ton weapons carrier and every time we spotted a dead American we jumped off, picked up the body and slung it any old way we could, usually by the arms and legs, onto the back of the truck.

As we hefted each twisted, frozen corpse onto the truck, I invariably turned away, averting my eyes from the glazed, blue, bloated faces of the dead, each grotesquely etched with the filth of war, many with open eyes reflecting the terror and violence of their last moment on earth. It was almost as if I could reject death, push it away and not let it intrude deeper into my life, as fragile as it was hour by hour.

The bodies, frozen stiff in every position imaginable, were stacked haphazardly higher and higher like cord wood until we couldn't throw them any higher. Then it was back to the field mortuary where we emptied our load and started the process all over again.

Everywhere we searched we found bodies, floating in the rivers, trampled on the roads, bloated in the ditches, rotting in the bunkers, pretzeled into foxholes, burned in the tanks, buried in the snow, sprawled in doorways, splattered in gutters, dismembered in mine fields and even literally blown up into trees.

We didn't try to identify them; that was someone else's responsibility back at the mortuary. We just located them, picked them up, piled them as high as we could and then dumped them off. Since the bodies were scattered everywhere, it didn't take long to get a load.

We didn't bother with German corpses.

While working this detail, I found that I soon considered American and German dead the same. A corpse was a corpse no matter what color his uniform was, and war was war. When I returned to my platoon two days later, I again wondered what was happening to me that I could become so blasé, so indifferent about death, especially those involving our own people. Oddly, no thought was given to the families of the dead or even to the dead themselves. Mental sensitivities were totally turned off as we numbly went about our job—find them, load them, get rid of them.

It had not been an assignment that I particularly relished, but in the Army you learn to say "yes, sir" and do as you're told without any thought or emotion no matter how revolting the order might be.

During my absence, my squad had gone looking for shelter and had found more than it bargained for in the form of a centuries-old chateau perched on the side of a small mountain and totally unmarked by the war. The chateau reminded me of the grandeur I had experienced in the Scottish and English countrysides.

When I entered the chateau, an elegant fireplace, ornate windows, marbled stone floors and rustic, hunting-lodge decor greeted me. Rejoining my buddies, I was greeted warmly by two rather plump, wholesome Belgian girls who welcomed me with feminine enthusiasm and hospitality. As soon as I entered what had once been a banquet hall, I immediately headed for the roaring flames of the fireplace to warm myself. It was the first time in many months I could actually sit quietly beside a fire and not worry about some German seeing the glow of the flames.

Seeing this and realizing I was half frozen, one girl disappeared and then reappeared moments later with a large mug of piping hot chocolate. Not believing my eyes, and slightly apprehensive about this unexpected friendliness, I sampled it cautiously. As I sipped it slowly, retaining it in my mouth as long as I could, I reveled in my glorious new-found fortune. Remembering a quote I had learned in school, I asked a French-speaking member of the squad to tell our Belgian hostesses the cocoa was "nectar from the Gods." They smiled appreciatively.

To demonstrate more American-Belgian good will, I went outside and had my picture taken with the two girls. Somehow, the picture wound up in the possession of *Stars & Stripes* editors and it was published, even back in the States. I wondered what my mother's reaction to it was, if she really believed I was fighting a war. The snapshot showed me being kissed on the cheek by one of the girls while the other one held my rifle.

The squad was told it would remain in Grand Han for several days, that it was, in fact, a brief rest period for us. Counting the time in Holland, northern Germany, the Roer basin and the Ardennes, we had been on the line nearly two months.

Unofficial word was received that the crisis in the Bulge campaign, for all practical purposes, was over. We were cautioned not to relax our vigilance for, even though we had the Kraut temporarily on the run, the war was still very much on. Actually, it wasn't so much that such information was being disseminated to us through normal channels but rather just a gut feeling, an instinct that we all shared. The Germans who had been stopped at Marche had been forced to split their armies and improvise their sputtering campaign along alternate routes. This had allowed Allied forces to cut these fragmented enemy divisions into small, disorganized groups. Our 9th Army, under Lieutenant General W. H. Simpson, had pushed southward from the north and General George Patton's 3rd Army had linked up with it from the south.

In the case of the 84th Infantry Division, the linkup came on January 16 near the small village of Engreux near the Ourthe River when a 33-man patrol from the 334th Regiment greeted a tanker from the 41st Cavalry, 11th Armored Division, Third U.S. Army. But though thousands of German troops and hundreds of vehicles were being encircled and captured, the main German forces managed to escape to Germany with their weapons, tanks and equipment intact. We would meet them again later.

Naively, I thought of peace, of returning home alive, of hot food, a soft bed with sheets and perhaps even a real toilet to sit on rather than the slit-trenches we had used since early November when we arrived on Omaha Beach. But all these thoughts amounted to absolutely nothing. I was about to find out the war was a long way from being over.

I pulled a supply detail one afternoon and was told I would be one of nine spare truck drivers used to pick up food at a supply depot about 20 miles away. I was assured the depot was well within Allied lines and I would not have to load the truck, just drive it if need be.

As the convoy traveled toward our destination, I took a few minutes to admire the beauty of the Ardennes Forest. For miles there was no evidence of the war, just the majesty of towering pines, craggy mountains and swift-flowing rivers. I didn't realize I was being lulled into a sense of false security by the scenery. It also didn't occur to me we hadn't been passing any American units in quite a while. But after all, there was nothing to worry about for the lead truck had a map and we were barreling right along.

A loud explosion somewhere in front of us made our driver slam on his brakes. On the ice-slicked road, he was not quick enough and we slammed into the rear of the truck in front of us a split second before the truck behind us rammed into us in a chain reaction pileup, throwing me violently against the windshield and then back against the seat.

I slumped to the floor dazed. "Jump! Jump" I heard a voice bellow. Without hesitating I fumbled for the cab door handle and fell headlong into a ditch.

Out from behind practically every tree in the forest German soldiers appeared firing at 18 truck drivers cowering in a roadside ditch. None of the drivers were shot so I can only assume the Germans were not trying to kill us but rather firing over our heads to intimidate us. So overwhelming were the odds, there was no realistic thought of resisting. Quickly I buried my P-38 in the snow, for to be found with it meant instant execution. Then we stood up meekly as a group with our hands over our heads and surrendered.

You can imagine our fright when, after a few minutes, the situation settled down and we recognized the black SS tank corps uniforms with the small silver skulls on the lapels and remembered that they had a reputation for taking no prisoners.

The first thought that entered my mind was a mental picture of Malmedy, where a mass slaughter of American prisoners by SS troops had occurred just a couple of weeks earlier. We were lined up and searched for weapons. Quickly, our watches and other valuables were snatched from us. While being herded into the woods for what I was sure would be our mass execution, I counted nearly 100 of them. In the woods, I saw what had caused our lead truck to explode: neatly camouflaged Mark V Panther and Mark VI Tiger tanks.

I was ashamed and dejected in these last moments of my life for surrendering like a coward without a fight. I was about to die without saying good-bye to my family; they would never know what happened to me. And surrendering without a shot, regardless of the odds, surely was not a hero's way out.

The tanks started to grind their way toward us through the trees and I instantly realized this would be how we were to die, crushed under the treads of a German tank or machine gunned where we stood. It was easy to figure out that 18 American truck drivers would only be in the tankers' way, slowing them up.

But instead, we were forced at bayonet point to watch as the tanks swung into position and their 88s started destroying the convoy, one truck after another at point-blank range. The dense, acrid stench of burning trucks added to the deafening, frightening scene exploding all around us.

Never before or since have I felt such hopelessness and despair.

After the German elation subsided, we were prodded painfully with bayonets onto the German tanks where we sat watching the tank crews prepare to move on. An SS trooper with a Schmeisser slung around his neck guarded us. The commander of the tank I was sitting on poked his head from the turret, looked at us with contempt and then burst out laughing. He yelled a remark at the foot soldiers, something loosely translated as "Take a look at these sad sack Amis."

Looking around at our sorry-looking bunch, I almost had to agree with him. What once had been cheerful, reasonably well groomed GIs had by now been reduced to a bunch of forlorn prisoners in baggy, dirty uniforms. This was the German's day and he was making the most of it.

Our helmets were taken from us and discarded, but we were allowed to keep our wool caps. The pungent exhaust fumes blown into our faces brought on instant nausea and near asphyxiation while low-hanging tree branches slapped painfully at us trying to sweep us from the tanks as we moved through the forest. Flames shooting from exhaust vents set fire to bushes along the way, leaving a trail a blind man could follow. I hoped someone would find this trail and rescue us, but I knew within me the chances were extremely thin.

We would not be missed, for I had seen no sign of American positions or entrenchments anywhere for many miles. After crashing through the forests for about an hour and carefully avoiding roads where they might be spotted by observation planes, the tank column halted and we were prodded off and instructed to sit in a circle in a small clearing.

One soldier who spoke guttural English ordered us to dig foxholes for the tank officers and crews, which we did with considerable effort. When we started to dig some for ourselves, he instantly stopped us and yelled, "Keiner Hohlen" ("No holes"), and then with arm motions told us that we could stretch out on the ground for the night.

Blowing snow started to fall and as it whipped against our faces during the night, I began to think the odds were improving that we might not be executed after all but rather relegated to a prisoner Stalag for American POWs. Simple logic dictated: the longer they kept us alive, the better our chances. I was afraid to tell any of the other prisoners what I thought for fear of raising their hopes and then being wrong.

Sickened by hunger, I couldn't even find a K-ration dog biscuit in my pocket to munch on. Eventually, one of the SS troopers approached our huddled, shivering group and offered us a pot of Kartoffel Suppe (potato soup).

"Essen" ("Eat"), he snapped. He motioned at the kettle and said sharply, "Trinken" ("Drink").

We each sipped some of the soup and then passed it around. When the guard threw a piece of black bread at us, indicating it was for all of us, we each broke off a small chunk. The soup was potato-flavored hot water for the potatoes had been removed and obviously eaten by the Germans. When we finished, the same German soldier retrieved the kettle and disappeared again into the darkness.

The bitter cold night made my feet throb again with pain. When I awakened, the other prisoners were huddled together murmuring amongst themselves, a welcome sound for during the night no one had spoken. We knew that at least some of the Germans spoke English, but our captors still didn't know that I spoke and understood some German.

Breakfast consisted of more potato soup and a piece of hardened cheese that a German threw in the snow before us. He wanted us to grovel. I took a bite and passed it on. My sense of taste had left me but I knew that anything I could put in my stomach would stave off exhaustion.

Trying to pick up bits of their conversation to find out what they had planned for us, I watched the Germans eating around a fire nearby and I noticed their food was the same as that given us. At least what little they had they were willing to share. This was another good sign—they might not be planning to execute us. Maybe we'd be liberated after all.

Shortly after daybreak, the column started pushing forward again through the trees, this time for nearly two hours. From the erratic course being followed, it appeared the tank commander was probing first one way and then another trying to find an escape route back to the Fatherland.

When the column finally stopped again, some of the SS troops started taunting us in a game of psychological warfare. They formed a circle around us with burp guns and rifles pointed in our direction and then kicked snow in our faces or shoved rifles and pistols in our faces yelling, "Toten" or "Schlachten!" ("Death, kill"), and then laughing hysterically.

One time when this charade ended, a slightly built German in his late teens lagged behind the others. When he was sure he was not seen, he took a loaf of bread from underneath his coat and threw it to us. In perfect English, he said, "Maybe this will help. I used to live in New York." Later, we heard a commotion near the tanks and the young German was being marched back to our group.

"They found out about the bread and I am to be shot. Always remember, there are good Germans." These were his last words before a volley from a quickly mustered firing squad cut him down. Then the execution squad left him lying in the snow beside our group, pivoted smartly on their heels and walked away. I had seen countless men die but never one murdered so methodically by his own people. I overheard a group of officers discussing us. Some wanted to kill us, while others felt that if we were murdered, they too would be shot if captured. The latter group was overruled and the decision was to eliminate us for we were slowing the tanks down and there was no real reason to keep us alive.

Now I was really terrified. I told the others, who were already on the verge of fleeing in panic. Some wanted to run, hoping they might make it to safety, while others wanted to fight the Germans with bare hands until they were shot.

While we continued to deliberate amongst ourselves, a group of officers walked toward us, pistols drawn. One officer barked out, "Auf Stehen" ("Stand up").

In one last desperate act, I stammered, "Ich wollen zu sprechen," ("I want to speak"). Surprised, the officer, a major, held up his hand and nodded to me. "Sprechen," he ordered. I told him they were surrounded by the 2nd Armored Division and that they, like the SS, took no prisoners. I asked them if they had heard of the "Hell on Wheels" division and then I told him I could guarantee them they wouldn't be killed and would, in fact, be fed hot food if we were not executed.

With a lump in my throat so big I could hardly swallow, I reminded them it was 18 Americans for 100 Germans. "Achtzehn fur ein hundert" ("18 for 100"), I repeated.

After a short discussion, the major came back and said they would surrender if I kept my word about their not being shot.

"But how do we know we won't be killed for destroying your trucks?" he persisted.

"Das ist krieg" ("That's war"), I answered quickly, trying to think of answers in anticipation of the questions.

He asked how I knew we were surrounded by the 2nd Armored Division. I pointed to two hills near us and told him the armored division was using them for artillery observation. He looked first at one, then the other.

As if my desperate spiel had been heard by the Lord Almighty, an American artillery shell whistled into the woods behind us, then another in front of us. An observer somewhere had spotted the Germans and was bracketing our position. The next round, I knew, would be on top of us.

I ignored the Germans, their guns and everything else as I sprinted for the nearest tank. I threw myself beneath it to escape the shrapnel that was flying everywhere. I figured the tanks offered better protection than lying out in the open. The Germans had already scattered, finding whatever instant shelter they could from the shelling.

When the barrage stopped, the 17 other American truck drivers, all of whom had remained exposed on the open field, had not suffered a single scratch nor were there any German casualties, tanks or men. The Red Legs (artillerymen) had expended a lot of shells but, by the fortunes of war, hadn't hit anything of value. The American artillery coming precisely when it did, when it was most needed to save the lives of 18 GIs, still remains one of the greatest unexplained coincidences of the war for me.

The German major stood in front of me, unbuckled his chrome-plated Luger and handed it to me. The surrender was official. The SS troopers and tank crewmen were lining up and stacking their rifles into tripods in the snow beside each tank.

When I told the group of frightened truck drivers that we were being freed, one GI dropped to his knees and blessed himself while the others jumped around, slapping each other on the back. As soon as the last German had put his weapon down, we started reclaiming the possessions that had been taken from us and, at the same time "liberated" a few additional ones of our own. We took as many weapons as we could carry and destroyed the rest. I told the major to have a meal prepared but he informed me they had no more food. This, I'm sure, had weighed heavily in their decision to surrender.

The next problem was how to return them to American lines, for we had no idea where or how far away they were. The German major pulled out a map and pointed to a coordinate. "Vielleicht dorthin" ("Perhaps there"), he suggested the American positions might be. But, like us, he couldn't be certain. His guess was as good as ours, we figured, so we started out on foot leaving the four tanks behind.

For the first time in a long time, I felt a little like a hero, but medals were normally reserved for officers who spent much of their time finding ways to write up citations for each other. The vexing problem of finding our way back to the American lines was solved after a couple hours when someone yelled, "Shut up!"

We all stopped and listened. We could hear tanks. Around a bend in the road, moments later, appeared advance units of the 5th Armored Division. Instantly, seeing the large number of Germans in the road, they started firing at them. I screamed and jumped around in the road until they stopped, but the commotion of the tank fire had produced dozens of olive drab uniforms from the woods on all sides. I looked at the German SS major and he nodded.

Some of us climbed onto the tanks that were headed for the 84th's sector and as I rode along, looking at the German SS POWs marching smartly in front of us, I thought back to Sherman Allen, the South High School teacher who had taught me the language that had saved

18 American lives. (As an aside, Allen beamed with satisfaction when I looked him up after the war and related how we had been captured, held prisoner and then released after one of the biggest con jobs of the war.)

When the captain in charge of the tank column asked how we had been treated, I told him that I had promised the Kraut major safe passage to a POW pen in exchange for our lives. He assured me no harm would come to them while under his protection.

For a moment, I thought of telling the captain about the incident where the SS officers had executed one of their own whose only crime had been to offer us a loaf of stolen bread. But then I thought better of it. No matter how brutal and senseless the punishment had been, it had still been an internal decision made by a duly appointed superior officer in a foreign army, not ours.

I relayed the captain's promise to the Nazi SS major and gave him a note with my name, unit designation and signature saying we had been humanely treated while his prisoners. He smiled, clicked his heels to attention and gave me a "Heil Hitler" salute.

I ignored it for he was still an SS officer who I was sure had committed his share of atrocities in Belgium. But with the note, I felt I had carried out my promise. He too seemed satisfied when I read it to him in German. Soon, the armored detachment arrived at Grand Han and the first one to greet us was Joe Everett with "Where the hell you been, Blunt, shackin' up somewhere?"

"Yeah," I answered, "Shacking up with Krauts and have I got some stories to tell ya when I wake up."

With that, I collapsed onto my sleeping bag and slept beside the fire. News of our escapade had spread by now and no one disturbed my sleep. When I awakened, my stomach hurt and only then did I remember we had not eaten anything for three days but potato-flavored hot water and some horrible-tasting, moldy black bread. I can still remember the first hot meal I ate after being released from German captivity. It was plain hot macaroni, slices of dry cheese, hard-crusted white bread, pineapple slices in sugary syrup, cold sliced beets and coffee sprinkled with powdered milk—truly a king's feast. An understanding mess sergeant insisted that I eat a second helping. I devoured it without argument.

Then I opened a late Christmas package from home and gorged

myself on candy, Cracker Jack from Thomas's store in Shrewsbury, animal crackers, fruit, dried meat, popcorn and gum.

Because of the slight interruption in my life caused by the German tankers, it was time to catch up on my letter writing home. Still governed by what I perceived my parents' emotions to be, I glossed over the hard facts and painted rosy images of life while traveling on the Continent. I touched on the subject of my various exploits but never went into details. I knew my parents were probably suffering every time they listened to a news broadcast or picked up a paper, so I felt there was no point in alarming them further. It was a practice I followed throughout the war. Some day I would write a book about it all, I thought, and release the memories that were already disturbing me so deeply. With that goal in mind, I continued to accumulate a more private daily chronicle, a barracks bag full of impressions and recollections written on any foolscap I could find.

I tried for another short nap but soon Everett was tugging at me. "C'mon, Blunt. It's time to wake up and die right again." As usual, that was his signal that it was time to eat more Army chow.

After the meal, word came we would be on the move again in a few minutes. It seemed as though that was all we ever were told, that we would be moving out again. Until I had been drafted into the Army and sent on a European vacation, I had never known how desirable it was in life to be settled in one location and given an opportunity to become acclimated to one's surroundings.

The trucks rolled slowly through the Ardennes forest closer to where the Germans were being bottled up. We were told we were going back on the line, but this time the report proved false. It appeared that we were just not being allowed to lag very far behind. That was OK with me; I had had about as much action as I wanted for a while.

We entered the town of Regne, where I quickly staked out a two-story house, mostly intact, for a temporary billet. I say "quickly," for the best accommodations—a couch, chair, perhaps a bed or even some rubble-free floor—went to those who claimed them first. It was almost comical to see hordes of heavily burdened GIs scrambling frantically from the back ends of trucks to the nearest houses—or any building, for that matter—all trying to be first to find a place to sleep.

I climbed to the second floor and found a stove and kerosene lamp. After warming the room, I delved again into my seemingly bottomless food packages from home before dozing off.

Combat GIs, it was said, always sleep with one ear and one eye open. I don't know how long it was afterwards when I was awakened by a strange squalling sound. I bolted upright, rifle in hand, listened again and then, flattening myself against a wall, moved cautiously into one of the other rooms.

There I found a Belgian woman had just given birth to a yowling baby boy and I hadn't even known she was in the house. At the sight of my menacing rifle and grubby countenance her eyes widened in terror. I quickly called for a medic and then gave the new mother a candy bar. Relieved, she asked my name and said she would name the baby after me.

I mentally scolded myself for becoming so careless, so militarily sloppy, that I hadn't even checked out the house for possible other occupants before relaxing and sleeping. This inattentiveness could well cost me my life someday. I went back to sleep and dreamt that I was being suffocated by a blinding light that was burning me with its heat. Fighting to wake up, I opened my eyes and found the nightmare was real: the whole room was ablaze. Somehow, the lamp had fallen off the bureau where I had placed it for the night and the burning kerosene had turned the room into sheets of fire.

I was able to free myself from my sleeping bag, grab my rifle and gear and throw them out a window. Then I dove out after them, landing with a jarring thud in a snow bank. I gathered up my gear and stumbled away from the building as other GIs in the building came flying out the doors. In all the confusion, it took me a moment to remember that a woman and her newborn baby were still inside.

Several of us ran back into the building by a back door away from the flames, made our way through the smoke-filled darkness to the upper floor where we wrapped the mother and her newborn in a blanket and led them out safely, just before the flames reached their bedroom. For the remainder of the night, we moved in with another squad, where I kept everyone awake coughing most of the night from lungs badly irritated by smoke. Medics took the woman and her infant son somewhere for shelter and I never saw them again.

Our unit was alerted we would be moving out again at 0400. It was getting to be that we spent only a few hours, sometimes only a few minutes, in each town as the division relentlessly pushed eastward toward the German border, now only a short distance away, we were told.

Minutes before the departure time, I propped myself up against the wall of a nearby building and went back to sleep to wait for the convoy. The 0400 jumpoff dragged on to 0500 and, after an hour's nap, I awoke somewhat rejuvenated.

During the short motorized trip, I fell asleep again and slid off the wooden bench seat without waking up. The rest of the way I slept doubled up on the floor. When the convoy finally stopped, I crawled off the tailgate with legs numbed by cut-off circulation and promptly fell on my hind quarters in the snow, my rifle and gear flying every which way.

This brought roaring laughter from the squad, and the gloom of the night move was broken by another example of what might be called Army humor. In the military, especially during combat or other trying periods, tension and frustration were kept in check by laughing at others and their misfortunes. It was accepted behavior. You either laughed or were laughed at, and to take offense was not allowed.

As always, we raced into the nearest building and claimed it as ours. We were told hot food was available at a farm house field kitchen about a quarter-mile away. I got my mess kit and joined a stream of men heading for the kitchen. On the way, I passed a sign saying Bovigne. At least I now knew where I was, as if it really mattered. I could see a building with white smoke spiraling from its chimney and a long line of standing GIs snaked around a corner toward us. Falling in at the end of the line, we were moving up one-by-one closer to the promised land of chow when we heard someone shouting for a medic.

We all bunched around a man sprawled in the snow, his head cocked to the side at an unnatural angle. It was one of the anti-mine squad members. A medic came running and even without touching him, called for an ambulance. It was obvious the man's neck had been painfully injured when a seven-foot long icicle, nearly a foot in diameter, had fallen off the mess hall building and hit him on the head as he waited in the chow line. We tried to comfort him with worthless words until the meat wagon arrived and took him away, but how could we explain away such a freakish accident? Surrounded by death in practically every form imaginable, and he had been put down by a damned icicle.

One by one, the squad was being reduced by the war. I wondered when it would be my turn to get it. Most of us felt it was only a matter of time. On the way back to my billet, I passed a church and with ghoulish curiosity looked behind it for the inevitable atrocity scene. This time, there were no slaughtered civilians but instead the neatly stacked, frozen bodies of about 30 German soldiers two rows high. Some were peacefully asleep while others had been horribly mutilated. Apparently, we stacked our dead like cordwood on trucks while the Germans piled theirs against churches for eventual burial. I felt a strange pleasure in gazing down at them, and wondered about divine retaliation for some of the murdered civilians I had seen.

On a side street, I discovered a German field ambulance tipped over, its body pockmarked with schrapnel and bullet holes. The vehicle, prominently marked with Red Cross insignia, had obviously been machine gunned. The body of the driver was slumped awkwardly over the wheel, and hanging out a rear door was the body of another German soldier, his head buried in the snow, his legs still partially inside the compartment.

The ambulance also contained three more uniformed bodies, killed while apparently being transported to a field hospital. I was posted for guard duty that night and, as my normal luck would have it, I pulled the 0200 to 0400 relief, the coldest, loneliest shift possible. This relief meant getting a couple hours sleep, then standing guard duty for a couple more and then ambling back to a cold sleeping bag for two more hours before being told to "shag butt" if you wanted breakfast.

As I walked my post, my mind was captivated by thoughts of home. I took a pipe and some crushed apple leaves (a tobacco substitute) that I had found on a dead German, and in the shelter of a doorway, I lighted it. I thought it would make me feel older, that smoking a pipe was something that men did. After punishing my lungs for a few minutes with the foulest, most rancid tasting smoke ever, I realized I was willing to wait a little longer to grow up. I threw the pipe away and never tried it again.

Totally preoccupied with my thoughts, I had not heard, until the sound was almost upon me, running feet coming at me. I pointed my rifle at the sound and was confronted by a panting company runner living up to his title. We were moving out again within five minutes. It seemed like there was no end to the on- and off-again routine of trying to chase and keep up with the German in his reluctant flight home.

Again, as I had done so many times before, I grabbed my gear and propped myself against a wall outside the billet to wait for the trucks. But when they didn't arrive, we were ordered out on foot at 0700, having gained three more hours of bone-chilled, but still sorely needed, sleep. The trucks were supposed to be waiting for us concealed in woods nearby but, in typical Army SNAFU fashion, they weren't there and we were forced to march until about noon through the forest.

Soon after the hike began, we were able to fall in behind a detachment of Sherman tanks and I found I could warm myself slightly by walking in the heat radiated by the motor. I tagged along like this for several miles, limping with each step, but the warmth felt good.

In the distance was a town almost obliterated by war's violence: Houffalize on the Ourthe River, southeast of Marche where segments of the 84th had initially stopped one salient of Hitler's advance.

In Houffalize, we joined other elements of the 84th and the 2nd and 5th Armored Divisions. GIs wearing unfamiliar shoulder patches were also walking around the town. They were from General Patton's Third Army that had fought its way up from the south to meet General Simpson's Ninth Army pushing down from the north.

The linkup between the two had been made, we were told, and it was a time for celebration. The German in his desperate push to the sea had been stopped, pushed back and finally routed, and, proudly, we had been partially responsible.

With the linking of the two armies came the gradual realization that I had fired my last shot against the Germans in Belgium, agonized through my last snow-filled Belgian foxhole, limped my last Belgian frozen mile and gone hungry for the last time in Belgium. And hopefully, had also witnessed my last civilian atrocity in Belgium. Told we could take a 10-minute break, I slumped into a nearby snow drift and fell asleep.

The long-missing truck convoy finally arrived, loaded us up again and we were on our way to the last stop in Belgium, Werbomont, where we were told we would remain long enough to clean up and rest before returning to Germany. In the billet I was assigned, I found a large mirror and looked at the strangest face I had ever seen: mine. My sunken eyes were blood-shot and ringed with dark lines. Covering my cheeks and jaw was a six-week-old scraggly black beard matted with mud and encrusted with fatigue. Deep furrows criss-crossed my forehead and I stood there wondering whether I would ever again look like the person I once remembered.

Clean uniforms were being issued next door and hot water was available for bathing and shaving. The eventual transformation was remarkable.

I removed the filthy rag dressings and vigorously scrubbed my feet with soap and water. Clean for the first time since being evaluated in the field hospital at Marianburg, I was able to obtain some bandages from a medic and rewrap them. Some of the blistered sores had broken open again and were bleeding from the march from Bovigne to Houffalize, but in general, my feet appeared slightly improved. Once this was done, it was time for the last alteration to my appearance, a haircut. Incredibly, amidst all the carnage of war, I found a barbershop with a red-headed, buxom, middle-aged woman barber dressed in a revealing, skin-tight orange sweater. To say she was amply endowed would be a gross understatement. As she leaned over my hair and shaved me, she almost smothered me by pushing her immense breasts against my face. Unfortunately, I was too young then to appreciate my predicament.

In Werbomont, I met cordial 18-year-old Maria, in whose home some of us were temporarily billeted. She insisted on waiting on us hand-and-foot; nothing was too good for the American liberators who had driven the hated Germans from her town. She made me promise to return to Belgium someday to visit after the war. But thinking that the war was practically over was premature, for the shattering sounds of buzz bombs continued overhead almost every hour. The dreaded truck-like sounds instinctively made us head for the cellars; V-1s were as unpredictable and indiscriminate as enemy artillery.

A notice was posted on a tree near the temporary company CP that a band concert by the division band would be held that night in an abandoned brewery at the edge of town. At the appointed time, I ran down the street, past the line of GIs already headed for the brewery. Sore feet be damned, I wanted a front seat just like days past with my father at the Plymouth Theater back home.

As I entered the building, I was nearly bowled over by the sound of full-sectioned arrangements. I sat there enthralled, jiggling up and down to the beat and envying the musicians who appeared so neat and clean and who, without doubt, had one of the most desirable jobs in the Army.

Suddenly, in the middle of the concert, a chant started from the audience: "We want Blunt. Get Blunt up there." The leader stopped the band and asked who Blunt was. Everyone pointed at me. I should have been deeply embarrassed by this interruption of the concert, but instead I felt special, even honored.

The leader asked if I was a musician and if I wanted to sit in. Foolish question. I was given a pair of sticks and told to go to work. I adjusted the drum set and kicked off a tempo for Woody Herman's "Woodchoppers' Ball." The band arrangement culminated in an extended drum solo for the last chorus. In the parlance of the music world, I was "Knocking myself out of this world."

When the concert was over, I left the brewery beside myself with excitement and I couldn't wait to write home about my musical experience. My January 26, 1945 letter home was simple and to the point. Boldly across the V mail letter form, I scrawled, "FLASH, FLASH, FLASH, I PLAYED, I PLAYED, I PLAYED. More details when I come back down to earth. I played with a band tonight, that's all I can say. Love, Your Son, Bud."

I'm sure my parents shared my excitement, especially my father. When he eventually read my letter for he would, at that moment, know that somewhere in Belgium his son was flying high—at least for a few minutes. For it was he who had always been able to come up with enough money for two admissions for the name band presentations week after week at the Plymouth Theater when money had been so tight during the Depression. And it was he who had accompanied me so many times to jam sessions at the Saxtrum Club in the Harlem district back home. I'm sure my father took my letter, closed his eyes and was there beside me, as always, when I sat in.

Our rest and rehabilitation period had stretched to eight days when word came on February 3rd we were going back to the Roer River sector of Germany, where we would prepare for the eventual push for the Rhine.

It was pouring rain when we loaded onto the trucks for the long haul back north. I claimed the pile of duffle bags and stretched out trying to sleep. About 12 hours into the trip, the convoy passed through Aachen, the first large German city on the Siegfried Line that had been taken by American forces.

As the column of trucks continued northward, the weather moderated slightly. Several hours further and the convoy stopped in a small city largely undamaged by the war. The sign said we were in Terwinselen, Holland. I remembered the name for it was near Heerlen, the town we had stayed in briefly before jumping off into combat from Marianburg two months earlier.

My squad was ushered into a dance hall containing pool and ping pong tables, electric lights and a radio. We were told it would be our billet until we moved on again. I grabbed a pool table for a bed and piled my gear on it.

It didn't take long before I met Netta, who for four days tried to wipe the memories of Belgium out of my mind. She showed me everything about the town, including windmills, tulip gardens, dikes, reopened stores, gift shops and a theater. She dressed and treated my still raw, blistered feet and her treatment must have been magic, for by the time I returned to Germany I could walk naturally almost without pain. I showered daily at the nearby coal mines and exchanged more cigarettes with the miners for silver jewelry as I had done when the 84th first arrived in Holland.

The Bulge was behind us. All that remained were the tortured memories of civilian atrocities and a winter that had been almost beyond human endurance. I didn't know at the time that the mental scars caused by what I had seen, endured and done would remain with me the rest of my life. And little did I know that there were many more wounds to come before the war finally ended—wounds that never heal and that can painfully sear the mind.

11

The Roer Breakthrough

In war, one learns something new every day, often every hour.

Orders were received February 5, 1945 that our push eastward toward Berlin, temporarily interrupted by the Ardennes breakthrough, was about to continue. We had been given a few days' rest to catch our collective breaths but now it was time to get back to work.

The squad assembled in front of the pool hall and boarded a convoy of freshly washed trucks, this time driven by black soldiers from the Red Ball Express, a supply-line truck network that kept us supplied with the implements of war brought in from the French ports of Cherbourg and LeHavre. I had been treated cordially by people in the past when they learned I was a combat infantryman, considered by many a venerated group, but the reception and respect offered us by these drivers was something special and unexpected.

A foot soldier's role is the rottenest job in the Army. He lives and eats in filth, and fights and dies in filth. At the same time, however, he is generally looked upon as the toughest, bravest, fiercest bulldog in the entire Army—although some airborne paratroopers might take umbrage to that premise. Out of respect, Lieutenant General George S. Patton Jr. once called infantrymen "The Queens of Battle, The Old Footsloggers." And he was a tanker.

The biggest drawback the combat infantryman had was his self-deprecating image. When someone treated him with respect and courtesy, his gratitude overflowed.

Through the dark, the trucks rumbled along the narrow, winding streets of Terwinselen and out into the battle-ravaged countryside.

In the distance could be heard the faint, familiar thudding of artillery. The road was so scarred by artillery fire, the convoy could barely navigate without driving across the adjoining fields. We jostled our way along mud-slicked roads, kilometer after kilometer wondering within ourselves what the campaign ahead would be like. One thing was for sure: it surely couldn't be any worse than the Bulge.

The undercurrent of artillery was becoming a constant roar and we knew we had arrived at the front. Normally, in these cases, the truck drivers stopped the convoys in some rear echelon area and the troops hiked the remaining three or four miles to the battle area, but not this time. The black drivers kept wheeling their rigs past the 155mm "Long Tom" emplacements and eventually past the shorter-range 105mm howitzers.

It was past midnight and the roads were almost impassable quagmires of Dutch and German mud. Several times we were compelled to push mired trucks out of water-filled craters. Every Kraut in Germany must have heard the whining of our wheels but our drivers stubbornly persisted in taking us as close to the front lines as the roads allowed.

"This is as far as you go," our driver finally yelled back at us. As if to emphasize his remark, artillery shells were swishing one after another over our heads.

I jumped off the tailgate and landed ankle-deep in mud. I was getting to the breaking point of futility and frustration of trying to cope with mud in France and Holland, snow in Belgium and now mud again in Germany. I had only had my clean, newly pressed uniform a few hours and already it was covered with muck. It was becoming obvious dogfaces were not supposed to look like the rest of the Army.

I asked the first GI I saw wandering around where the front line was. "You're standing on it," he replied as he continued on his way. "The outposts are over there," he said pointing to foxholes about 50 feet away.

"Where are we?" I persisted.

"Lindern, on the Roer River," he shouted back.

There wasn't much left of it after the fanatical resistance the 335th Regiment had met there before the division had been redeployed to Belgium. The taking of Lindern on November 29, 1944 had been one of the fiercest, hand-to-hand battles the 84th had encountered up to that time.

Even though the Germans had been driven from the town seven weeks earlier, it was still considered hot (dangerous) and the entire area west of the river would have to be contested again, for in many areas the Germans had moved back in while we were away.

I was impressed with the black drivers' bravery when I realized they had taken us all the way to where the bullets were actually whizzing. Some, in fact, even tried to wrangle ways to remain with us for a few days to join the actual fighting. But it was still a strictly segregated Army in those days and their opportunities to fight were limited. Instead, black soldiers were usually relegated to driving trucks or serving in other noncombat capacities.

In the rubble of a nearby demolished building, I was able to clear a space large enough to curl up and allow sleep to blot out some of the exhaustion of constantly being on the move. As I dozed off, I hoped I would get a package from home, that my feet would finally heal, that I could find some hot food somewhere and maybe even some new souvenirs to add to my collection. When I hoped, I always hoped big.

Someone rolled the guard duty roster dice the right way and I was able to get about six hours of uninterrupted sleep my first night in Lindern. Nonetheless, my rest was eventually terminated abruptly by the same reveille call the Germans had invented during the Bulge: wake up artillery.

To escape the shelling, I headed through a doorless opening leading to the cellar and plunged headfirst about eight feet, landing with a bone-jarring thud on the cellar floor. As I picked myself up, I looked at the door opening and found the cellar stairs were missing. While trying to pick myself up and clear my head, I was able to yell a warning to the others and one by one they jumped down without injury to the protection of the building's two-foot-thick concrete foundation.

Luckily, choosing the cellar for protection was the prudent option, for minutes later the building sustained a direct hit. In the language of today, someone was rattling our cage. The intense barrage, which lasted about 20 minutes, belied reports that the Germans were suffering from ammunition shortages.

I ventured a peek outside and the same GI I had talked to the day before was back again. "See what I mean?" he yelled. "You don't walk around much here. Lindern's the hottest town on the Roer. You jump from house to house if you want to stay alive for long."

I got the point right away.

"Get back inside," he yelled. With that, another artillery shell exploded in the street. "It's a favorite trick of the Krauts to let us think it's all clear and when we start walking around again, they lay in a few more. You play your cards close here."

He said the Germans still had the town under direct observation and every time they saw anything move, they cut loose with an 88. Later, I learned the chow tent was on the other side of "Screaming Meemie Alley," a narrow street zeroed in on by the Germans. Again, it was a matter of the "quick and the dead." During our brief stay in Lindern, we all became accomplished short-distance sprinters.

German troops, only a short distance away in a row of pillbox bunkers, also had the town in their field of harassing machine-gun fire. When the 84th had been called upon to abandon the Roer Basin sector in order to reinforce the troops being overrun in the Ardennes Forest, units of the German Army had moved back into the previously American-held towns. Now these troops were fighting a delaying action to slow down the American advance toward the Rhine.

"What else do we have to look out for?" I asked the Lindern veteran.

"Mines. They're all over the place. The fields are covered with them."

I passed all this information on to the others in my squad and we quickly accepted the fact that if we wanted hot food three times a day we would have to run the gauntlet across "The Alley."

I made it across OK for breakfast my first day and then returned to the billet to catnap for a couple hours. When I awoke, I knew it would be a good day, for another package and a couple letters from home had arrived. The arrival of mail was a very special event for a GI. It allowed him a few minutes to withdraw into his private shell and close out the sordidness of the war around him. These few private moments were our only precious link to the sanity of our earlier lives.

Mail call in combat was different from that back in the States, where the company clustered around a mail clerk standing on a box and yelling out each name as he came to it in the mail sack. Then he scaled the letters—or threw the packages-through the air in the general direction of someone screaming "Here" back at him.

At the front, on the other hand, the company mail clerk generally hand-delivered all the mail to the billets where he knew each soldier was living. He even knew each man's bedroll. If he found a man sleeping, he placed the mail quietly beside him. If the recipient was not there, the clerk left his mail on the man's sleeping bag. Often, you woke up and found these most cherished surprises beside you. These packages of love from home, which were like receiving Christmas presents every few days, were my inspiration and strength to keep going.

Actually, I found that after bolting across "The Alley" a few times, it had become a sort of sport, us against them. Each time we made it safely across, and as far as I know, everyone always did, it brought on laughter for we knew we were driving the Kraut gunners crazy trying to get one of us. Every foot race with death brought a Mauser bullet whacking against a building close to your head, usually chipping off chunks of masonry or splintering wood from door frames. Actually, it became a most thrilling and exciting game we played with the Germans each day.

Bored with always being on the receiving end of enemy fire, I legged it at full speed one day to a building on the outskirts of town facing a row of pillboxes on the far side of a broad meadow. I figured if I was lucky, I could get a few shots off at them. As I have said, killing had become a challenge, even a need, and I found myself seeking fulfillment.

As I threw myself into the building, I literally bumped into a badly decomposed German corpse. Startled, I recoiled in horror. I hadn't realized just how jumpy my nerves had become.

I located a small hole blasted in the wall at ground level. To snipe, you lay on your belly instead of standing at windows and doors as the Germans usually did, for these were the first two targets on which an enemy zeroed in when returning fire.

I waited and watched, hoping to spot a walking target. When after an hour there were no signs of life across the sugar beet fields and, satisfied it was safe, I foolishly walked fully exposed in a low crouch out to the nearest orchard away from German pillbox range. There, I found a foxhole containing two rotted German bodies. Holding my breath against the smell, I searched them for souvenirs but found nothing more than a few worthless Reichsmarks, a fountain pen, some black bread and cheese, pictures of their families and their Soldat Buchs.

While I was gazing at the pictures of their women, parents and children, I felt a strange sadness, and for those few moments in a Lindern orchard I remembered that these unrecognizable, bloated chunks of rotted meat had once been human beings with loved ones. I wondered whether their families knew yet that they were fatherless or husbandless. Somehow on that particular day, I could not subject these soldiers to the final indignity of stealing their personal, cherished belongings. I respectfully put them back in their uniform pockets and walked on. As I walked, I felt a twinge of remorse for all the families I had destroyed with bullets. The men I had slain had been only targets to me, not people, and for a few moments I worried about the killing lust that I knew had built up inside me. I tried to convince myself that I was only impartially doing the job I had been trained to do, but still, I was experiencing troubled emotions. For some unexplained reason, at that moment I identified with the two rotted corpses after I had pictorially met their families.

I was well aware that my conscience, carefully tended through my familial and religious upbringing, was in conflict with my recent actions. But I was powerless to resolve the differences. Circumstances had forced me into a life over which I had no control; but my concern was that I wasn't even trying to control it, just going along with it—and, even more distressingly, sometimes enjoying it.

I looked up. The sun suddenly seemed to have lost its warmth for me. I returned to Lindern, unfulfilled.

In a hedgerow near the edge of town, I found another decaying German soldier, his head hanging from his neck by a few shreds of skin. He was holding a Panzerfaust, a German tank grenade launcher that apparently had misfired and blown up in his face. The constant varieties of death, the sheer gruesomeness, again held me spellbound.

I had been in combat a little too long and was becoming dangerously careless in my behavior, for I had wandered around in the orchard aimlessly looking for souvenirs and now found myself in the middle of another mine field. I had been warned but had not paid attention, and I mentally chastised myself, knowing full well that soldiers who ignored warnings didn't live long in combat.

Most of the mines were "Schu Minen," small, square, wooden anti-personnel concussion devices with a half-pound of explosive and a detonator. The top telescoped over the explosive charge when stepped on, thereby activating the firing pin and setting off the mine. To hamper detection, the mine contained no metal.

I froze and looked around. There appeared to be hundreds of them and, at first glance, I couldn't figure out a route by which I could retrace my steps. I wondered whether this time I had pressed my luck a little too far. On hands and knees, I began to probe with my fingers for I hadn't even brought a bayonet with me. I was able to remove a few mines but most of them were frozen to the ground. Cautiously, I crept backwards, probing gently as I went. One-by-one, I carefully lifted the covers and removed the firing devices of about 30 mines, eventually clearing a narrow path back to the company area in Lindern.

One of the mines looked almost new and showed no signs of being weatherbeaten, so I removed the detonator and fired it harmlessly into the ground. After unwrapping the paraffined paper I discarded the now-harmless block of explosive and shoved the deactivated mine in my jacket pocket as a souvenir to send home.

Back at the company area, I borrowed a bar of brown laundry soap from the company kitchen, cut it to the size of the mine charge and replaced the detonating pin. You couldn't tell it from the real thing; I walked over to the CP, found Captain Bowen and shoved the Schu Mine under his nose.

"OK if I mail this home Cap'n?" I asked casually as I "accidentally" dropped it on the floor. I found that some officers in the Army simply didn't have a sense of humor.

The next day, I decided to expand my souvenir search area even farther, so I followed railroad tracks that led to a cluster of small buildings, including a rail station, burlap bag factory, garage, machine shop, grist mill and several houses. But I didn't find much; obviously other loot hunters had been there before me.

Climbing a nearby banking to look around the countryside, I found the wreckage of an American A-20 light bomber in a field several hundred yards away. After taking a picture of the plane with a cheap German camera I had taken from a German prisoner earlier, I headed back to Lindern.

Along the way, an uneasiness, sort of an unnatural feeling, came over me, as if my instinct was warning me again. I hit the dirt and looked around warily. Stretched out before me was a row of some of the most expertly camouflaged pill boxes I had ever seen.

Armed with only a carbine, a couple clips of ammo, a pistol, trench knife, two grenades, some nitro-starch and a candy bar, I started to sweat. I was, for the first time, seeing the real German Siegfried Line. The pillboxes extended as far as I could see.

Being alone in the face of such awesome defenses, I ran panting and puffing, crouched over, all the way back to Lindern.

When I told the others about what I had found, they informed me the 102nd Infantry Division had captured 92 already abandoned pillboxes while we were fighting in Belgium. I felt a little foolish for being so jumpy and letting abandoned fortifications spook me so.

The Germans, having evacuated the whole network of boxes when faced with the advancing Allied forces, had pulled back across the Roer where they were now content to sit back and take pot shots at us while they waited for our next move.

A rough hand on my shoulder was the alarm clock that told me it was my turn for guard duty. I draped an overcoat over my shoulders and stumbled out into the cold stillness of the murky night. I leaned against a door casing and stared into the fog. After a few minutes of staring at nothing, I began to realize the rest in Holland had affected me. I was alone and getting jumpier by the minute. As my nervousness got worse, I looked at myself and wondered if I was actually becoming afraid of the dark. Feelings such as this usually went unadmitted to one's self in combat, but it was becoming quite apparent to me.

To be totally immersed in the horrors of war over a long period of time and then suddenly transplanted temporarily to the relative tranquility of a rear area, only to be abruptly returned without any mental preparation to combat again, strains the nervous system's ability to compensate for the upheaval.

In combat a man, in time, usually becomes immune to the gut-wrenching fear than envelopes him; his responses to crises become automatic. His mind becomes dulled by the physical and emotional stresses of war and he regresses to the primal instinct of survival at all cost. But once taken from this violent environment and reverted, even temporarily, to peaceful, non-threatening surroundings, his instincts and reactions are pushed to the background and a normal living mode takes over.

If that man then is rudely reinserted into the ultimate terrors of war, his built-up inner defenses often cannot make the adjustment immediately and he can easily become paralyzed with fear. The habit of bravery born of necessity can desert him.

This, I was afraid, was happening to me. The proof was apparent when I recoiled when suddenly encountering German corpses, by my growing fear of mines, my almost constant preoccupation with death and now by my growing apprehension about what was possibly lurking in front of me in the fog.

I began to worry, for the one thing I didn't need at this time was for my nerves to break down. I reasoned that I had done quite well controlling my emotions so far, and with the war seemingly only with weeks more to run, I didn't want to unravel this close to the end of hostilities.

As I stood at my guard post, the low, vibrating truck-like rumble of a buzz bomb overhead intensified my nervousness. The walls of the building I was leaning against trembled from the vibrations transmitted by this V-1 rocket. The fog made the rockets, which I had dubbed "messengers of death," sound as if they were only 100 feet or so in the air over my head. One after another they came, their flames tinting the fog a faint, eerie red and then droning off in the distance, leaving me alone again with my thoughts.

I ducked into a doorway and lit a match to check the time. The watch showed 10 minutes to go before my relief was due. Adhering to the standard practice of many GIs I knew, I pushed the watch ahead those 10 minutes and walked back to my billet to wake up the 0400 guard. After he shuffled grumbling out the door, I put my head on my helmet and figured I could perhaps get a couple hours of sack time before morning.

With hot oatmeal in my gut, all uncertainties about my mental state disappeared. Darkness plays strange tricks on people, I reasoned, and soon afterwards, with my confidence restored, I was off again exploring. In what was apparently a last desperate maneuver by Hitler's commanding generals, the V-1 firings were being intensified and they continued to rumble overhead throughout the day.

No matter how many of them I saw, I still stopped and watched each one with morbid fascination. They were ugly and fearsome, but they personified a crude but awesome power not seen before in conventional warfare. Even though I feared them for the devastating damage they caused upon detonation, I begrudgingly admired the scientists who had developed them, one of whom I would interview 15 years later as a newspaper reporter.

The toll of dead Germans in Lindern, lying all over the town in every twisted position and form possible, was reminiscent of Matthew Brady's pictorial history of Civil War battles. I suppose any combat veteran would say that one war is the same as any other, that only the uniforms change.

Another sound that quickly became part of a combat infantryman's life was the approach of German Me-109s on a strafing run. These planes had a sound all their own and if a GI wanted to live long, he learned to recognize that sound and react to it fast.

In Lindern one afternoon, I heard that all-too-familiar sound and looked up quickly to see from which direction they were coming. Two of them, the lead plane and his playmate, had already swooped downward from the east and were headed straight at me. I dove at the closest house and hid under some fallen rafters, the only mantle of protection I could find. The pilots, flying with reckless abandon, pulled out of their dives a split-second before slamming into the earth.

Their approach was through an almost impenetrable curtain of ack-ack and .50-caliber machine gun tracers. Thousands of bullets arced through the sky searching for their targets but when they couldn't find them, they gracefully fell back to earth defeated.

I watched through a shell hole in the wall of the house as the planes' wing guns spat a stream of slugs into the ground and richocheted off buildings all over town. Violently, patches of earth erupted all around me and, seconds later, the planes were disappearing behind the town in a swooping arc as they climbed with a whining roar back to altitude. The pilots, it seemed, had no specific target that I could determine; we had no tanks in the town or ammo dumps; just a couple companies of bewildered GIs.

A few GIs had jumped onto trucks with .50-caliber machine guns mounted on their cabs to try to return the planes' fire, but the Messerschmitts were out of range before the ground fire could be brought to bear.

"Medic! Medic!" someone was hollering down the street. Once the planes disappeared back toward their airfields and the "all clear" had been sounded, I ran toward the shouting. An officer was lying in the mud near the 3rd Battalion CP.

"The medics can't help him now," I heard someone murmur. The officer had remained on the street to watch the fireworks display and, by another freakish accident of war, he had been hit in the chest by a spent bullet falling from the sky.

The next day I decided to explore more closely the abandoned pillboxes I had seen previously. I entered one and was instantly miniaturized by its mammoth size. The boxes easily covered three acres and had been built into a series of small hills totally hidden from aerial observation or detection. On the ground, the boxes could not be seen until someone was practically on top of them and by then, if they were occupied, it was usually too late. Trees grew from their roofs and tall pasture grass almost covered the artillery and machine gun firing apertures.

I tugged at the two-foot-thick concrete slab that had served as an entry door. Inside was a monstrous room, empty except for row upon row of steel cots suspended in tiers from the walls. I counted 40 cots in each room. Hundreds of artillery shells and "potato masher" grenades were still stacked there and I knew our demolition engineers would move in eventually and destroy them. The main chamber where the 88s were located contained empty racks for dozens of rifles and machine guns; there were facilities for enough supplies to sustain an extended defense—or attack—had the occupants wanted to. I felt strangely out of place standing in that enormous abandoned enemy fortification, one that only weeks earlier had been filled with Kraut soldiers trying to destroy us.

I peered out of the firing ports and saw what their eyes must have seen: the American occupation of Lindern. I stood beside an 88 and peeked through machine gun slots fantasizing what it must have been like to be a German soldier there.

I scratched around for souvenirs but there were none that weren't readily available on the battle field. With that I left the dank, stagnant air of the pillbox and walked back into the sunshine. I wondered why they had retreated without a fight from this important section of Hitler's vaunted Siegfried Line that had been two decades in the making—unless it was as the Unteroffizier prisoner in Belgium had told me: they already knew their war was lost and further sacrifice of life was needless.

Still wanting to explore further, I continued walking slowly toward a town I could see in the distance right on the banks of the river and directly across from the German positions. The last few hundred yards were spent repeatedly watching the town with field glasses I had taken off a dead German officer in Belgium. Each time I checked, I detected no signs of life so I stood up and started to close in, somewhat warily, on the nearest buildings in this seemingly abandoned town.

After brazenly walking down the main street, I climbed to the attic of a bombed-out school, a great observation post from which to see across the Roer. The attic was strewn with shattered slate roof tiles, splintered wooden rafters, old text books and pre-Nazi German flags.

On the east bank of the river, I could see German soldiers wandering around in the open, apparently confident we weren't interested in them. It didn't occur to me that wandering around alone in unoccupied territories was unacceptably foolhardy. I had been captured once, and I probably wouldn't be so lucky a second time. But for some reason, that thought had not entered my mind before starting to explore this nameless riverfront town.

Through the binoculars, I could see that the entire area beyond the river had been flooded. The fast-flowing Roer was normally only about five feet deep but the Germans had opened the Henbach Dam to the north of our position and the depth had risen to 11 feet. The usual 60-foot wide river had been greatly widened by the flooded lowlands that stretched to the eastern horizon.

At an estimated range of about 200 yards, I fired off a clip at the figures walking around unconcerned on the east bank of the river. I might as well have been shooting a pop gun at them, however. They ignored my rifle fire and went about their business as usual. They probably hadn't even heard my rifle fire.

Our division intelligence learned later from German prisoners that the troops waiting for us on the other side of the river were from the first battalions of the 59th and 103th Volksgrenadiers Divisions. At least they were Wehrmacht; perhaps they would not fight with the ferocity of the SS troops we had run into throughout the Ardennes campaign.

I was to soon find out just how wrong I was about their ignoring me. A couple minutes later, they laid two 88 rounds into the town, one of them less than a block away from the school in which I was hiding. I stopped the sniper foolishness right away.

When I returned to Lindern, I learned that the 1st and 2nd platoons of LOVE Company had been severely mauled during fighting in nearby Mullendorf. They had been dug in near the village when their position was overrun by a sudden counterattack. I heard the news remorsefully, remembering all the friends I once had in those platoons. Hitler's supermen, as battered as they were, were not going to give their homeland up that easily.

The company runner came by, informing us a movie was being shown that night in one of the rear-area towns. I grabbed my gear and jumped onto the nearest truck headed that way. "Saratoga Trunk," starring Gary Cooper and Ingrid Bergman, proved to be a great morale booster, for it took our minds off the war and transported us into a fantasy world for a couple of hours.

I awakened the next day to more of the grim routines that punctuate war and that insidiously eat away at a man's spirit until he is existing, not living—mud, dank cellar habitation, 88 barrages, rotten chow, guard duty, dead Germans, rockets, mines, machine guns, mortar attacks, strafings, buzz bombs—just another normal day of infantry ground combat.

In Lindern, the Krauts added a new twist: Nebelwerfer rockets that whined like banshees in the air. The principle behind them was to add another psychological weapon to their arsenal, rather than waste more foot troops. The rockets seldom caused any casualties and we soon learned to ignore them. They more or less amounted to a bark rather than a bite.

Orders came down that we were to strip all divisional ID from our uniforms, patches, rank designation—everything. For no plausible reason (the Army seldom had persuasive reasons for anything it did), divisional brass didn't want the Germans to know who we were. I never did find out who our top echelon brain trust officers wanted the Germans to think we were, the French Foreign Legion?

This strict secrecy, I figured, meant we were heading across the Roer—and I was right. Pontoon bridges were being built at Linnich to span the Roer but as soon as the engineers stretched them across the river, the Germans blew them up for they already knew we were coming and had moved in heavy mortar, artillery and infantry reinforcements to greet us. The only thing they didn't know was when, but then again, that didn't matter much for they had had plenty of time to get ready for us, whenever we decided to come.

Propaganda leaflet artillery shells began to shower down on Lindern. They welcomed us back to the Roer region after having done such a "splendid job" in Belgium and said that superior forces would be waiting for us. So much for keeping our identity secret.

With all the waiting, I was getting itchy and bitchy, a GI's prerogative. There was an old saying in the Army that a bitching GI was a happy GI, but I never believed that old military saw. When I was bitching, I was far from happy. But I knocked off my bellyaching fast when Joe Everett shut me up by reminding me that each day we didn't have to cross the river was another day we lived.

The only diversion I could come up with to fend off this boredom born of waiting for something to happen, was to correlate into booklet form the dozens of pages of journal notes I had scribbled since shipping overseas. The diary of daily events, observations, opinions, impressions and emotions, coupled with a detailed written map of the division's route across the continent, would enable me to better interpret and relive my experiences in the event that I survived—and the chances were getting better every day that I would.

On February 21, we were briefed and told the crossing would come in two days. It would be our first such river assault and it was being called "Operation Grenade." On the 23rd, the softening-up artillery barrage started at midnight and continued until we jumped off at 0400.

Strategy dictated that we had two minutes to sprint across a two-foot-wide, bouncing, swaying pontoon bridge and secure a position on the other side. German fortifications across the river were known to be strong and armament heavy. Looking at my watch, I knew that in six hours I would be across the river or dead.

I tried to grab some sleep but thoughts jumbling around in my head prevented it. The "Red Legs" had been cannonading the Germans entrenched on the far shore of the Roer for three nights to simulate a river crossing but each barrage had only been a diversionary sham. This time, though, it was for real and they were shoveling shells past their gun breechblocks as fast as they could handle them.

We hoped the Germans would think it was just another routine night barrage and stay huddled in their holes.

About an hour before the river crossing was to take place, the ground we were standing on started reverberating from the intensity of the artillery bombardment. As the jump-off hour approached, we started to move through the town and across nearby fields toward the west bank of the river in more or less mob formation.

The night was foggy and depressing, which helped to conceal the troop movement and perhaps offer us some element of surprise. But it did little to alleviate our feeling of impending doom.

Slogging through the mud, I lost all conception of time and distance, but eventually I became aware through the blackness that we were filing between two rows of ruins. When the ground sloped downward I sensed we were approaching the river. The town, I was told later, was Linnich, where engineers had been trying to establish foot bridges for us. There was very little of the town left that we could see.

When we finally halted, the column had become a crowd and we milled about aimlessly, resting whenever we could and waiting for further orders. Our job as mine removal specialists was to cross the river with riflemen from 1st Platoon of Anti-Tank Company to clear the landing area of mines for the foot troops coming afterwards.

The Corps of Engineers, we could make out, mostly from the sound, was feverishly trying to establish a narrow foot bridge across the river for us. According to plans, the remaining reinforcing assault troops coming behind us would paddle across in 12-man, squad-size pontoon boats.

Strangely, I felt no fear as I waited for the orders to cross, just an apprehensive desire to get it over with. The first rays of daylight revealed geysers of mud and debris being thrown into the air on the far bank of the river by our exploding artillery shells. During the American bombardment, the German artillery batteries that had harassed us so much back in Lindern were not returning the fire. Several minutes later I learned they were conserving their ammunition for our actual crossing.

German bunkers and breastworks were being destroyed and timbers could be seen being tossed like matchsticks into the air. Occasionally, a shell landed in the river, sending up a fountain of water that, for a moment, shielded our view of the German entrenchments.

Orange flashes of exploding shells were burying themselves in the earth, making the ground erupt violently as if rebelling at being disturbed. Suddenly, without warning, the dawn was silent.

"Move out! Move out! Move out! This is it!" a muffled voice started yelling. I wiped the mud from my carbine and ran blindly toward the bridge. As I did, the solid footing of earth gave way to exaggerated swaying and bouncing. I knew I was on the foot bridge.

I slung my rifle and grabbed for the rope handrail as water started gushing into my boots. Crouching and running as fast as my tottering equilibrium would allow, I felt as if I were running in slow motion. The other bank of the Roer seemed so unobtainably far.

Midway across, I came to a hurdle in my path. It was a GI, head hung in the water, whose war had ended on the footbridge. I skidded to a stop, stepped gingerly over him and then kept going. Another body was in the water wedged against the bridge by the swift current.

The bucking footbridge did its best to throw me into the river but I clung hard to the rope. German 88mm shells and mortars were now exploding in the water all around us, but I was scarcely aware of them for I was trying to contend with a buckling bridge that was fighting me every step of the way.

Behind me I could hear our division's anti-aircraft guns pounding away at waves of Messerschmitt-109s and Focke Wulf-190s appearing from the east to strafe and bomb us as we tried to cross and establish a beachhead. From the squadrons of planes appearing from the east, the Luftwaffe seemed to be throwing everything it had left at us.

The banshee-like whine of diving planes, together with the body-battering concussion of shells and mortars exploding only yards away and the constant uninterrupted volume of ear-shattering artillery all around us blacked out all thought, all emotions, all reflexes. It was if we were trying to function in a black void of time where reality ceased and eternity took over.

On the other side of the river, I could make out GIs already engaged in hand-to-hand combat with the Germans. I reached the other shore, sprinted a few yards to the right and threw myself into the mud.

With a resounding thud, a German mortar shell landed on the bridge. Several GIs blown into the water were desperately trying to swim the last few yards to shore. Those of us who had made it across were lobbing grenades into a trench running along the river bank. A burp gun almost within touching distance cut loose, spewing out a hail of bullets over my head. I threw a grenade at the sound of the chattering gun and was rewarded with a shower of mud by the explosion. But the gun was silenced. Up and down the line American grenades were taking their toll.

I crawled frantically to a nearby bunker and rolled a grenade inside, but it was a waste of taxpayers' money—the Germans there were already dead. In all the excitement, I came across another German and pumped several shots into him before realizing he too was already dead. When the trench appeared to be empty of enemy soldiers, I peered over the parapet and saw a town a few hundreds yards inland with Germans scurrying back and forth.

I cautiously looked around. GIs were running and crawling everywhere around me. A tenuous beachhead had been established and we were clinging to it by our fingernails, waiting for the inevitable German counterattack. Behind me, the bridge had been repaired and American troops were pouring across, a most reassuring sight. A Sherman tank and a jeep hove into view from a treadway bridge a few yards downstream.

The devastation around me was total; not a tree had been left standing. As far as I could see in every direction, artillery had laid barren the entire countryside.

I rifled through the pockets of the German with the burpgun my grenade had killed and took his Soldat Buch. I also took a stick "potato masher" grenade from him and tucked it under my jacket.

Orders were passed along to dig in and hold the position while the infantry advanced. Finding a ready-made hole with a dead German in it, I pushed him to one side and squeezed in beside him to wait, for it was easier than digging a foxhole for myself. In the hole I found a badly rusted .32-caliber pistol that was so old it wouldn't even fire, so I thought. I pointed it at the bottom of the hole and pulled the trigger, jumping a foot when it blasted a hole in the mud no more than an inch from my right boot. Again feeling stupid for displaying such an unmilitary disregard for firearms, I tossed the gun into the river in disgust.

During a slight lull in the fighting, I decided to disarm the German concussion grenade I had found. I removed the powder head, punctured the seal with my trench knife and poured out the charge. Then I unscrewed the cap on the other end, pulled the activating string and placed the grenade outside the hole until the detonator cap went off with a harmless pop. Then I knew the grenade was safe to keep as a souvenir.

We were told our platoon had crossed the river without a casualty and now we were to hold our positions while the foot troops pushed forward toward the town I had seen in the distance. The best way I knew to secure a position, militarily speaking, was to catch a short nap. Fortunately, we were not needed to sweep for mines in front of the advance troops as we had expected to do.

By midday, the push inland had started and we slogged through the mud to the nearby town of Rurich, where I had observed the Germans earlier. Already the massive Allied assault toward the Rhine River was grinding forward. Advance units were spreading through Rurich and, without even slowing down, were advancing beyond it.

Anti-Tank Company's mission was to mop up any bypassed pockets of resistance and clear the area of possible snipers and stragglers. One by one, we worked our way through the shattered buildings but our only reward was six artillery-stunned Wehrmacht soldiers, all battered into near-speechlessness. We herded them together and pointed them in the direction of the bridges back to Linnich while telling them that as long as their hands were folded over their heads, they would not be bothered by American troops. So, without any GI guards, the small band of prisoners walked to the rear, arms dutifully over their heads, more or less on the honor system. But not before we had stripped them of all valuable "prizes of war."

They were as sorry a bunch of Kraut soldiers as I had seen during the whole war. After checking out their unit identifications, it became obvious they were not Wehrmacht soldiers at all, but rather, more of the disorganized Volksturm troops we continued to encounter during the Roer and Rhine river breakthroughs. These Volksturmers were merely untrained civilians in military uniforms but many were still fanatically loyal to Adolf Hitler and, as such, still had to be considered dangerous. As we caught our breaths in Rurich, we knew that "Operation Grenade" had been a success. If the American Army could manage to continue the momentum of our advance across the Roer Basin, the war would surely wind down in a matter of months, perhaps even weeks.

If only we could have known the push eastward would accelerate greatly in the next fortnight, our exhausted morale would have shot skyward. But the future cannot be forecast, and we had to be content with merely grinding out the kilometers one at a time, as any foot soldier was expected to do.

12

The Rhineland

Before pushing inland, I paused to take pictures of the foot bridge upon which I had crossed the Roer River and of a column of about 50 German prisoners carrying their dead and wounded on crude wooden stretchers on their shoulders. Their numbers reinforced my hope that German resistance here in northern Germany would be lighter than we had encountered in Belgium.

It was simple logic: the weaker the resistance, the farther we could penetrate into the heart of Germany each day. And the more ground we gained, the closer we would be to Berlin, the end of the conflict and the sparing of both American and German lives.

But I already had learned that in war no beachhead is ever truly secure. There is always the imminent threat of an enemy counterattack. The Bulge—where often for every kilometer we gained, we were pushed back two—had been ample proof of that.

Rumor had it that the price the 84th paid in casualties had been high even though German resistance had been lighter than anticipated. In Rurich, we were told to get indoors and stay out of sight pending further orders. We were still within sight of the Roer and the closer we pushed toward Berlin, the harder the German was expected to fight for his homeland. Since blind obedience is the best course of action in the army—at least when it is convenient—I obeyed and found a rubble-free corner of a building where I could get a few more minutes of precious sleep.

A bellowed "Let's go!" brought me back to my senses. I climbed into a three-quarter-ton weapons carrier waiting for us on the street and this time was lucky enough to get the cherished tailgate seat that offered fresher air and a faster escape if an emergency arose. If I wanted out, I wanted out in a hurry. The memory of the slow GI killed during the convoy strafing days before was still fresh in my mind.

We were fighting, for the most part, on the flat sugar beet fields of northern Germany and we soon realized that the gently sloping hills that disturbed these plains had been put there by the Nazi regime, not nature, for these hills were usually more cleverly concealed plllboxes.

As the weapons carrier lurched along the road, a shell burst behind us. Before we could yell a warning to the driver, another 88 hit, this time closer. We were in an open field of fire and were being tracked by German artillery or a tank.

Ignoring the shell craters in the road, the driver rammed the accelerator to the floorboard and we grabbed anything we could to hang on in the back. The next shell landed almost beneath us, lurching the truck sharply into a field. But despite a shredded tire that instantly started to burn, the driver kept the vehicle under control. Maintaining his speed as the Germans continued to track us, he outraced them and eventually screeched to a halt behind a protective building on the outer perimeter of the village. From the spasmodic machine gun and rifle fire, we were able to tell our troops were still trying to take the town. We sat in the truck watching and listening as the infantry and tank firefight to occupy the cluster of houses seemed to shift back and forth.

We searched for the German artillery that had chased us across the open field but couldn't locate it. Both American and German tanks could be heard grinding through the village before us, taking pot shots at each other. Occasionally, GIs could be seen leaping from one rubble pile to another as they darted through the streets. It was house-to-house combat, the final resort of the infantryman when all other assault methods failed. Eventually, our troops were pulled back, artillery called in and the issue was soon settled.

I worked my way forward a short distance to get a better view of the fight. "Get back here, Blunt, where you belong," the platoon lieutenant cursed. "I'm sick and tired of always having to look for you." I glared back at him and obeyed, climbing back into the truck almost defiantly as he continued to fume and ream me out.

If the good lieutenant was finding me recalcitrant at times, it was probably because he couldn't accept the fact that I was possessed of an independence that bordered on disobedience of all laws, natural or otherwise—not to mention a single-mindedness that could best be described as all-consuming. He and I were never in the same Army—or world, for that matter.

Once the fighting in the town died down and we were able to enter, we found that billets had already been designated for our squad. When we entered ours, we found a table of hot food, including a platter of steak, in the kitchen. The Germans had pulled out so quickly, they hadn't had time to finish their meal, so we, always trying to be helpful, finished it for them like a bunch of scavengers.

Beside the kitchen stove, we found a pair of highly polished boots. Somewhere there was a barefoot German soldier running around cursing us. "They're coming back!" someone hollered from the street. We ran from the building, "advancing to the rear," as it was called, and finally stopped to regroup at the edge of town where we waited to see what would happen next. A short time later, when the firing subsided again, we returned to our billet to find the Germans had re-occupied the house, cooked some more food and had taken it with them. And, we noticed, the barefoot soldier was no longer barefoot. The boots were gone.

"Where are we, anyway?" I asked one of the men in Baker Company, some of whom were also sharing our building.

"Doveren, or something like that."

By daylight, we were better able to survey conditions in the town and like every other city or town we would see in Germany, it had been reduced to rubble. A few snipers remained and occasional artillery continued to shower us with death, but these were considered more a nuisance than a danger. The Germans had given us Doveren, but they had made sure we paid a dear price for it.

To move around in the town necessitated a series of duck-and-run maneuvers, for short uninterrupted sprints in the open invariably invited sniper bullets. Timing a run was not a safe answer because the Jerry was also timing them and he already had his rifle sighted in and his finger on the trigger.

When it came time to head for the chow tent, you took a deep breath and literally ran full tilt for your life. Each time I tried it, a sniper bullet smacked into a building right behind me. Then I'd crawl to the next open space where it was the same routine all over again: pause, take a deep breath, jump up, and try it again, often with another bullet whistling past my head. One time, when I made it safely back to my billet, I brazenly and foolishly stuck my head out a window and thumbed my nose at the sniper.

Eventually, our tormenter was located, captured and sent to a rear-area POW pen. He was allowed to live, for as far as we knew, he had never hit anyone, just played his deadly game with us.

From the attic of our billet, I could see more than a mile into German territory. What a wonderful place for an artillery observer—or an American sniper. With the crack of dawn each day, I climbed to the attic and placed the enemy territory under surveillance, watching for any sign of movement by the German troops. Every day the hunt was on. It became a game with me. Then I spotted him, a German Wehrmacht soldier at a distance of about 500 yards hiding behind a large tree. Occasionally, he peeked around the tree before ducking back behind it. He did this several times as I watched, not daring to move a muscle for fear he would see me.

Without warning, an 88 slammed into the building from which I was watching. The explosion almost tore my head and ears apart; I was showered with roof slate and mortar. The observer behind the tree had to have spotted a reflection off my field glasses and called up an artillery strike to send me over a "hello."

Figuring my observation post was no longer a good place to be, I crawled backwards to leave. A sharp pain shot through my leg and my pants were stained with blood, this time the real thing, indicating I had been hit by shrapnel. Feeling a lump on my leg, I dropped my pants to examine the wound and found a fragment buried beneath the surface. I dug at it with my trench knife and once it was removed, I put it in my jacket pocket as a bloody souvenir. I poured some sulfur drug from my firstaid kit on the wound and bandaged it.

As I limped back to my billet, I became determined. Now the war had become personal and strictly between the Kraut behind the tree and me. He had won the skirmish that day but there would always be another time, and that one would be mine.

Again, as in Belgium, I didn't put in for a Purple Heart. I didn't want to upset my parents, and besides, I didn't want to cheapen the medal by accepting it for such a minor wound.

I told one of the squad members, Irving Firschein, a zoology student from Brooklyn, what had happened and he became interested in my American sniper scheme. The next day we were up early and in the attic with rifle and field glasses to help guide my aim. For almost an hour we watched for targets of opportunity even though the chances of hitting one at that range were minimal.

Just about the time we were going to call the venture off, there he was again, concealing himself behind the same tree, his green Wehrmacht uniform blending almost perfectly against the background. Now I was certain he was an artillery forward observer and he would be the perfect target. But the distance made it an almost impossible shot.

Each time his head appeared, I cut loose with a round, with Firschein correcting my windage and elevation. But I couldn't see the point of impact, so, after a couple of clips, I resorted to an all-tracer cartridge load.

I watched each red streak richochet off the tree or dig into the ground, but each time I was missing. Finally, I held my breath and squeezed the trigger slowly.

"You got him! You got him!" Firschein started singing. Then he went into a detailed account of how the German had been thrown backwards when the bullet struck him and had then plopped face-first to the ground. We watched as other German soldiers scattered away from the tree but they too blended into the background and made for poor targets. I really wasn't interested in them very much, for I already had my quota for the day.

Doveren became quiet and for as long as we remained there, we were subjected to no more artillery shellings.

After a breakfast of canned cheese, hard biscuits and cold lemonade, I decided to look for the artillery observer I had shot the day before. I wanted his Soldat Buch. This one would be a real trophy but it would mean penetrating rather deep into enemy-held territory. After about a hundred yards, I found it would mean traversing a mine field laced with barbed wire. To make matters worse, the whole route was across an open field. Every Kraut in Germany could probably observe me.

Not knowing any better and motivated by my intense desire for the dead Kraut's identification book, I picked my way through a heavy concentration of anti-tank Teller mines that had been scattered across the beet field. They had, for the most part, been sloppily covered with straw to conceal them, an indication they had been put down with extreme haste as the German troops pulled back.

It is said that God protects the innocent. Apparently he also protects the stupid for I made it safely across the field and when I arrived at the tree, the Germans had apparently pulled back for there was no one in sight anywhere.

They had not bothered to remove their dead from the battlefield for there he was, the observer still lying there face down. I rolled him over and found my bullet had hit him in the forehead and had taken most of the back of his head off. His shattered face was matted with dried blood and it wasn't until I looked as his Soldat Buch that I knew what he had once looked like. He looked to be in his teens. After relieving him of the book, I left him there to rest in the silence of death.

When I returned to the company area, the lieutenant was looking for me. The word had already circulated about the "American sniper" caper and he wanted to congratulate me on my marksmanship. Funny person, that officer. One minute he was chastising me, the next minute praising me. I didn't bother to tell him I couldn't duplicate that shot again in a hundred years. I showed him the Soldat Buch with the German's picture. He shook his head and looked at me, as if irked at my bloody enthusiasm.

Later that afternoon, the company runner began yelling that we were pulling out again. The only redeeming factor of constantly being on the move was that each time we climbed back into the damn trucks we were getting closer to Berlin and this fact alone had to be our sustaining strength.

The truck convoy proceeded along a flat road flanked by tall poplar trees and eventually we passed a roadside sign designating the group of shattered buildings we were approaching as Baal. As quickly as I could, I found a remote building and sacked out for a few more minutes of sleep. I was always careful to notify the company runner where my billet was in each city or town, especially if I were living alone somewhere, for if he couldn't locate me and the company should pull out without me, leaving me alone and vulnerable in a German civilian-infested town, it could really spoil my day. In the morning, I discovered that an Anti-Tank Company GI had been killed by an artillery shell in the town and I hadn't even been disturbed by the explosion. Another letter the captain would have to write to grieving parents or a wife somewhere back home.

It was obvious the tempo of the war was picking up, for our stays in each town were becoming shorter and shorter. This could only mean we were pushing ahead harder and faster and with dwindling German resistance. For every kilometer put behind us, the chances escalated that more American soldiers would return home alive.

During the next troop movement, the truck stopped after about an hour to give us a break and, while stretching my legs around the convoy, I noticed a World War I-type trench that extended outwards into a field. It was close to the road so I jumped into it and landed almost in the laps of three dead GIs, all victims of German artillery. There had been no indication they were there. One of them had been disemboweled. Another had a leg practically blown off and the third had an arm hanging only by threads of skin.

It was evident they had tried to dress their wounds in the few moments before they bled to death for I found bloody compress bandages and empty packets of sulfur drugs scattered about the trench. But it had been a losing battle to stem the bleeding; most of it had poured onto the bottom of the trench, painting the mud a dark brownish red.

I lost my appetite for souvenir hunting and returned to the convoy. My optimism had been wiped away in that second I had leapt into the trench. The war, as long as one shot or one artillery shell was being fired, was still not over, no matter how fast the convoys were moving forward, no matter how close we were getting to Berlin.

On February 27 we rolled into the city of Erkelenz, where we met our first German civilians. A major breakthrough was in the making and the 84th was leading the way for the whole Allied effort in the dash for the Rhine. The division had covered 30 miles in six days, taking nearly 3,000 prisoners. Before the division reached the Rhine, still another 20 miles ahead of us, the number of prisoners we captured would climb to more than 9,000. And, on top of that accomplishment, the 84th would also be credited with knocking out 112 enemy pillboxes and bunkers.

In Erkelenz, I stopped a girl on the street and asked where we were. She replied we were in the Rhineland and that the river was close. But that was as far as we were going, she stated pompously, for "Der Fuhrer's" new secret weapons would drive us back to France and we would never reach Berlin.

This was the first time I had heard Nazi propaganda being mouthed off at me firsthand other than from Axis Sally. It disgusted me. I poked her angrily in the stomach with my carbine to join the other refugees evacuating the city fleeing west. As she walked away, she glared back at me over her shoulder. I stood there smiling superiorly at her and then, as a parting shot, I blew her a kiss.

We were told the 84th had swung north after crossing the Roer instead of concentrating its effort due east, which would have been the shortest route to the Rhine.

The reasoning behind this strategy was two-fold: to confuse the German high command into perhaps committing its troop concentration where the most logical push should come, and second, to probe for weak spots in the German defenses in the areas the reinforcement troops had vacated. The strategy apparently worked. We were really grinding the kilometers behind us each day.

No sooner had the convoy gotten on the road again than our truck was violently thrown up into the air with a deafening roar. Duffle bags smothered us and men fell on top of each other like jack straws.

I was knocked over the tailgate and onto the ground by the blast. I couldn't focus my eyes. Someone lifted me up and said, "This one's OK." After several minutes, my vision cleared and I learned the truck had hit a Riegal mine. The truck had been demolished and was lying on its side. The only casualty was Firschein, whose ear drums had been damaged. A meat wagon took him away but he would rejoin us later in Rheinhausen where he would make a company name for himself catching frogs in the Rhine River and sending them back pickled in jars of schnapps to a museum in Brooklyn.

The close call with the mine made me realize that I wasn't the only one who got careless at times. The convoy commander had put hundreds of GIs in peril by barreling over roads that had not been first cleared of explosives. In officer manuals, that would be called taking a calculated risk, an acceptable strategy as long as the determination was made by an officer.

Now the squad was down to only a handful. After trying to relocate our gear, we doubled up with another Anti-Tank Company truck. Later, a few miles down the highway, our driver screamed "Hit it! Hit it!" through the cab's rear window. We dove for the ditches just as an Me-109 screamed past us on the first of several strafing runs.

Furious that all I could do was bury my face in the mud, I jumped up onto the truck cab, swung a .50-caliber machine gun mounted there around and yanked back on the bolt. When the fighter made another run, just above the tree line, I started firing. Other GIs down the line were doing the same.

The plane was coming in dead on and I could see I had a perfect field of fire so I held the gun steady and let the pilot fly right into my stream of tracers. The striped fighter shuddered and started to trail a plume of black smoke as it peeled off to the right and slammed into a nearby field.

Several of us bolted from the convoy toward the burning plane and found the pilot lying unconscious near the wreckage. Even before he came to, I had grabbed his Mauser pistol from its holster, his helmet off his head, his fleece-lined leather gloves off his hands and was tugging at has flying boots. When he opened his eyes, he was surrounded by a ring of rifles and other GIs had relieved him of his goggles, leather jacket and flight suit pants. He must have thought he was fighting the United Souvenir Hunters of America.

The pilot didn't appear so invincible standing there barefoot and half naked in the mud and snow. I tried to speak to him but received only a torrent of arrogant insults in return. Mixed into his tirade, I could make out the words, "Amerikanische Schwein Hund" ("American pig dog"). When we all started laughing at this denuded Aryan Luftwaffe warrior, his glowering expression darkened and his contempt for us was clearly evident. Jubilantly, we all ran back to the convoy with our prizes of war knowing that this "superman" would probably never threaten us again. To us, he hadn't even been deemed worth taking prisoner.

I would never know whose bullets actually knocked the Me-109 out of the sky but I had seen some of mine hit home and I knew I had helped. Later, one of the GIs in my platoon gave me a picture he had taken of me atop the truck firing the machine gun.

The convoy rolled on, destination, as always, unknown. After a while, it stopped to give us a chance to relieve ourselves, this time beside a graveyard offering a rather macabre sight.

A "blockbuster" bomb had landed in the middle of the cemetery leaving a crater into which a building could fit. Scattered throughout the sides and bottom of the hole were the remains of graves and the buried dead from apparently many generations, for there were skeletons of the ancient, the taut-skinned frames of the old, the decomposed remains of the more recent and the almost perfect cadavers of the recent dead.

The smell was overwhelming. I felt like I had stumbled upon the tombs of Egypt. I had never seen death in this form before; all over the sides of this enormous crater were scattered bones. It made me wonder about subjects I hadn't thought about before—like, what happens to us after we die. I was now seeing the answer firsthand for myself.

It sombered me and I walked away, leaving these German souls to their now disinterred and disturbed sleep. As we rode along, I began wondering about heaven and eternity There were so many questions to which I didn't know the answers and I realized now that, even after death, there is sometimes no peace. I suppose what I had seen was all part of growing up.

Suddenly, thinking back to the Luftwaffe strafing a few miles back, I started laughing, drawing quizzical expressions from the others. "We're towing a whole bunch of flak wagons. Where were they when the Me-109 strafed us?" I asked. The whole truck had a good laugh.

The bone-rattling ride continued but no one complained for it was still better than walking. During one highway break, I spotted a farm on the far side of a field. Turning to "Joe Loot" Everett, I said, "C'mon, Loot. Food." We hopped off the truck and away we went to forage. As we cautiously entered the farm house courtyard, rifles at the ready, we faced a scowling German farmer.

"Lebensmittel?' ("Food?") I asked him. "Eier?" ("Eggs?").

"Ich habe gar nichts. Gehen Sie weg" ("I have nothing. Go away"), he protested.

I shoved my M-1 against his gut and yelled back just as loud, "Sei ruhig!" ("Be quiet"). He glowered viciously at us.

Everett and I searched the barn and the farmer's vegetable cellar, returning with arms and pockets full of eggs, pickled beets, flour, potatoes, smoked ham, some pilfered German army chocolate and other staples from the farmer's well-stocked larder. Everett milked a cow and filled his steel helmet and our canteens with warm milk.

I yelled to the convoy and as a horde of men came running, the farmer became apoplectic. One of the GIs fired a shot in the air to intimidate the old man, who stood his ground screaming curses at us. When the mob from the truck convoy finished looting the farm, the farmer was a little hungrier that winter but the conquering forces wouldn't be. To the victor went the spoils. A few minutes later, we moved on. But this time we were chomping happily on our liberated edibles.

I felt little sympathy for the farmer. My stomach had not once been truly filled since leaving England and to satiate my persistent hunger was the most important thing to me. Having their countryside and homes ravaged was a price the vanquished had to pay in wartime.

At each break along the way, I jumped off the truck, kindled a fire and tried to boil eggs in my helmet beside the road, but inevitably each stop was too brief to even heat the helmet up slightly. This was the same helmet that a few days earlier had served as a toilet in a Belgian foxhole but, when truly hungry, you don't worry about unnecessary details.

Before bedding down for the night in the next village, the name of which I believe was Wegburg, I was finally able to cook some of my liberated ham and eggs on a stove and enjoy one of my more memorable meals. In the morning, I found an abandoned bicycle and went for a ride, which was a major accomplishment on Wegburg's mud-filled streets. Everett found a horse wandering around a nearby pasture and promptly mounted it bareback. What a strange sight we must have been, Everett on a plow horse, me on a wobbly bicycle.

Together, we went to a nearby farmhouse where the occupants stood silently by the door waiting for us to start looting. I told then we meant them no harm. At this, they started jabbering between themselves, both scattering in different directions. She came back moments later with an apron filled with eggs and he appeared around a corner of the house with a bottle of schnapps (German whiskey).

I went for the eggs, Joe for the liquor. When I hesitated momentarily before accepting the eggs, the woman understood and ran back into the house to cook some up for me. To say they were delicious would be an understatement for they had the woman's touch, something that cannot be duplicated any other way.

Then in a strange twist of war, the couple insisted we stay for the night. Fearing a trap, we declined. But they persisted and we finally agreed. Tempted by the offer of real beds, neither of us thought about the consequences of being left behind by the convoy. The wife made up beds, complete with linens, in the attic, but since this was too much for us to accept at face value we set up a flimsy system of standing guard. The wife warned us to stay alert; a few German soldiers were still active in the region.

We slept soundly and were awakened by the woman asking whether we planned to sleep all day. The time was 0530, the beginning of a farmer's day. She already had breakfast, a wash basin and razor waiting for us in the kitchen.

We ventured outside and could hear rifle and machine gun fire in the distance. As I gazed around this peaceful farm, I realized we were once again caught between two worlds: of war and tranquility. I had heard that the Rhinelanders were friendly, hospitable, outgoing people and now I was starting to believe it.

I asked the farmer if he knew what was going on with the distant firing. "Just some Amis fighting with German soldiers," he replied, somewhat disinterested with it all. His world was his farm, and his attitude was a striking example of German isolationism.

After eating and shaving, Everett and I checked out the fighting, Everett saying he was tagging along only to protect me from myself. Cutting across a pasture, we were joined by another anti-tanker who, like ourselves, was goofing off.

Crouching low in a ditch as we ran, I stumbled upon a mortally wounded Wehrmacht soldier lying on his back. Half of his face and skull had been blown away. Only one eye remained and it was watching me. I drew down on him with my carbine but realizing instantly be was no threat to me, I lowered it again. That one eye held me in its grip and I couldn't move. The German kept looking at me deplorably. Like so many other wounded I had seen, this man had also been disemboweled by a massive gut wound. The one remaining eye blinked at me repeatedly. From the bloody foam drooling from what had once been a mouth, I could make out one whispered word over and over: "Schiessen, schiessen." ("Shoot, shoot.")

I put my carbine to his head but no matter how hard I tried I could not put him out of his misery. Some unknown force was preventing my finger from squeezing the trigger. I must have remained transfixed on this man's pleading eye for several minutes before lowering my rifle and continuing running along the ditch to the town.

When I retraced my steps from the town back to the convoy an hour later, he was dead. Before the war burned itself out, I asked a chaplain whether I would have been right in committing a mercy killing. His answer was, "No. If God had wanted him he would have taken him." That was the only explanation I would ever get but somehow it seemed totally unsatisfactory.

We sprinted to the closest building and crouched in a front room where we could see the street. Suddenly a Schmeisser machine gun erupted from beneath us at some unseen target. There were Germans in the building where we had sought refuge but, for some unknown reason, they had not yet heard us. We tip-toed across the floor and waited for the next burst of fire. When it came, Everett quickly opened the cellar door as I pulled the pins on two grenades and rolled them down the cellar stairs.

When they exploded and the smoke billowed up the stairs, the other anti-tanker leaped into the cellar and cut loose with his "grease" gun. "C'mon down. These guys are loaded with loot down here," he hollered up at us. He was right. On two machine-gunners and a lieutenant we found a pair of Lugers, three P-38s, a grenade launcher, a Leica camera, field glasses, jewelry, knives and a Nazi armband. It was a lucrative day for Everett, Blunt and the other GI whose name I never got. We divvied up as much as we could carry and started back to the company area. I never found out who the Germans in the cellar were firing at, and why we were not subjected to return fire.

After first checking for possible other Germans still in the cluster of houses, we returned to the farmhouse. Everett gave the farmer the horse and I gave him some American cigarettes. I offered the wife a Hershey bar, and she was absolutely delighted. She had never seen or tasted one before.

Then it was time to return to the company area to face the music for being AWOL. We knew the punishment would probably be severe but the farmer's wife's meal and the good night's sleep had been worth it. And besides, we had all that good loot to ease the pain.

When we asked around, we found that no one had even missed us even though we had been gone for two days. We bartered our loot with others in the platoon and then settled back in as if nothing had happened. I must say, Everett and I sure loved to take chances, but if we kept it up much longer, we were sure to get caught eventually.

Orders came through that troops were needed to reinforce EASY Company in an attack on the nearby city of Dulken. It had gotten to the point that when such orders came down the lieutenant looked at me first. In my youthful enthusiasm and ignorance, I was constantly doing foolish things, like volunteering for practically every detail that came along. Word had filtered back that many booby traps had been found in the city so at least we were going to work in an area where allegedly we had some expertise.

The approach to the city was a 400-foot-wide open field offering no concealment whatsoever. In the distance, we could see factory chimneys still smoking. Tanks were lumbering toward the city and they would provide the only protection we had. With my new binoculars, I could see white sheets and flags hanging from practically every window indicating that at least the civilian population would not be a problem. But since I also knew Germans had in the past offered to surrender under a white flag and then had come out shooting, I remained skeptical of surrender flags.

A truck-mounted public address system rolled up to the edge of the city and blared out in German, "People of the city of Dulken, you have 10 minutes in which to surrender yourselves. Those who remain behind may be killed because in 10 minutes we will start an artillery barrage that will destroy your city. Then we will attack and those found behind will be treated as soldiers. This is your last chance. All civilians must leave the city. Take whatever possessions you can carry and come this way. You will not be harmed."

The announcement was repeated over and over again. As the minutes ticked away, a handful of bewildered civilians straggled toward us. Then the numbers swelled. When they reached our position, they were directed to the rear by German-speaking GIs. We were the first Americans they had seen and most of them appeared frightened. More and more came through our ranks carrying battered suitcases or sheets and blankets filled with their meager belongings.

Many of them appeared to be Wehrmacht soldiers taking the easy way out for they were of conscriptable ages between 18 and 50. Hitler was scraping the bottom of the barrel and Volkssturm troops were becoming more evident each day. But we didn't challenge those who may have been active-duty soldiers because this was just another form of surrender—only this way without bloodshed, and without the civilian population realizing that they were capitulating.

The refugees were methodically searched for weapons and then motioned to the rear. Occasionally, a weapon was found and that person, man or woman, was diverted to a POW pen. Eventually, the flow of refugees stopped and the loudspeaker gave the last warning before an intense howitzer barrage pounded the city for about 20 minutes.

When it stopped, a solitary German soldier crawled out of the rubble and limped toward us, one arm held feebly up in the air. The stump of his other arm, badly shattered, hung limp at his side.

I started in his direction but the commander of the tank I had been walking behind waved me away. Then, without hesitation, he deliberately veered the tank toward the soldier and ran over him with his tank treads. The badly-wounded German soldier looked to have been a teenager. It was as barbaric an act of war as any I had ever seen committed by the Americans. I was finding out that cold-blooded murder was not just the province of the Germans.

The tanks pounded away with their 76mm cannons. Every GI in sight was hammering away with M-1s at every door and window. I did the same, even though I never actually saw any targets to shoot at. The sounds of battle were deafening and powder smoke from the cannons enveloped me, making it difficult to breath, or even see, for that matter. The ground in front of the tank erupted in a showering fountain of dirt. The tankers spotted the 88 before we did in a bunker so the duel began.

The tank turrets traversed slowly and I hightailed it for cover—the tank had suddenly become no place to be just then. The Shermans won after several rounds were fired and a squad of GIs moved in to mop up what was left of the hastily built bunker.

The American fire on Dulken was far heavier than the return fire we received from the Germans left behind as a delaying force. The American rationale, I presume; was that this close to the end of the war, ammunition was far more expendable than soldiers' lives. Pound the city into submission first and eliminate the opposition before sending in the troops, was the theory. It was a good, conservative theory, one I hoped the Army would continue to use.

As the isolated sniper fire lessened, I started a house-to-house search for booby traps, the job I had been sent there to do. I came across a sidewalk air raid shelter and was preparing to throw a grenade into it when I heard a woman's voice.

"Kommen Sie heraus" ("Come out"), I commanded. First a hand appeared in the opening, followed by a terrified elderly woman holding her arms in the air. I asked her who else was in the shelter and if any German soldiers were in there. She assured me there were only "Alte Frauen und kindern" ("Old women and children"). She told them to come out but no one appeared. Cautiously, I entered the shelter and found the occupants huddled in a corner trembling and crying. I looked at their wrinkled faces and I felt a little ashamed for doing what I had been contracted to do back in September 1943: soldiering.

I softened my voice and told them there was hot food behind the American lines or, if they wanted to, they could stay in the city for the Americans had already passed through and they were no longer in any danger.

The old woman's tears came when she realized she and the others would not be shot. I think she was also greatly relieved to hear an American speaking German, even though haltingly. Before walking away, I threw a candy bar to the small children still crying in the shelter. I had more and they had nothing. "Gott sei Danke. Gott sei Danke" ("Thank God, thank God"), she kept murmuring as she tried to kiss my hand. In a gesture of youthful chivalry, I let her.

I kept up my search but found no booby traps. The city was mostly deserted, at least where I was looking. I worked my way down one of the streets as other GIs continued mopping up. As one of them in front of me walked past a house, an old woman leaned out a second-floor window and poured a tub of scalding hot water on him. As he screamed in pain, his buddy across the street, in a lightning move, shot her. She tumbled to the street with a sickening thud. I just stepped over her and kept walking without even looking down at her. I was learning that Nazi fanaticism came in all ages and genders. I had reached the stage where now even the killing of old women didn't bother me.

In one of the partially demolished buildings, I climbed to the top floor to start working my way down room by room. I heard no sound but still I sensed that someone else was there with me. That instinct, born of months in combat, was warning me again. I inched toward one room and violently kicked the door open, jumping inside as I did so. In a blur, I scanned the room and saw only a blanketed figure in a bed on the far wall. With carbine at the ready, I moved closer.

Under the blanket was a man who appeared to be in his 90s and obviously on his death bed. His face was wasted, his cheeks hollowed and eyes dimmed with time. The sight of this helpless old man completely took the fight out of me as I envisioned my own grandfather who had died only eight years earlier.

"Entschuldigen Sie mir Mein Herr" ("Excuse me, sir"), I whispered and walked softly away leaving him to his oncoming death with dignity. I knew there was nothing else I could have said to him; the war raging around him had already said it all for me.

Deep in thought, I stumbled over the rubble to the next house, again to look for possible booby traps. As the saying goes, you never hear the shot that hits you. As I entered the front door, a violent blow punched me in the side, spinning me around and dumping me in a heap on a pile of shattered masonry. A sniper had been following me in his sights and my preoccupation with the dying old man made me careless in a city that had not yet been declared safe.

As I lay in the rubble collecting my thoughts, another bullet slammed into the door jam over my head, throwing splinters of wood into my face. This time I reacted fast and rolled inside the building. Instinctively, I felt for the wound. I couldn't understand why there was no pain, just a dull ache as if I had been walloped hard in the side by someone. There was no wound. The sniper's bullet had severed my cartridge belt and hit my M-1 ammo pouch. The cartridges had been flattened and twisted but not one had exploded. Another close call with death. I carried the clip with me until the war ended but eventually it became lost. I remained momentarily interested in the shattered ammo clip in my hand as I pondered what a close call it had been. Foolishly, I ignored the sniper, another careless mistake.

I crawled to a window and shot nervous glances out at the street. I even dangled my helmet out the window on a piece of wood as a ruse but the cagey sniper didn't bite. I heard the roar of a Sherman tank approaching and I yelled at the sergeant crouched in the turret.

"Sniper, sniper over there," and pointed at the building across the street. He heard me and instantly "buttoned up" his turret.

I hadn't noticed at first but the tank was equipped as a flame-thrower, similar to the British "Crocodiles." The tank turret slowly ground to its right and in the next moment, the building across the street disappeared in a massive sheet of fire. I watched the building consume itself to a pile of burning debris. But I also knew that a sniper would most probably move to the cellar and wait the fire out. Then he would resume his deadly game.

When it was safe, I climbed over the rubble and, not finding a charred corpse inside, tossed a grenade into the cellar. I didn't bother to check if anyone was there. Back in the street, I found other elements of Anti-Tank Company entering the city. They informed me EASY Company had been assigned to occupy Dulken until further orders and I was to rejoin my old outfit.

The squad had taken a billet in the cellar of a former coffee mill where the dampness penetrated our bones and our handwarming candles were most welcome. Looking around in the flickering candlelight at the faces of the other squad members, I smiled at what a bunch of "sad sacks" we were, but we were buddies, we had shared a lot and that was all that was important. We were now only a few and I wondered how many of us would see the end of the war. Then I blew out my candle and tried to sleep.

In the morning, we found it had snowed and turned quite cold during the night. We were given K-rations and, as crazy as it might sound, they hit the spot. It is amazing how good dry cheese and cold lemonade tastes on a winter morning when you have nothing else. The Army always went to great lengths to assure us of a well-balanced diet.

In an attempt to bolster our morale and pride, a written commendation was passed on to each of us individually through the chain of command on March 15 from Ninth Army Headquarters (Lieutenant General W. H. Simpson), to the XIII Corps Headquarters (Major General A. C. Gillem Jr.), to 84th Division Headquarters (Major General Alexander R. Bolling), to Regimental Headquarters (Colonel Lloyd H. Gomes), to Battalion Headquarters (Lieutenant Colonel William T. Barrett), to AT Company Headquarters (Captain John C. Bowen), to Anti-Mine Platoon Headquarters (Lieutenant William L. Ray Jr.) to Blunt's Headquarters.

The citation, in part, read: "The 84th succeeded in the course of a very few days in making a name for itself by reducing the enemy strongpoint of Geilenkirchen, thereby facilitating the advance of the Army to the Roer River and the speedy installation of bridges and expeditious seizure of key towns east of the Roer River . . . during "Operation Grenade," thereafter the rapid advance despite an extraordinarily exposed left flank . . . and never losing its momentum from the Roer to the Rhine rivers . . . and superior performance". . . etc., etc., on and on ad infinitum. Like the old Army saying of that era, the unit commendation and ten cents would buy me a cup of coffee back in the States.

I tried to catch up on my correspondence home and my daily diary notes. But my hands were too numb to hold my German fountain pen and scratch paper, so I put them away for another day.

13

The Kraut on the Run

With only a few minutes' warning, we were on the move again, this time haphazardly, as if we didn't know where we were going. And it turned out we didn't—we had inadvertently intruded into territory that had not yet been wrested from the Germans. During the breakthrough from the Roer to the Rhine, the situation, as it had been so often during the Bulge fighting, was quite fluid. We seldom knew where the enemy was, or even where we were. For the most part, the Germans were in full retreat, but throughout their flight they kept stopping and confronting us with pockets of stubborn resistance.

We were moving eastward so fast and with so many salients that on numerous occasions we were penetrating the enemy's rear areas and leaving our flanks dangerously exposed. Had the Germans at this phase of the war had more military strength and equipment, they might well have turned the tide of battle in this 50-mile stretch of their homeland between the two rivers. But they didn't, and the American forces were fanning out helterskelter on a wide front in every direction wherever they faced the lightest resistance.

The cold, penetrating March dampness, the constantly wet uniforms and the lack of proper rest or food were gradually wearing me down. One exhausting truck convoy after another, one rubble-pile bed after another on top of weeks of cold food were too much for my system. There were times I went into uncontrolled fits of shivering that lasted for hours.

It was during one of these trembling episodes that I apparently lapsed into unconsciousness, for I remembered nothing until I came to some time later all wrapped up in blankets on the floor of a meat wagon with a medic sitting on the rear compartment wooden bench above me.

I tried to sit up but couldn't. I hurt all over, but at least I was warm for the first time in days. "What's the matter with me? I'm OK, I just don't feel well. Just warm me up a little," I protested.

"You've got pneumonia, buddy," the medic said. "We took you out of the truck when you passed out."

"How bad is it?"

"Not too. It's just coming on. I've got you all doped up."

I don't know how long I remained in the ambulance but one time I looked out it was light, another time it was dark.

"How long have I been out," I mumbled.

"Two days," he answered.

"Where are we?"

"Beats the hell out of me."

"Have I eaten?"

"Nope. Feel like a K-ration? It's all I've got."

I tried to eat it but my arms were too heavy to open it and my jaws ached too much to chew.

"How long will I have to stay here?" I kept on.

"Until you're all better. Maybe a couple more days."

The ambulance was like a limousine compared to the "six-by-six" trucks in which I had covered half of Europe. I drifted off to sleep again. When I woke up, the ambulance had stopped and the sun was shining brightly outside. A head popped in the back door, asking cheerily, "How ya feeling, Blunt?" It was good old Joe Everett again, my ever-faithful companion. He told me the convoy had advanced almost 20 miles while I was "out of action." I struggled to sit up and found myself in a motor pool with smoke coming from a kitchen a few feet away. With Everett helping me, I made it to the chow line.

"Sick man coming through," Everett bellowed. The chain of GIs parted respectfully for us up at the front of the line. The menu of the day was plopped into our mess kits and we wandered off to find a quiet place, away from the others, to slop down our slop. Bucking an Army chow line is a well-defined, time-tested science that takes great talent honed by years of experience. Joe and I were two of the best in the ETO.

The 84th had taken 1,461 Germans prisoners during the Battle of the Bulge. In this dash for the Rhine River, the division was credited with taking 7,306 prisoners, a sign of the vastly different type of warfare we were facing here in the Rhineland.

Hitler's defenses were falling like dominoes, and the resolve of his troops was weakening with each day we pushed them deeper into their homeland. Some German units fought even more fiercely as they were pushed deeper into the heart of Germany while others, apparently convinced of the futility of further resistance, surrendered readily and often in entire unit groups. The Germans were being squeezed unmercifully by American, British, Canadian and Australian forces from the west and the Russians from the east. They were literally in a geographic vice with no place to retreat to. The fervor and fanatical loyalty to Hitler's leadership was now practically nonexistent and most German commanders were merely trying to survive and save what remained of their troops.

However, as Germany's "Lebensraum" (living space) shrunk, the resistance, in direct proportion, became more fanatical in a few instances. Nonetheless, we could practically smell the end of the war.

One of the more positive by-products of our sprint to the Rhine was that most of the villages we passed were now left mostly intact and the roads were largely undamaged. Forests were not being destroyed and the beet fields would grow bumper crops again.

Also missing were the heavy toll of dead bodies and the carnage of burned-out German or American tanks and vehicles along the roads, sure signs the German army was still in full retreat. A war was being lost, an entire nation being brought to its knees. But, thankfully, hundreds, perhaps thousands of lives were being spared. It was already too late to salvage an entire generation of Germany's male population, but at least there was still time to prepare for the next one.

The convoy was coursing its way along a cobblestoned street in another typical German town when suddenly it halted, backed up fast, hung a U-turn and sped back from whence it had come. When I suspected we had taken a wrong turn and wound up in an enemy-held town, I was right. Everybody breathed easier again and started to tease the driver.

"I was only following the other guy," he alibied with a big grin.

We continued on. After two more grueling hours we pulled into

Monchen-gladbach, just west of Dusseldorf. From the degree of destruction, it was easy to tell that a fierce battle had taken place there. From all the bullet-pocked buildings, we knew there had been heavy street fighting before the town had been taken.

Mess personnel handed out more K-rations to us as we emptied out of the trucks. I was hungry enough so that the rations tasted good. Perhaps I was becoming hooked on them, for this was the fourth time in as many days that these abominable rations had hit the spot. Continuous hunger over a long period of time does funny things to people's stomachs.

While walking along one of the city's deserted, demolished streets, I came across what to me was a sad sight: a music store that had sustained a direct artillery hit. Drum sets, violins, horns and pianos were scattered everywhere. I picked through the rubble, found two Zildian high-hat cymbals from Constantinople, shoved them in my barracks bag and moved on. After the war ended, I was able to use them during my months of occupation duty in southern Germany and eventually bring them home, where I played them for many years in civilian life.

White flags and bed sheets were draped as signs of capitulation from practically every window in the city, not unlike those we would see in every city and town in our path from the Roer to the Rhine to the Elbe rivers, where the Germans finally capitulated totally and all shooting ceased. Civilian resolve was collapsing as fast as that of the Wehrmacht.

When dealing with civilians, except for a couple of old women, I never once met a Nazi the whole time I was in Germany, either during or after the war. Strangely, the Nazi was universally the "other guy." Monchen-gladbach was only a rest stop for us. Soon we were rolling again, only this time I was in a Jeep with a company lieutenant on another billeting detail. My basic knowledge of the German language made me a handy guy to have around when it was necessary in each city or town to locate adequate quarters for the platoon. My job was to evict the occupants from their homes once we had found what we wanted. It was considered a choice detail, for it meant I invariably wound up with first pick of the houses—and the souvenirs.

It was March 3, 1945 as we drove across a broad field and approached the major industrial center of Krefeld, practically on the

Rhine River. From its appearance, it was considerably larger than Geilenkirchen, the largest city the 84th had taken so far. I asked a civilian whether there were still German soldiers there and was told, "Nein. Nur Amis" ("No. Only Americans").

As our jeep probed its way cautiously into the city on a major boulevard, we were practically swallowed up by a blinding flash. Artillery—either theirs or ours—was still shelling the city.

The Jeep was riddled with shrapnel; only the windshield had saved us from serious wounds. With the lieutenant screaming for the driver to take evasive action, we zigzagged and careened around corners until we found a side street not under the direct observation of the 88 batteries. I reminded the lieutenant that he had assured us that Krefeld had been cleared and there was nothing to worry about. If looks could kill, his expression would have done the job.

After we caught our breath and got the lumps out of our throats, we realized this shelling was probably an isolated incident. Our thinking was confirmed by the number of civilians crowding the sidewalks in business suits, women bicycling with shopping bags hanging from their arms and even a few cars driving on the streets. Just your everyday, normal German city.

Without realizing it, I was seeing in full flush the carefree attitude of the German Rhinelanders. They laughed a lot, loved to party and were even somewhat receptive and outgoing toward Americans. As in Dulken and Monchen-gladbach, white surrender cloths were hanging from most windows. The lieutenant and I entered an ornate apartment building and started knocking on first-floor doors, each time being greeted by civilians who couldn't comprehend that we were Americans, the first they claimed to have ever seen.

We told them to evacuate, that we were taking temporary possession of their homes. They didn't seem to mind too much and reappeared a few minutes later with their paltry belongings over their shoulders. We told them they would probably be allowed to return to their homes in a few days when we moved on.

One woman, however, shook her fist at me and hurled invectives at both of us. In other words, she was swearing up a storm. A hard slap on the ass stopped her yapping. Once again from the street, she continued to curse us. When I put my rifle to my shoulder and pointed it in her direction, she took off down the street as fast as her fat little bandy legs would carry her. The other residents thought this was quite funny. I figured the irate woman with the disturbed attitude must have been an "auslander" (foreigner). I was learning to love the Rhinelander sense of humor.

I informed the lieutenant of what the residents had said, that we were the first Americans they had seen. This disturbed him. We both hoped the Germans had, in fact, retreated to the river. If not, the enraged woman's cursing would summon them from five miles around. We found the empty apartments suited us well, and decided to take over the entire building for Anti-Tank Company. I was ordered to find the most elaborate room for the company CP. It was on the second floor—but I claimed it for Everett and myself. A much smaller, more ordinary room on the first floor was set aside for Bowen and the other officers.

When Everett first saw his luxurious new accommodations, complete with soft beds, sheets, radio, drapes, electricity, bathtub, working toilet, paintings, ornate pastel tiling and carpeting, his mouth fell open. The first thing he did was bounce on the bed to make sure it was for real.

"Not bad, Bluntie old boy, not bad. You're learning," was Everett's only comment. From him, this was high praise.

Actually, the best find of all after months of "slit trenches," "four-holers" or behind-the-bush relief, was not the soft bed but rather a real toilet that worked. It was heaven to have some place to sit and meditate. The whole time we stayed in Krefeld, the company brass never caught onto my "coup de guerre." Everett said he was very proud of me, another glowing compliment. After a solid night's sleep, I stepped outside to check out the city. An MP came chugging by in a miniature Volkswagon sedan about the size of the English Austins seen in the States. I stuck my hitchhiking thumb out and squeezed in beside him. We cruised the city until the "liberated" car ran out of gas, after which I hoofed it back to my billet.

Fortunately for us, German resistance in Krefeld had been light and the fury of war passed by the city quickly, leaving most of it undamaged. The streets were now filled with American soldiers, but for the most part they were ignored or tolerated by the German populace.

I pulled billeting detail again, for as quickly as our luxurious respite began, it was over and the company was heading for the town of Mors. As in Dulken, Monchen-gladbach and Krefeld, we found a sea of white cloth hanging from practically every building.

As usual, I was left alone in each city or town we entered to "protect our interests," namely billet sites, until the platoon could be moved forward.

I entered a private home and informed the occupants we were taking possession temporarily. The couple, appearing to be in their 60s, outwardly didn't seem to mind and the husband started questioning me right away about the progress of the war. As I brought him up to date, he sat quietly, shaking his head almost dejectedly. He told me he was a retired Wehrmacht soldat. As we talked, it became obvious he had long since resigned himself to Germany's failure to win the war.

As a gesture of his acceptance of his Fatherland's fate, he confided in me where he thought an SS officer who had committed atrocities against his own people was hiding. Casting caution aside, I located the house, kicked in the so door and leaped inside. The house was abandoned but the officer, in his haste, had left behind an ornate, chrome-plated ceremonial dagger, complete with gold tassel. It was a most welcome addition to my loot collection and well worth the trouble of having searched the house. Before pulling out of Mors, I gave division MPs the address where the SS officer lived and I heard later he had been arrested.

We remained in Mors for four days, and I had ample opportunity to discuss the differences between American and German culture with the old man who had informed on the SS officer. I'm sure we both learned a lot from the stimulating "unterhaltungen" (conversations), making the world a little smaller, in a manner of speaking.

The order to move out came just in time, for some of the "midnight snack cooks" in the squad managed to blow up a stove and heavily damage the billet. Except for the fact the building had been the home of the old couple, this didn't bother me for it was the third time I had narrowly escaped from burning and exploding sleeping quarters. I hoped the old Wehrmacht soldier and his wife would find other suitable housing.

During this period of our push to the Rhine, the war was being waged by other outfits somewhere else and, frankly, I was relieved that at least temporarily, we weren't involved. I had had enough fighting to hold me for a long time and now I wanted to slack off and watch it from the sidelines. Minutes dragged on into hours and as we pulled into a small village, the jouncing resignation of those in the back end of the troop-carrier truck was interrupted by the distant rumbling of artillery. As soon as we stopped and unloaded, I yelled to the first civilian I saw, "Wo sind wir?" ("Where are we?")

"Rheinhausen im Rhineland," he shouted back, waving with a smile.

I found a room with a couch in the first building I entered, a one-story stone structure, almost on the banks of the Rhine. The first familiar face we saw was the squad's zoologist from Brooklyn, Firschein, who had rejoined the mine-removal platoon after his ear injuries. No sooner had he seen the river than he was off frog hunting for rare specimens for a New York museum. One afternoon not long after his return, I found him walking blissfully along with a thermos bottle filled with German whiskey and containing two pickled frogs he said were native only to the Rhineland and which he claimed would be valuable additions to the museum's collection.

The squad used to tease him about his rather unusual hobby. Everyone stopped laughing, however, when he received a lovely, engraved certificate of appreciation from the museum for his research contribution. After that, we treated him with great respect. To each his own.

The chow tent was about 200 yards away and our orders were that only one or two men at a time were to be seen on the streets so as not to draw artillery fire or allow the enemy to assess our occupying troop strength. Our first breakfast in Rheinhausen, our first hot meal in weeks, was pancakes, bacon, coffee and bread. The town was small, with rows of simple one- and two-story homes formed in a square in the middle of a vast flat plain. It was a peaceful village and the occupants accepted us without noticeable malice.

Army life returned fast. Guard duty rosters were posted as soon as we arrived there. I was called to the company CP where the captain asked me to find a civilian woman who could launder his uniforms. I chose a nearby house that had several entryways and inside I found a middle-aged woman and a raven-haired daughter, about 13 or 14, whose beauty instantly riveted my attention.

The mother, who seemed honored to have been chosen as a laundress for the Amis, assured me she was the best in the village. As the mother washed and ironed the captain's uniforms, the daughter, Inga, asked dozens of questions about America.

Figuring that laundering uniforms did not constitute fraternization—which the Army had already declared strictly "verboten"—I brought my own uniforms to Inga's mother for laundering. Later, the company commander informed me I was to face a special court-martial for consorting with the enemy. Placed under house arrest until the trial, I could only think of the shame I was bringing upon my family.

Instead of sympathy and understanding, others in the company kidded me about not being a real soldier until I had at least one court-martial on my record. The way I felt, I would just as soon not be a "real soldier" if that is what it took to be one.

Bowen admitted he felt partially at fault for sending me into a German civilian's home in the first place to get his uniforms cleaned. He said he would help me any way he could during the trial. He also told me a certain 2nd lieutenant, a mere PX officer and not even a line officer, was pressing the charges in order to get promoted to 1st lieutenant. Bowen said he had tried to convince him to forget the whole incident but this sad excuse for an officer was adamant in using me as a stepping stone to a silver bar.

Before departing the billet for the trial, I shoved a drum stick up my sleeve for moral support. Just feeling it there would offer me strength, I thought. I was scared.

When I entered the makeshift court room, I was faced by two colonels, two majors and two lieutenants. Bowen sat near me. The panel asked my name, rank and serial number. Then I was advised not to testify against myself.

One of the colonels read the accusatory specifications against me: that "Private First Class Roscoe C. Blunt Jr., Serial Number 31390582, did on 20 March 1945 and again 21 March 1945 fraternize with German civilians in violation of memorandum, Headquarters, 84th Division dated 23 November 1944, Subject 'Fraternization,' by visiting the home of Egne Novotne, 6 Fresareder Strasse."

My mind was so befuddled with embarrassment and apprehension, it hardly recorded what was being said. When the voice reading the charges stopped, I pleaded not guilty. I was asked why I went there. I looked at Bowen and he nodded. I told the court he had asked me to find a laundress for his uniforms.

The presiding judge, a colonel, asked what I did there while the uniforms were being cleaned and I answered, "I talked to the woman's daughter about America." The court asked why I engaged in conversation with the women. Slightly exasperated by this question, I asked the colonel if I was expected to sit there and stare at the walls while the clothes were being washed. From the expressions on the court panel's faces, I knew my retort had been the wrong one and had not pleased the presiding officers.

The hearing lasted about an hour. Bowen, true to his word, tried to intercede and assume some of the blame for my actions. The intervention apparently was to no avail for a week later, on April 2nd, I was found guilty on both counts and sentenced to six months hard labor and forfeiture of $40 a month in pay for the same period.

Bowen, still feeling that I had gotten a raw deal, appealed my sentence and it was reduced to three months labor, without confinement, and a fine of only $120. But to someone earning only $50 a month, that fine was still a lot of money. Later on during my stay in Europe, I was able to find a variety of other ways to make up the money taken from me by the Army.

Again, Bowen apologized for the severe penalty and said he would make the labor as light as possible. He suggested KP, for there I would have first crack at the hot food every day and there would be no more C- and K-rations.

It sounded good to me but it was all a big charade. After a couple days of kitchen duty and a few pots and pans scrubbed, I was back with the mine-removal squad and no one seemed to care. But I also had the added advantage of being able to sneak back to the kitchen looking for food any time I wanted by just saying I was supposed to be working there. I did it often and it always worked.

The bucking PX supervisor was promoted a couple weeks later.

One day in Rheinhausen, I heard a shout so I went up and found a Red Cross truck parked on the main street. Two women in rumpled uniforms were distributing hot coffee and doughnuts. All you needed to obtain them was a dirty combat uniform and 20 cents in invasion marks. I had established a principle of not paying for a supposed charitable offering in Greenock, Scotland and I felt compelled to maintain the same policy in Rheinhausen.

Even though I supposedly was on KP punishment, I could never escape guard duty. The night was clear and cold, as it usually was after midnight, and the moon on the river was serene. As I casually walked about my duty station, secure in the knowledge that infiltrators or raiding parties would not come back across the river once they had reached the comparative safety of the other side, I gazed at the stars and my thoughts crossed the Atlantic to home. I was convinced I was destined to be a musician—I still harbored ambitions to be the best drummer in America some day—but I wondered what else I would do. Hell, the war was practically over. A guy had to plan ahead. It was a beautiful Rhineland night for quiet reflection.

Word was passed down from division that the 84th had been the first Allied division to reach the Rhine in northern Germany and had taken more prisoners than any other outfit on the continent. It made me realize my division was more distinguished than I had given it credit for. I couldn't know it at the time, but the 84th would set many more records in the months to come.

The squad started to horse around. We had been resting and getting stale on the west bank of the Rhine for nearly three weeks while the big brass figured how to get across it. Food boxes from home, usually accompanied by a dozen or more wonderful letters, continued to reach me. Animal crackers or Cracker Jack can do wonders for low morale. A can of fruit cocktail is like a lobster dinner. A tin of Spam can be fantasized into steak. The loving thought that deprived my family of much-needed ration points and the tenderness with which these many packages were sent were my strength.

As I walked a guard post the next night from midnight to 0400, I noticed a shiny object on the ground. It was a four-by-six piece of cardboard with a vial attached. The instructions on the back told German civilians it was a delayed-action incendiary bomb, and that it could be used to sabotage American vehicles. I looked around and found the ground littered with these potential bombs that must have been dropped by the recon plane I had ignored a short time earlier.

I notified the sergeant of the guard and then sprinted to the CP where I woke up the captain. Quickly, he ordered the whole company awake to search the village and recover as many of these incendiary chemical vials as could be found. Within minutes, men were scurrying everywhere with boxes, sacks and flashlights.

We must have found them all, since there were no incidents of sabotage while we were billeted there—or perhaps the Rhinelanders were too busy being "gemutlich" (agreeably pleasant) to worry about sabotage. Off and on, I did some kitchen time. The company executive officer concurred with Bowen that I had gotten a bum deal at the court-martial and he made sure I had plenty to eat during my imposed sentence. As officers went, he was OK. Anyone who kept my stomach full couldn't be all bad.

I heard the division band was performing back at Krefeld and hoped I would get another opportunity to perform with them. But it was not to be. The Army, with its usual efficiency didn't find out until after the war tended that I carried a Number 435 (bandsman) classification on my military records.

Promising to return it before we pulled out, I liberated a small short-wave radio from one of the townspeople, which enabled me to listen to Axis Sally broadcasts, always a source of amusement in the company. When atmospheric conditions were right, I could also faintly pick up the BBC in London for music and the latest war news.

As the squad crowded around the radio, a tank rumbling by brought us to the windows. We were being reinforced by elements of the 5th Armored Division, an indication that something big was in the wind. It could only be the river crossing we had all been waiting for.

A German plane came threatening out of the sky at the town and, just as suddenly, banked around and retreated back across the Rhine. As we picked ourselves up off the ground, we were showered by more propaganda leaflets, the same ones showing half-naked wives in the arms of their supposed lovers. The leaflets made excellent tinder for our morning fires.

I swear the Germans across the river heard our laughing, for moments later we were under another artillery bombardment, this time by shells containing more propaganda leaflets extolling the virtues of surrendering to the Third Reich.

The leaflets promised no more cold food, no fear, no more dodging bullets, no more foxholes, no more artillery, no more snow or mud. The leaflets made it all sound so wonderful, most of us could hardly resist the temptation to defect to the other side.

It was only a matter of days before we were restricted to quarters for what we all hoped would be the unfolding of the final phase of the war. If we crossed the Rhine successfully, the back of Germany's military might would be broken forever. We were about to attempt what Hitler had convinced his people was impossible: to breach and penetrate the area east of Germany's largest natural obstacle.

If anyone was to make possible the impossible, it was the 84th.

14

Germany's Last Barrier

There wasn't much conversation at the "last supper." A pall of uncertainty and apprehension hung over most of us as we counted the hours ticking by. Crossing the Roer had been a bitter, bloody fight orchestrated by some of the most intense artillery fire experienced by man. The Rhine was much wider, more strategically important, better defended. It was the do-or-die campaign for the German Army, the last defensible position before Berlin. But, how could it be any worse than the Roer had been?

The questions uppermost in our minds were: How many times can one go back on the line and still come out again in one piece? How long was it before someone's luck runs out? Was this going to be the end of the line for any of us? As I loaded my gear onto the six-by-sixes, the last remembrance of Rheinhausen was hoping that some day I could return because, court-martial notwithstanding, those had been happy days for me.

Nightfall came quickly and the convoy headed north along the west bank of the river under full combat restrictions: no sound, no lights, no talking. I looked at my watch. It was a little after midnight, April 1, 1945. "Happy Easter," someone on the truck chirped up. The remark came as a surprise. Most of us had forgotten. The road became rougher and the temperature dropped sharply, making us all shiver—partially from the cold, I thought, and partially from the anticipation of what lay ahead.

I was puzzled that we had received no briefing whatsoever. This was not like the Army, for as lousy a communicator as it was, we were

usually told something. All we knew for a fact was that we were part
of the 13th Corps and we were on the move again and, according to
Axis Sally, heading across the Rhine. The answers we sought would
soon be forthcoming, for eventually the convoy slowed to a crawl and
we could see for ourselves where we were.

I peeked under the canvas hanging from the rear of the truck and
observed another strange sight. As it had been in Geilenkirchen, the
whole landscape and sky was lit up by huge antiaircraft floodlights
that cast an unnatural, eerie blue mode everywhere, turning shattered
trees into silent sentinels and transforming shadowy buildings into
macabre, ghost-like silhouettes of death.

These lights surely could be seen forty miles away by the Germans,
so why not hire a brass band to announce our arrival? In the distance
I could see a Corps of Engineers treadway bridge across the river and
I realized someone else had already done our dirty work for us. A
crossing had already been made, a beachhead apparently established
and we were going to ride across the river without a fight, probably to
reinforce troops on the other side.

I was greatly relieved. Although I didn't consider myself a shirker,
I also knew full well that man's destiny is determined strictly by how
far fate is pushed—and I had been pushing mine pretty far, hard and
often.

From the heavy concentration of anti-aircraft and artillery batteries on both sides of the river, it was obvious that counterattacks by
German planes, tanks and infantry were expected at any time. For
years we had been taught to conceal, deceive, sneak, hide and camouflage, and here we were riding down Broadway for all the world to see
and hear. This could only mean the enemy had been pushed some distance inland away from the river.

The convoy swung creaking and groaning onto the bridge and the
soft swaying of the river could be felt. MPs were everywhere raising
arms up and down, flagging us through, urging drivers to "Go! Go!
Go!" as fast as they could negotiate the narrow steel treads across the
bridge.

Even though we were surrounded by a massive troop buildup, I
still felt exposed while crossing the bridge. Our truck lurched up an
incline on the east bank of the river and promptly became mired in
mud, churned up, I presumed, by the first tank companies to cross.

Off to our right stood a ghost-like monolith: the remains of a huge masonry bridge, its center span collapsed into the water. Its support pillars had been blown away and now what had once been an architect's dream lay in ruins in the swirling brackish waters of the Rhine.

The bridge had been destroyed by the retreating German troops to slow our advance, a futile maneuver for nothing could stop the American juggernaut powerhousing its way almost recklessly toward Berlin. Almost as soon as we hit the far bank of the Rhine, the German artillery started. We jumped from the truck and landed in water-filled shell craters. In my haste, I neglected to grab my rifle when I dove off the truck and now, pinned face-down in the mud, I couldn't go back after it.

Somewhere down the line, non-coms were yelling to get back onto the trucks, that we were going to make a run for it. I was so covered with mud and river muck, I kept slipping off every time I tried to climb back on board. Finally, strong hands reached down and lifted me aboard as the truck started to roll forward. Weaving and careening around shell holes, we drove toward a glowing red horizon. Before us, a whole city was burning and we were heading into the flames.

I thought I had seen total devastation in France, Belgium and western Germany, but nothing compared to the city we were approaching. To say every inch of it was burning would be accurate, for there in the city of Wesel man had accomplished the ultimate obliteration.

As we moved slowly through the city, flames searing both sides of the convoy, I dubbed it "the city of the burning dead" in my diary notes. In the Catholic religion there is reference to "man's hell on earth." As we advanced slowly through Wesel, flames scorching our truck's canvas sides, I had found hell on earth, and I was in it.

I had seen the name Wesel on military maps and I knew we had traveled about 15 miles due north from Rheinhausen. From the same maps, I had measured the distance from the Rhine to our next major objectives: the Weser River, slightly more than 100 miles ahead of us, and the Elbe River, only 250 miles east. According to the map, it was then only 65 more miles to our ultimate destination: Berlin.

I spent my time studying the map of Germany's northern plains and trying to calculate the remaining distance divided by the 50 miles we had just traversed in the past nine days. If my arithmetic, never one of my strong points, was correct, I figured that at the rate we had been pushing forward, we should be able to reach the Weser in 18 days the Elbe in 45 days and then Berlin in 54 days, give or take a few hours. In my mind, I was projecting that the war would be over in a month and a half. I didn't dare transmit these private thoughts to anyone for fear of being accused of lunacy.

History proved my calculations incorrect. The 84th actually covered the distance from the Rhine to the Elbe rivers in precisely one month. As I said, math was never my forte.

The 5th Armored Division continued to cut a path into Germany's heartland for us, and the 102nd Division was backing us up. The 84th's assignment was to support the armor and roll over all resistance while the 102nd Division brought up the rear mopping up after us and eliminating any small pockets of resistance we had bypassed in our frenetic advance. Our regiment penetrated almost 10 miles inland to Warendorf before encountering some light resistance. The following two nights—April 2 and 3—the 333rd and 335th regiments were in a virtual race northeastward almost 60 miles inland to the outskirts of Bielefeld and Telgte, respectively. The 84th was still advancing on a broad front and in many areas was only meeting token German resistance.

Close behind the armor and infantry battalions, we found that whereas we had advanced sometimes as little as 10 miles in a day between the Roer and the Rhine, we were now capable of covering 60 miles in a day. The mighty German war machine was crumbling faster and faster each day the war was prolonged.

Only the battered remnants of the Wehrmacht and a few straggling Volkssturm conscriptees appeared to be in our way. The SS divisions, once Hitler's pride, were no longer in evidence. What was now facing us were only the dredges of Hitler's once awesome military might that had struck terror in the hearts of nearly a dozen European nations since 1939. And now they were sharing the same fate, for a similar massive, inexorable Allied might was striking back at them with the same ferocity they had once displayed. We were part of a military force that was practically invincible, seeming to grow even more powerful with each passing day.

The resolve to defend one's homeland is strong and we eventually encountered elderly women with pitchforks, men brandishing rusted-out World War I vintage rifles that would no longer shoot, and children with knives and clubs. We were occasionally confronted by those resorting to Werewolf tactics whereby cables were strung across roads to behead anyone riding on motorcycles or Jeeps.

Some of these cables were hung higher off the ground to decapitate anyone standing up in a troop carrier. The barbarism of modern warfare expanded as we received the repulsive order to shoot these defenders on sight, regardless of their sex or age, if they were armed and threatening us.

In reality, there is no basic difference between a rifle in the hands of a 10-year-old girl or in those of an experienced Wehrmacht soldier. One can kill just as suddenly as the other.

By dawn, we were driving over flat plains of sugar beet fields interspersed with marshes, lakes, smooth-sided valleys and belts of rounded-off hills. Militarily speaking, the terrain would offer no major obstacles to tanks, walking infantry or the thousands of vehicles needed to sustain a war's thrust.

During a roadside break, small fires sprang up along the convoy as men tried to warm themselves. During this drive, I tried to stomach C-rations that had been issued to us but they continued to stick in my craw, bringing on instant nausea. As I had done so many times before, I dug into my duffle bag for the contents of my most recent package from home to sustain me.

Without stopping, we whizzed through two small villages, both untouched by the fighting, a sure sign the Germans were still in full and uncontrolled flight. After 24 hours of sitting practically motionless in the rear of a jouncing truck with only a few 10-minute roadside stops all the way from Wesel, the truck finally stopped and 12 muscle-sore men tumbled out.

I pulled the first guard tour and started a slow limping gait for four hours in front of our temporary billet while the others slept or tried to find food. I was kept company by the inevitable buzz bombs rocketing their way westward toward civilian destinations.

Even before my tour was up, we were ordered back into the trucks for another move and the only solace was that even though each move totally disrupted our eating and sleeping cycles, they also brought us that much closer to war's end. As we pulled out again, sleet and freezing rain started to fall. I remembered the spirit-killing march of France, the extreme pain of the Belgian winter and the soul-consuming terror of combat in between. But this truck confinement between the Rhine and the Elbe equalled them all as far as discomfort and exhaustion were concerned. Of course, I could have been walking all these miles instead, and then I would of really had something to complain about.

Company brass had distributed copies of *Star & Stripes* relating an incident in Stuttgart in southern Germany in which 18 GIs had died from drinking "buzz bomb" rocket fuel as a substitute for liquor. Amazed at the stupidity of such booze-craving GIs, we all got the message. I had seen men squeeze Sterno heating jelly through a woman's silk stocking to get a few drops to drink, but "buzz bomb juice" was just too much.

Seventy-two hours elapsed before we were told we could leave the convoy for a much-needed rest. There was no town in sight so we all fell to the ground and tried to sleep in ditches beside the trucks. What seemed like minutes later, a company non-com came along kicking the feet of each man, telling us to climb back on board. Hours had no meaning nor did kilometers and scenery. Twelve hours became 24, and 36 became 48, and I have no recollection of them for I was, I still believe, unconscious most of the time. The human body gets to a certain point of needing rest and then it rebels and collapses.

On April 4, we were in Bielefeld, a small city in the heart of Germany's northern central plains. Here and there we could hear the mopping-up sounds of occasional rifle fire and grenades. Soon, we were pulling past smouldering German and U.S. tanks beside the road. The resistance obviously was stiffening the closer we got to Berlin— and with it, we observed an increasing number of combat dead.

Without warning, the truck slammed to a stop and we were told to "deploy and form a fire line." We were meeting a small pocket of resistance and it had to be cleaned out. The lieutenant, Everett, another GI and I crawled along a ditch toward a machine gun nest that had been raking the convoy and causing multiple casualties.

The lieutenant handed me two grenades he had been carrying and, adhering to the old "delegate and disappear" officer tactic, told us to take out the nest while he supervised from back in the ditch. Machine gun slugs were tearing up the edge of the defile in which we were crawling and no matter which way we moved, forward or laterally, the wildly ricocheting bullets chased us.

We were out of effective grenade-throwing range and the stalemate dragged on. Then I felt a hand on my shoulder. It was our black truck driver who had appeared out of nowhere with a Browning Automatic Rifle. He took my grenades and said he would show us how it was done. I tried to tell him he would get his stupid head blasted off if he tried, but he just stared back at me in contempt.

Disregarding the bullets spraying all around us, the driver stood up and ran toward the machine gun emplacement, firing the Browning from the hip. Miraculously, he managed to get unscathed to within a few feet of the bunker even though the German gunners were concentrating their fire solely on him.

In almost a single sweeping motion, he threw the grenades into the bunker while hitting the ground. Simultaneously with the explosions, he jumped inside and emptied his 20-round BAR clip into the three German gunners. Then he picked himself up and casually sauntered past us without a word as if he were on his way to church, and returned to his vehicle. Whoever this Quartermaster Corps driver was, he had earned the respect of an entire convoy of white GIs who were on their bellies observing the caper. He was one of the true heroes of the war and none of us ever found out his name.

With each short "piss call" break, fires were started as men continuously tried to get warm. I had been trying to boil an egg the past 100 miles or so and had barely managed to get the water in my steel helmet even lukewarm.

In desperation, I poured the water out and broke some eggs into the helmet to try frying them. A gooier mess one never saw but when they turned to charcoal, I scraped them off with my trench knife and ate them anyway. Even burned to a crisp, they tasted better than cold C- or K-rations.

We rolled into the only-slightly damaged town of Herford. As we milled around stamping our feet for warmth, a fancy horse-drawn carriage came around a corner followed by what appeared to be a whole battalion of German soldiers surrendering themselves to us. At the head of the column was a colonel who stopped and handed his Luger to our company commander. I was quickly summoned to interpret. His men, he said, had not eaten for two days and they just wanted to return to their homes. He gave the captain a portfolio of military maps and other pertinent data.

He said they were all that remained of the once-proud Hermann Goering Division and they had recently been redeployed from the Eastern front to fight the Americans on the Western Front after the Russian campaign had been lost. He also expressed relief that he was surrendering to the Amis rather than the hated Ruskies, whom he said he feared.

Bowen instructed me to tell them to walk to the rear to Bielefeld and once there, to disband and find their way home. When I translated this to the colonel, a sudden outburst of emotion swept through the German ranks. Their bitter war in Russia was over and they had survived. Now their American war was also over and they had beaten the odds twice and survived.

They swarmed over us with pictures of their wives, mothers and children while others tried to embrace us or, at least, shake our hands. Seeing this emotional display by so many hundreds of Wehrmacht soldiers completely unraveled the hatred that had been welling up inside me since I had witnessed the atrocities in Holland and Belgium.

But I knew something they didn't: that their homes and towns had been reduced to smashed mortar and stone, their families had become refugees wandering hundreds of miles from city to city like nomads seeking food or shelter, and that, for most of them, there would be nothing to go home to. It would probably take years for them to be reunited with their loved ones and to reacclimate themselves to post-war Germany.

15

Liberation

During the next troop movement, the convoy stopped abruptly in the middle of nowhere for no apparent reason. We couldn't hear a fire-fight nor see any traffic tie-up. As we waited patiently for the column to start up again, a mob of people, without warning, swarmed around the rear of our truck. They were all trying to get at us, babbling in foreign languages I couldn't understand. Some were trying to climb aboard and kiss us. For a moment, not knowing who or what they were, we braced to fight them off.

One of the GIs in the truck was jabbering with them in Polish. The truck had suddenly been turned into a cacophony of languages. They were slave laborers from a nearby concentration camp. Over and over they asked whether anyone in the truck spoke Polish, Serbian, Dutch, French, Russian or Czech. None of them spoke English. It took a few minutes to sink in that the pictures of concentration camp prisoners we had seen in newspapers and magazines back in the States were true. Now these pictures were surging all over us.

As fast as they could talk, they told us of starvation, of working 20-hour days until many collapsed and died, of mass killings and open graves with corpses covered with lye. Every one of them was intent on telling their individual stories as fast as they could to the world, or, for that matter, to anyone who would listen. It was crucial to them, even before finding food for their decimated bodies. They were consumed by a need to talk, and the longer they crowded around us with joy, the more we learned of the boundless limits German cruelty.

Many of the liberated concentration camp prisoners did not take part in the jubilation, but rather stood respectfully at attention, their hands saluting their liberators silently. The majority merely stood stunned with their heads bowed unable to react either mentally or physically to their liberation.

Was the war over? Was Poland free, Belgium free? Had Germany surrendered? Was France still occupied? Were we in Germany to stay? Was the Russian Army coming too?

They clamored almost hysterically for any news from the outside world. No matter how fast we tried to answer, to use sign language or to shake or nod our heads, we couldn't keep up with the frenzy of questions. Some of them had been locked up and tortured for years and had no idea what had been going on in the world during that time. As we tried to answer every question, our responses set off groups of prisoners dancing in the muddy road between the trucks.

Not realizing they were holding up the whole war effort, they practically carried us to a nearby pine grove where a mass grave contained the skeletal remains of more than 400 slave workers of all nationalities.

The stench of death was overpowering. The rags hanging from the emaciated concentration camp inmates told only part of the horror story, of the appalling filth, the inhuman cruelty and starvation that had been perpetrated upon them. Captured by these inmates who were feebly demanding only that the world be told of the horrendous atrocities committed there, we were brought to another grave site in woods behind the camp where the remains of 2,000 more slaves had been buried in long, open trenches by bulldozers.

They told us of another guard who had hung two Russian inmates and, on another occasion, had arbitrarily shot an American aviator who had been critically beaten by German people after parachuting into a nearby village.

Next, they took us on a forced tour of a long, one-story wooden barracks in which 60 men and women had lived. Most slept on the earthen floor without blankets and many had died of tuberculosis and pneumonia. Most of those surrounding us were covered with lice, and ugly sores festered on their bodies. Their gaunt faces and sunken eyes told us what their mouths couldn't.

In one of the barracks, I found an emaciated woman cowering in a corner, her face to the wall, her arms covering her head. A large tattered rag that served as a blanket was draped over her. The Polish-speaking GI was able to ascertain that she was a nun who had been thrown into the SS guard barracks to satisfy the physical needs of an entire company for more than a year. She had been reduced to an insane mute living out her life in tortured memories.

We emptied out every C- and K-ration crate we could find in every truck and fed them, reasoning that even if we missed the next meal of rations, we never could be as hungry as these wretched souls standing before us.

We spotted a German officer walking briskly away from the camp on the road to Herford. We stopped him, confiscated his .32 caliber Mauser pistol, and turned him over to the prisoners who erupted into a violent mob scene when they saw him.

He had been the commandant of the camp and had, on one occasion in an act of intimidation, shot a Russian slave five times with his pistol in the face and chest and then threw him from a barn loft. The camp inmates related how they had been forced to take his body by wagon to the woods for disposal. In an example of instant justice, we left the major to the crowd who I assumed would beat him to death. I didn't bother to stay around to watch.

I broke away from the crowd as soon as I could. The stench was more than my sensitivities could stand and I was afraid I was going to break down emotionally. I thought I had seen everything in Belgium that war could spawn, but what I was looking at now was almost beyond human comprehension. I was learning fast that there is absolutely no limit to what man is capable of doing to man. The name "Rehren" on the concentration camp entrance sign would stay with me the remainder of my life.

Soon the convoy was on its way again, but over and over it was stopped by mobs of newly freed slave workers wanting only to touch our hands as they passed from truck to truck. It was impossible to move forward without running over them. Several miles down the road we passed another concentration camp, this one in flames. The freed slaves there were purging their past with fire. Many of the inmates had already started the long foot journey to the west, toward freedom and, for some of them, to their homes in Holland, Belgium and France. At the same time, thousands of others were trudging eastward as far as their diminished strength allowed, looking to retrieve their futures in Russia, Poland or Czechoslovakia. As we drove past them, we tried to scrounge from our barracks bags even more rations or cigarettes that we could throw to them. These people added a new terminology to the American vocabulary: DPs (displaced persons).

During our entire campaign eastward from the Rhine River, our division had repeatedly been forced to stop, usually for at least hours, sometimes for days, to wait for British troops lagging behind on both flanks. A Canadian Mapleleaf paratrooper told us the British were meeting almost no resistance on our northern flank, but were nevertheless unable to move forward except at what seemed to us a snail's pace. Their reluctance in battle always seemed to be leaving our flanks dangerously exposed and vulnerable, and increasing the chances of costly counterattacks from the retreating Germans. This reluctance to be daring, or even aggressive, in battle, added to a general feeling of resentment toward the "Limeys." I could readily understand this, for I had actually seen the Brits stop in the middle of an attack near Geilenkirchen and indulge themselves in a spot of tea. They never seemed as bold or innovative on the battlefield as American troops. The lack of British initiative slowed down our breakthrough for almost a week and, I felt, had been responsible for a needless waste of American lives.

Between the Rhine and the Weser River, the skirmishes with the Germans were hit-and-run affairs, day in and day out. During one such firefight, we were deployed in a field and ordered to advance on a nearby town in full frontal formation. One GI, passing by a house, found a large jug of Schnapps, a potato-based whiskey, and passed it around. Potent stuff. When the attack finally got underway, a line of pie-eyed GIs were weaving and stumbling their way across the field. Mortars rounds were dropping all around them and machine-gun fire was raking the meadows, but still the drunks staggered on undaunted. Seeing this incredible invincibility, the Germans pulled back quickly and there was not a single American casualty.

As part of a support platoon, we were at the rear of the attack when it disintegrated. Without orders to the contrary, we continued on to the edge of a small town where I entered a farm courtyard at the outer perimeter of houses and farms. The fire fight was over and it was time to relax my guard a little. I figured the Germans were probably still running. As I walked into the courtyard, a bullet splattered against a wall beside my head just as I caught a fleeting glimpse of a gray uniform disappearing behind a building.

Instinctively, I jumped backwards. I had seen him and he had seen me. Now the standoff would begin. With my luck, there had to be a diehard in the village. The advantage was mine, however, for he was probably alone and I had dozens of GIs somewhere close by.

We traded shots but it was no contest. He apparently was unaware that American GIs were armed with semi-automatic rifles rather than the clip-loaded, bolt-action Mausers they carried. As I fired a round, I stayed sighted-in on the corner behind which he was hiding. Sure enough, his head and rifle lunged out again after my shot and I quickly finished the duel. As he pitched forward, I fired another round into his head for good measure. Ammunition was plentiful and I didn't believe in taking chances—at least, not these kinds. I relieved him of his Soldat Buch and his watch.

The whole incident had taken only minutes and I continued the house-to-house search at a crouching run. When I was satisfied my section of the town was cleared, I rejoined the others. The sun was warm, so I sat a few minutes against a building to rest and catch my breath. I didn't even know the name of this small village in which I had nearly been killed. After the maddening stop-and-go travel of the previous day, our next move covered almost as much ground as we had after crossing the Roer River. Every time this happened, our morale and hopes soared.

In each small village and town we passed through, we saw groups of unguarded German prisoners sitting propped against buildings beside the streets. I wondered what was going through their minds as the almost endless columns of American troops and armaments passed through. On other occasions, we saw long lines of German soldiers who had been captured and then released with instructions to go home. None, as far as I know, had argued or complained for it was clearly evident that all the fight had been knocked out of them.

We were beginning to realize that any fighting from there on would be strictly going through the motions for the remaining Wehrmacht rank and file. The once-swaggering goose-step march with heads held arrogantly high was now a head-bowed shuffle as the vanquished tasted the ignominy of total, unforgiving defeat.

Many of the repatriated German prisoners begged for food along the route in search of their homes. In many instances, they were refused. The German people, as a whole, wasted little time or forgiveness on losers, men who could not produce the promised victory for the Fatherland. Many of these once-feared fighters were turned away when they merely asked for a place to rest on their long journey home.

But the Volkssturmers were still something to worry about. Their hero-worshipping, propagandized loyalty to Hitler made them individually unpredictable. Some merely went through the motions of putting up a defense while others were bent on becoming martyrs.

The exhaustion of war is insidious. It doesn't come on all at once, nor is it quickly relieved by a period of sleep. Its inception is hardly noticeable at first, but then it grows inside, paralyzing first the body and then the mind. It slowly builds and finally becomes solidified like old age and there is only wisdom, born of tribulation, to take its place. The convoy continued its buttocks-blistering path toward the Weser and Elbe rivers, stopping only occasionally to keep from killing its GI passengers.

At one stop, Everett and I ran to a nearby farmhouse to "liberate" some food. The farmer adamantly denied having any, but a carbine in his gut changed his story. Finding several cows and a flock of chickens, we filled our helmets with warm milk and eggs. Then, after raiding the farmer's sub-cellar, we loaded our pockets and overcoats with beets, Schnapps, ham and potatoes. More and more, we rejected the Army's contention that C-, D-, and K-rations constituted a balanced diet.

The farmer violently tried to restrain us from stealing his food, but a rifle round in the ground at his feet gave him pause to reflect. His hate-filled facial expression told it all, and we felt absolutely no qualms about stealing from him. The eggs were fried in our helmet, the meat eaten raw and the Schnapps was passed around. Anything to take the dust out of our throats and the edge off our hunger.

The many days in the cold back-end of a truck brought back the pain from my frozen feet, intensifying the almost agonizing beating to which I was being subjected. Kilometer after kilometer, the numbers of prisoners filing westward was increasing. Whole regiments were giving themselves up and it was evident that it was only a matter of time until Germany's final, complete military collapse.

During one rest break, a large group of men came running at us across a field, yelling and waving their arms. We figured just another bunch of DPs wanting to express their emotions at being liberated. But this time, something was different. These men were yelling in English and most were wearing olive-drab uniforms instead of the standard, striped concentration camp rags.

They were American prisoners of war, some taken by the Germans as early as the African and Italian campaigns. Many had been captured during the Battle of the Bulge. Like the slave laborers, they too were gaunt and undernourished. Some jumped on the trucks with us and wanted to fight the Germans again. Others just wanted to hear the news from the war front and from home. Battalion officers rounded them up fast and informed them there would be no more fighting in their futures, that they were going to be fed, given medical exams and treatment, processed, paid off and then shipped home as fast as the Army could arrange it. Many of the liberated GIs couldn't hold back their tears. Again, as we had done for the DPs, we emptied out every bit of food we still had left and gave it to them.

When we finally pulled into another of the many nameless villages we had seen, Everett and I tried to bed down in a barn beside the road but aching bodies and the cold prevented it. We decided to look up our old companies for a visit, me to LOVE Company, Joe to EASY Company. I found my old company and one of the first men I came across was a sergeant, one of the few I still remembered from the old days back in the States. He seemed happy to see me and know that I was still alive.

He told me very few of the originals who had shipped out with me from Camp Claiborne seven months earlier still remained. Thirty-two had been killed and more than double that number had been wounded. I was saddened when told one of those killed was someone I had buddied with back in the States. The sergeant said LOVE Company had lost a company commander and more platoon lieutenants than he could remember. Hearing this, I knew I had made the right decision in refusing the OCS offer back in Belgium. L Company's combat mortality and casualty rates had been extremely high, a condition that I knew existed in practically all infantry line companies. When the sergeant asked me if I wanted to go out on a recon patrol with him for old time's sake, I jumped at the chance to get away from truck travel for a few hours, even though I had not forgotten what had happened to me in my last recon patrol.

We fanned out and approached a wooded area to determine whether there were snipers there and, if so, how many. Once in the protection of the trees, we started to crawl. As soon as we started, the fatigue that had built up the past week from almost constant truck travel caused me to lag behind. I was out of rifle company shape.

The forward scouts detected a sniper position even before the first shot rang out. The point men were already in a fire fight and we were moving forward to cover them, for even though we were the hunters, we were also the hunted.

I spotted a German legging it across a clearing about 100 yards away. I emptied a clip at him, some rounds of which I was sure had hit him, but he continued to run until he disappeared into another clump of trees. Everett, who had rejoined me when he couldn't find his company, also pounded away at the fleeing German. He too, missed him.

Disgusted with my apparent poor marksmanship, I wondered if I should volunteer for rear echelon duty until I heard Everett muttering to himself, "Jesus Christ, Blunt. This damned defective ammunition is getting worse every day." Until then I had not known what was wrong. He broke me up, and the embarrassment of not being able to hit a running target at only 100 yards evaporated.

I reminisced a little with the sergeant and then it was time to return to Anti-Tank Company, where the others chided us for glory hunting instead of slacking when we had had the chance. I checked the German map I had been carrying and learned we had already crossed the Weser River, apparently during one of the nights without my even knowing it. Now we were on the road again, this time our destination being Hannover, Germany's 12th largest city.

I asked around about the Weser River crossing and was told the 335th Regiment's 1st and 3rd Battalions had made a successful crossing April 6, establishing a beachhead just north of the Weser Gebirge (mountains). Elements of the 333rd Regiment had gone across in support the next afternoon and immediately started pushing inland toward Eisbergen, about eight miles away.

I did some fast calculating and determined we had covered the 100 miles from the Rhine to the Weser in four days. If we continued at that rate, the war would be over by the weekend and we would be in Berlin. We continued northward toward Hannover where its inhabitants spoke the "Hoch Deutsch" (High German) I had been taught in high school. People throughout Germany understood High German but most spoke varying dialects and had difficulty understanding those from other geographic provinces.

On April 10th, as we approached the city, friendly artillery fire was winging its way over our heads, for Hannover was still under siege. From about a quarter mile away, we entered the city on foot as reinforcement troops, spaced at 10-foot intervals on both sides of a broad boulevard. Fires were burning everywhere and more dead littered the streets. Only one thing differed radically from the street scenes in the previous cities and towns. Here, the German equipment, field pieces and supply wagons were all horse-drawn. Burning ammunition carts were exploding and often beside them lay the corpses of the soldiers who had been pulling them.

The Luftwaffe was less and less in evidence now, as were mechanized vehicles. For the most part, men performed the tasks of horses. Each one of these realizations buoyed our spirits. What gasoline was available to the German Army was now steadfastly reserved for the few remaining tanks. It was becoming quite obvious to us that Hitler's "secret weapons" had been of little benefit to his war effort.

We found evidence of more and more defective artillery shells. The sabotage efforts of slave workers in the munitions factories appeared to be making a difference. The Wehrmacht had abandoned the use of its Nebelwerfer (rocket launchers) after too many had proven faulty and had blown up, killing the users.

Every day now, American troops were lifting a page from Germany's military manuals and were taking full advantage of the pincer movement strategy: encircle the enemy from two sides and entrap or eliminate him. Hannover was a vast city, and we infiltrated it for more than an hour before we reached what appeared to be the business district. No civilians were seen anywhere; obviously, they had been evacuated earlier. Like every city and town before it, Hannover was being systematically destroyed by American might.

We were told to form a skirmish line and clear the area for several blocks in front of us. When a German burp gun sprayed a building near me, I hit the ground and buried my head in the rubble. Each time

I tried to lift my head, machine gun bullets whipped at the pile of masonry around me, ricocheting in every direction. I was exposed to the German gunner and pinned down by him.

I caught a glimpse of movement across the street and saw a GI firing a BAR. He purposely showed himself to the German to divert attention from me momentarily. As he did so, the German's return fire cut him in half with machine gun slugs. In that precious moment the GI with the BAR had given me, I spotted the gunner and fired as many rounds as I could get off. He jackknifed out of a second-story window and fell to the street with a sickening thud, his helmet bouncing across the street. I jumped up, ran to the German gunner's body and emptied the rest of my carbine clip into him.

Then I ran to the other GI but there was nothing that could be done for him. His body had been ripped apart and his blood was trickling across a sidewalk and forming a crimson pool in the gutter. I was shaking with rage and gratitude at the same time. This man had purposely sacrificed his life for mine. It was with grim, slow movements that I returned to the German to get his Soldat Buch. I didn't even look at the picture.

Death was starting to hit me hard, for we were so close to the end that I wanted all the killing to stop once and for all. My brain had reached a saturation point of how much carnage and slaughter it could absorb. I realized the Allies would settle for nothing less than unconditional capitulation after the Germans had been totally vanquished, but I wondered if there wasn't some way we could bring this about through negotiation without more senseless throwing away of lives on both sides. I didn't realize it at the time but the voluminous massacring of so many lives was converting me from a hawk to a dove. Enough was enough, I thought. I couldn't take much more of it.

I edged my way around a street corner and was greeted by the sickening sight of two German boys about 10 years old, hung from a lamp post by the Gestapo for refusing to serve as Volkssturm defenders. We cut them down and left them to two mothers hysterically wailing and cradling the children in their laps as we continued on.

Words wouldn't come to us so we just walked away silently, leaving them to their private sorrow. The scene made me reflect on the Kraut teenager who had been cruelly executed back in Belgium for trying to feed hungry American prisoners.

The lieutenant told us to bed in for the night in an adjacent school. Guards were posted. After pulling my tour, I climbed to the fourth floor seeking a quiet night's sleep. Everett and two others were already settled in. Everett and I stretched out on the floor, the others in bunks along a wall. Sleep came fast as the sounds of the street faded. I don't know how long we had been asleep when the world caved in on us. A mind-shattering explosion knocked me senseless as the walls and ceiling caved in, burying us where we slept. I could neither hear nor see anything but gradually I sensed men walking around me with candles and flashlights probing their way through a thick, stifling cloud of gunpowder smoke, all the while pulling at debris.

I tried to get to my feet but extreme dizziness knocked me back down again. The room was filled with splintered timbers and masonry. Shadowy figures were stumbling around and yelling. Gradually, my senses returned and I realized that our room had sustained a direct artillery hit.

Everett and I on the floor had escaped unscathed. One of the GIs had a badly lacerated wrist from shrapnel and the other had disappeared. The shell had come through the wall and exploded in his bunk. All that remained of him were chunks of meat and flesh spattered all over the walls.

Everett tried to pick me up and drag me to a hallway where we met company officers who were quite unnerved by the incident. Through badly ringing ears I heard their hollow voices asking whether I was all right. As I struggled to respond, two men with a blanket removed the dead GI's remains. Their load was light; there wasn't much left of him.

In the kerosene lantern light of the command post, I vomited when I saw my uniform was covered from head to toe with the dead man's blood and flesh. I staggered outside and continued to throw up, crying in total frustration at fate. I had said good night to him only minutes before. I stood there pondering the same question I had asked myself over and over so many times before. Why had I been spared during this months-long series of close calls? These near-misses were becoming almost a daily routine with me. There had to be a pattern, a reason, but I just couldn't figure it out.

I wasn't prepared for what came next. It was one of the most emotionally shattering experiences of the war: we were told the pulverized

GI had been killed by a shell from one of our own tank divisions that had not been informed we were occupying this section of Hannover. Later, we heard that such accidents of war were referred to as "killed by friendly fire," a cruel misnomer if I ever heard one.

I felt my tormented brain collapsing into despair. This was followed by a period of deep depression. I couldn't fully comprehend then just how long these memories would haunt me throughout life. There were just too many of them, one piled on top of another. When would they all stop, and how much more insanity would I be forced to endure?

We had made our contribution to the war effort and now it was time to move on again. As the convoy closed in on the city of Braunschweig, we saw dozens of American, British and German tanks burning on the streets and fields. German and American dead were everywhere, hung out of windows, sprawled over piles of rubble, in doorways and in tank turrets.

It was obvious from the carnage that Braunschweig had been one hell of a battle. I gazed into the faces of the American GIs crumpled in the gutters and thought about how far they had come and how close they had been to the end. I felt deep remorse for these GIs and their families for their senseless deaths at this stage of the war. The ferocity of the fight for Braunschweig meant that German resolve was obviously stiffening.

Moving eastward again the next morning, I could only stare with dimmed eyes at the canvas wall of the truck. I had withdrawn into an emotional shell. Everett, sensing my grief, put his arm around me and we rode in silence the rest of the way. When the truck column halted, we were told we would be there for about an hour. A nauseating smell permeated the air we breathed. Off in a field I saw a row of wooden barracks of the type we had grown to know as concentration camp huts. A sign over a barbed wire gate read "Nord Stalag III." Nearby was the town of Ohrdruf.

The genocide of Jews and other foreign nationals was spread out before us everywhere we looked. Huts were filled with dead and near-dead skeletons that stared up at us with sunken eye sockets wherever we walked. These pathetic creatures were too far gone to speak or even move. Just their haunting eyes remained to stare at us without emotion.

A 12-foot-high fence strung with double rows of barbed wire enclosed the camp and beyond it were coils of concertina wire. Inside the primary wire fence stood a six-foot-high electrified fence, and between the two outer fences the ground was littered with shards of broken glass, rusted scrap steel and antipersonnel mines. The mine field, we learned later, was a favorite method of prisoner suicide. The Germans didn't try to foil these attempts for to do so meant more mouths to feed.

A railroad siding ran into the camp, and strings of boxcars were parked there with their doors open. As a few of the prisoners stood at the wire fence staring silently at us, most of us lowered our eyes rather than stare back. Many had had their teeth pounded out for their gold fillings by inhumane guards. It was difficult to differentiate between the living and dead skeletons stacked on wooden platforms that served as beds. At each row of bunks, I tried to tell them softly, "Wir sind Amerikaners" ("We are Americans"). It seemed so inadequate because most of these wretched souls would die before our medical teams could help them. We had arrived too late.

I entered the administration building—easy to identify, since it was the only structure in the camp constructed of brick—and found a prisoner seated in the commandant's desk chair. He stuck out his hand and I reluctantly took it in mine. I was squeamishly repulsed by his appearance and didn't want to touch him.

In a hollow whisper, he said, "Hello."

When I realized it was the only English word he knew, I conversed with him in German. He told me the German doctors at the camp had conducted experiments on his throat and he no longer had a voice box. I winced as I listened to his tales.

He showed me large scars on his arms and back where the camp doctors had performed skin grafts for plastic surgery and large scarred areas on his legs and buttocks showed where skin had been surgically removed for other experimentation.

Then, in an attempt at a joke, he said all this had been done while he still had meat on his body.

When I asked about the multiple scars on his shoulders and back, he repeated over and over again, "Das peitschen. Das peitschen" ("The whip. The whip"). He told of guard dogs who had ripped inmates to pieces and then eaten them. I wanted to believe the stories he told, but they all seemed just too incredible for me to comprehend. I asked him his nationality.

"Ich bin Deutscher Jude" ("I am German Jew"), he answered, a glimmer of pride still showing. As such, he had been considered an enemy of the Third Reich. I told him that in America, a Jew was treated as freely as any other citizen. He nodded silently in docile resignation. He took me to a concrete building with a tall chimney at the rear of the camp. As we approached, he slowed his pace and then stopped, obviously still terrified of the building.

"Das crematorium." He insisted I go inside and then tell the world what I had witnessed. While he waited outside, I entered it alone and instantly wished I hadn't.

Skulls, bones and ashes were everywhere and the smell was overwhelming. Fingernails had gouged out the walls and a deep pit contained the bones of what must have been hundreds of prisoners. The walls were a gruesome mural of smeared blood where many, when finally realizing their fate, had bashed their heads against the walls to render themselves unconscious or attempt suicide.

When I rejoined him outside, tears were streaming down my cheeks. Softly, he said in German, "Now I will show you the others, the more fortunate." They had been frozen solid and then thrown into vats of hot water in what had been primitive cryogenic experimentation. The German doctors had never successfully determined how long the human body could be frozen alive, for there had been no survivors.

In nearby woods, he showed me cremation pyres of railroad ties and skeletal bodies stacked in criss-cross patterns. The concentration camp guards had not had time to light the last pyre before being overrun by American troops. "This was how they disposed of the bodies," my Jewish guide told me.

Other bodies in the box cars were covered with powdered white lye to ward off disease and to make them deteriorate faster.

"You must never forget what you have seen here. The world must be told," he insisted. The date was April 25, 1945 and I can safely say, in his memory, that I shall never forget what I saw and inhaled.

Before we pulled out of the area, we observed that American MPs were, at gunpoint, herding German men, women and children, young and old, from all the surrounding towns, on tours through every inch of the camp to witness what had transpired there. To a person, every last one of them denied all knowledge of the camp's existence. Some, I was happy to see, were being forced by Army officials to carry the skeletons to graves where they could be properly interred.

I asked my Jewish guide whether there had been any humane guards at the camp. Yes, he said, but they were usually weeded out quickly, shipped out to less desirable details, and replaced by more sadistic SS guards. I told him American doctors were on the way. "They can't help now," he answered simply.

As I left to return to the convoy, his echoing last words were, "Vergessen Sie nicht" ("Don't forget").

As we moved out, G-2 (intelligence) units started coming in to interrogate these DPs and Jews who were considered prime sources of military information about German troop and armament strengths and locations, and even descriptions of enemy entrenchments and fortifications. After all, they had built most of them.

I had made a covenant with this nameless Jew and it was a solemn pact I have kept for over half a century. I haven't forgotten. I couldn't even if I wanted to.

16

Rendezvous at the Elbe

Soon after the convoy continued its journey and we had stopped at the small village of Weinhausen, I was offered a "good deal" that supposedly would enable me to get lots of sleep and good food.

Skeptical of the Army's "good deals," I hesitated. With some reservation, Everett, a new replacement to the company and I crowded into the back seat of a battalion colonel's Jeep and were driven to battalion headquarters, where we were informed our new duties were guarding prisoners as makeshift MPs. It did sound like a good deal, and for once I was pleased that we had volunteered for something non-hazardous and perhaps even enjoyable. We were dropped off at a large farmhouse and told to remain there for further orders.

The first prisoner placed under our protective custody was a frail, bespectacled, sneaky-looking civilian. He was the principal of a local school and also the local Gestapo Gauleiter—one of the most feared and hated officials in the area.

I instantly had some vengeful ideas for him. As I stared at him, I recalled the concentration camps and a plan of retribution came to me. When I told the others, they answered with sly smiles and nods of approval. I walked up to this known Gestapo official, stood only inches from his nose, and snarled in my best sinister voice, "Ich habe Ohrdruf gesehen" ("I have seen Ohrdruf").

His steely eyes widened for a moment and then narrowed to slits again but his stonefaced expression didn't falter. Even when I prodded him to a manure pile and jammed my carbine hard into his gut he didn't flinch a muscle. This was one hardcore Nazi.

I shoved him again and this time he fell backward into the manure. Still, he just stared at me without a trace of fear. This infuriated me, and strengthened my determination to break this heartless bastard. I picked him up by the collar, gave my carbine to Everett, and gave the Gestapo supervisor a right handed roundhouse belt in the face as hard as I could throw a punch.

He lurched backward again, blood from his nose smearing his face. I hit him again and again but still he didn't utter a word. "I'll make this son-of-a-bitch crawl on his knees and beg," I roared at Everett. I took the German's face and smeared it in the manure until he was in danger of suffocating. His face was cut, his nose was bleeding badly, manure clogged his eyes and mouth and by now his glasses were gone.

I dragged him to a barn wall and stood him up facing us. Then I methodically paced off 10 steps, counting each one out loud. "Eins, zwei, drei, vier . . ." I pivoted on my heel smartly and rammed a clip into my rifle, all the time glaring at the German. I theatrically elongated each move I made, for I wanted him to suffer maximum mental anguish. It was street theater at its best. Still, he refused to make a sound. I asked him if he had anything to say. He continued to glare at me, his eyes filled with hatred. Without another word, I fired a shot at the wall only inches from his head. He didn't even flinch. In mock-sarcasm, Everett and the replacement teased me about missing my shot. I took careful aim and put another round inches from the other side of his head.

At this, he wavered and almost collapsed. I knew that I was getting through to him at last. He fell to his knees and I let go another round in the dirt before him.

He staggered to his feet and tried feebly to once more assert his Teutonic superiority. His pathetic attempt to maintain his dignity made us laugh. I approached him and slapped him hard across the face. His eyes became mere slits of rage, but now some fright could be detected. I punched him hard in the stomach and then kicked him on the ground before pulling him to his feet and giving him a savage carbine butt blow in the stomach. Everett and I dragged him back to the manure pile, threw him in it and ordered him to "Bleiben Sie da" ("Remain there").

I beckoned the replacement over to the gauleiter and snarled, "Er ist ein Jude and er hat auch Ohrdruf gesehen" ("He is a Jew and he has also seen Ohrdruf"). "Er willen Sie haben" ("He wants you for himself"), I added. The German, hearing this, leaped up and started to run. I fired a shot at his fleeing feet and he stopped in his tracks. The purported Jew grabbed him and shoved him back against the barn wall. I kept yelling at him,"Er ist ein Jude, ein Jude" ("He is a Jew, a Jew").

The bullet, ricocheting off the courtyard cobblestones as he attempted to flee, coupled with the constant screamed threats, reduced the Gestapo prisoner to an almost comedic, dung-covered, incoherently-babbling spectacle. Roughly, we stood him up again. The guard who was being passed off as a Jew placed his rifle close to the Kraut's head, took careful aim and fired—on an empty chamber.

The loud click of the M-1 sent the prisoner back on his knees muttering and sputtering so incoherently I couldn't understand him. We threw him back on the manure pile and walked away. I had made him grovel and I was finally satisfied. My only wish was that my Jewish guide at the concentration camp had been able to witness my performance. He would have enjoyed it immensely.

Fortunately, the colonel hadn't witnessed any of our Gestapo prisoner treatment for he wouldn't have approved. Officers were like that.

By now, the POW count had risen to the hundreds and we spent each day patrolling a barbed wire enclosure that held them. There was little fear of their trying to escape for they were undoubtedly being fed better than they had in a long time. In probably the easiest and most productive loot haul of the war, I located the town's Burgermeister (mayor) and told him all weapons in the town had to be turned in to me immediately or he would be imprisoned.

One character trait about the Germans that worked to our advantage was that they had been indoctrinated since birth to obey an order. About an hour later, he returned with a blanket filled with pistols, antiquated rifles, knives, bayonets and swastika flags of all shapes and sizes. I thanked him and when he left we delved into the pile. Out of it, I retrieved a beautiful chrome-plated, pearl-handled .25 caliber automatic. It was a masterpiece of beauty and I now regret having sold it on the ship coming home for $65. Today, it would have been priceless to me.

During one of my explorations, I followed a sloping hill into an underground munitions factory, built to avoid aerial detection and bombardment. It was mammoth and included railroad sidings entering and exiting from both ends. It had been abandoned, perhaps when the slave workers had been liberated, but appeared ready to start up again on a moment's notice. I was certain our demolition teams would have a field day with it, or perhaps the Army would have some use for it.

Eventually, when the crunch of German prisoners that was mounting every day had been processed, interrogated and then sent home, we were reassigned back to Anti-Tank Company in Hildesheim. We tried to rest up but the Germans interrupted our sleep by counter-attacking with tanks. We took to the hills behind our billet and formed a skirmish line, climbing until we reached the top where we flopped on our stomachs. I laid out a row of grenades and extra M-1 ammunition bandoliers on the ground beside me.

The much lighter carbine was the weapon to have when marching, but in a firefight, nothing beat the M-1. Also, I had seen German soldiers take carbine slugs in them and keep coming. This seldom happened when they were shot with an M-1.

A crashing sound to the rear startled me. It was only a bazooka team coming through to establish forward positions. The tank noise grew as someone shouted, "Here they come!" Two badly scarred and rusted-out Tiger tanks emerged from the trees but no infantry could be seen accompanying them. The bazooka team fired off a round but it fell far wide of the lead tank, which instantly started spraying the ground with machine-gun fire.

I started to jump up and run but was stopped by the bazooka team high-tailing it past me. Without realizing what I was doing, I grabbed their abandoned bazooka and put it to my shoulder. Everett loaded me, tapped me on the helmet and I fired. The rocket round hit the side of the closest tank and glanced off before exploding into the ground. The tank kept coming; it was now only about 75 feet away. Suddenly the tank exploded in flame and smoke. The tank spun around and tried to pull back, but another round struck true and the tank began to burn. The turrets of both tanks opened up and their crews surrendered.

As Everett and I were lying on the ground trying to catch our breath and get our hearts started again, GIs from Anti-Tank Company appeared out of the woods trailing a 57mm piece behind them.

As they danced around celebrating their kill, I wondered if I would ever confess to Everett I had been on the verge of bugging out in the face of the tanks before the bazooka team did. We brought the weapon back to the company area and gave it to the captain, who figured the team must have been new replacements from some nearby line company. While trying to sleep I wondered why, after all these months, I had almost panicked. I admittedly didn't want to die this close to the end of a war that was practically over. But the problem was, someone had forgotten to tell the Germans. The company field kitchen caught up to us and we enjoyed one of the army's two standard breakfasts: pancakes and coffee or oatmeal, coffee and bread without butter.

The weather in northern Germany in mid-April was starting to moderate, allowing the canvas sides to be rolled up on the truck as we moved forward again. This offered us an opportunity to drink in what was left of the northern German landscape, and the fresh air was invigorating.

We marveled at the autobahn highways that Hitler had built years before in anticipation of the war he had planned for so long. The multi-laned highways stretched through Herford, Hannover, Braunschweig and Magdeberg, and all highways led to Berlin. Other equally direct roadways ran north and south throughout the country, making the autobahns, engineering masterpieces for their times, one of the most efficient highway networks in all Europe. These super highways had been built for the speed that helped assure the success of Hitler's Blitzkrieg. They were a welcome relief after being jounced around so roughly on the shell-pocked highways of France, Holland, Belgium and the Rhineland.

I vacated my usual tailgate spot and stood up facing forward behind the cab to let the wind blow in my face, much as I had done years before when my father had driven my sister and me for ice cream cones in a beat-up pickup truck in the middle of the night at Treasure Valley Boy Scout Camp back home.

Suddenly, I was jerked backwards abruptly and violently and sent sprawling by Everett. After bouncing off the floor, I came up ready to fight until he pointed out to me a steel cable stretched across the road that would have beheaded me had I remained standing. I had not even seen it, so much was I enjoying the passing scenery. The near-miss sombered me and I sat down again, grateful again to Everett who had spotted the cable in time. He had saved my skin numerous times before in combat and now he had done it again. Officers gave themselves medals in combat for all sorts of things, but "Joe Loot" never received one, even for saving a life. I never invented a medal to award him—just my friendship.

During our move, we began to see launching ramps at the edge of fields and hidden in wooded areas. We assumed they were for the German V-2 rockets and V-1 buzz bombs because here and there we could see camouflaged missiles of some sort. The convoy was moving fast and we were able to get only a fleeting glimpse of some of Hitler's secret weapons.

We entered the town of Seehausen, a few kilometers from the west bank of the Elbe River, and halted on a tree-lined street. We were assigned an abandoned farmhouse nearby as our next temporary billet. I ran to it, grabbed a bed and defended it from all comers.

I heard a voice calling my name. It was the company commander informing me the farmhouse would be the company kitchen site and reminding me I still had KP punishment to serve. A month had already elapsed, and except for washing a few pots and pans back in Rheinhausen, I had ignored the court-martial sentence completely. The KP was my guarantee of more hot food. I settled back into my bed and slept, secure in the knowledge that my fighting days were probably over—that is, if I wanted them to be.

After eating and scrubbing a few pans, my time was my own. That meant more souvenir hunting and countryside exploration. I wandered to a nearby house that had a shed at the rear. Alone with my thoughts, my mind slowly was pushing the horrors of the war behind me and I was thinking about the future.

Some of my free time was spent plinking away at the shed wall with my pearl-handled .25 caliber pistol and various other German hand guns. The explosions in the palm of my hand offered the excitement I was beginning to miss from the lack of combat. There was a slight reorientation transition going on inside me and I was having some difficulty adjusting to it. Excitement creates excitement, I had found, and boredom dulls enthusiasm.

But when the other GIs complained about all the noise, I stopped and packed the weapons away. My punishment in the company kitchen required about an hour's work after each meal, leaving me the rest of the day to explore the river.

On the way back to the company, I became quite jumpy. I was at least a mile and a half into territory that had never been declared clear of German troops. Beside a pathway I spotted a log structure in the trees—a machine gun dugout. I hit the ground and crawled toward it, damning myself for being so careless this close to war's end. My stomach was knotting up and I realized I was scared out there alone without Everett's usual backup. The dugout was empty and I reasoned it probably wasn't a bunker at all but merely something put there by some farmer or woodsman.

Getting jumpier by the minute, I looked up and down, back and forth to the left and right, in front and behind me as if searching for a sniper. It was a good thing I did, for through the trees I spotted a uniformed Wehrmacht soldier coming toward me. Before even determining whether he was armed, I flopped to the ground and started firing. I emptied a whole clip at him. I could see branches being snipped off and bark from trees flying. But no German. He had fled, armed with an intriguing story to tell his family some day about one of his close calls during the war. Like the German, I started to run and didn't stop until I was safely back in the company area.

The sameness of each day was broken up by radio broadcasts telling us that Hitler was dead by his own hand, and Benito Mussolini, Fascist premier of Italy, had been strung up with his mistress in a public square by his own people. I felt that at last, the war was only a formality, but until it ended, it was business as usual: souvenir hunting, pots and pans scrubbing, and devouring packages from home.

Four teenage German girls carrying babies walked into our camp one day asking for food. We fed them and played with the babies. Then we pointed the young mothers toward the west. They were fleeing from the oncoming Russian troops from the east because they had been told what the conquering Ruskies would do to them. We pooh-poohed their beliefs but the stories they had heard later proved to be true. During a Berlin visit some months after the war ended, I was to get firsthand accounts of the pillaging, looting, raping and carnage the Russians perpetrated in Berlin after it fell to them.

Before leaving, the girls told us their babies were illegitimate and had been for the "Vaterland." One girl displayed a lovely blue and gold medal awarded her for having five "pure Aryan" babies. I took the medal from her. They told us the national honor of having as many babies as possible prompted many wives to put themselves in German Army barracks, at the will of entire companies, to ensure quicker pregnancies. I couldn't help but think how proud their husbands would be upon returning from the war and learning how honorably their wives had also served their country.

I told the company commander I was getting restless working in the kitchen. He told me he never checked the kitchen and as long as he saw an American uniform working there, that was all that mattered. I hurriedly hitched a ride to the nearby town of Trebel, where others from my squad were billeted. The town was graced by a peaceful common not unlike those in New England. I located Everett and learned the Elbe River was only a couple miles away. He warned me there were still some small skirmishes going on and occasional German patrol action along the river.

Just fine, I informed him, for I was looking for a prisoner to replace me in the company dishwater. On foot, we headed for the river. After a half hour, we broke out into the open and found a panorama of activity before us. The fast-flowing river was clogged with small boats, rafts and chunks of wood; people were clinging to them and swimming frantically toward the west bank.

An American machine gun emplacement had been dug out near the water and the gunners were intermittently firing short bursts across the river at thousands of German troops massed there. We scrambled into a ditch when a few of them returned fire. I asked one of the gunners if I could have a crack at the .30-caliber aircooled machine gun. He moved aside with a wave of his hand and I sighted in on a group of Germans already partway across. The stream of bullets spattered little geysers of water all around them. Some turned back, but the others continued on despite being fired upon, ducking beneath the surface when they could. The fear of the Russians closing in on them was overruling their judgment. Some figured the machine gun bullets spitting around them posed less of a threat to them than the hated and feared Ruskies.

I turned the gun over to Everett, who fired a few bursts at the far bank, feeling that he too had made his small contribution to ending the war.

We crawled back to the ditch and watched the constantly growing swarm of humanity crowding the shoreline. Many women, fearful of their lives and the treatment they would receive at the lust of the advancing Russian troops, were climbing out of the water naked without any noticeable embarrassment. To one of them, a blonde about 20, I called out, "Wo gehen sie?" ("Where are you going?")

"Amerika," she answered without a moment's hesitation. "Vereinige Staaten" ("America. United States"). We stashed her into the bushes while I tried to find her some clothes. I managed to rustle up fatigue pants and a shirt. She dressed herself and tried to dry off. I gave her a K-ration and told her to stay away from the other Americans. She understood immediately.

About that time, a high-ranking German officer stepped from a crowded rowboat and was immediately taken into custody. Standing beside him was an attractive woman, also dressed in a Wehrmacht uniform. "Offizieren Matratze" ("Officer's mattress"), the blonde girl with us mumbled under her breath.

At just the appropriate time, a small band of German soldiers, their hands already folded over their heads, appeared from a wooded area. I pointed to one and beckoned to him. Wide-eyed, he walked hesitantly toward me. He spoke English and said he had been a radio repairman in the Wehrmacht. I asked him if he wanted some hot food but he would have to work for it. He almost jumped out of his tattered green uniform at the offer.

What a fine-looklng parade we must have made when we walked back to Trebel: a good-looking, water-soaked blonde in sloppy Army fatigues, six disheveled Kraut prisoners and two combat-dirty GIs. I entered Wegener's Gasthaus in the town and commandeered some clothes for the young girl. Then I claimed a pool table in the bar area as my bed. Herta Wegener, a woman in her 40s, welcomed us as she would any other guest for the night.

I brought the six prisoners back to the company kitchen at Seehausen, dressed one in one of my uniforms and put him to work. The two Louisiana cooks didn't particularly like the idea but they kept their mouths shut. Besides, it was the closest they had been to a German since we landed on the continent. The other prisoners were released and told to find their way home. The prisoner who spoke some English stayed with me, for he would be useful to me later. He slept under my protection for several weeks as we moved through Germany after the cessation of hostilities. We argued constantly over who was the better soldier, the American or the German. We were better equipped, he conceded, but they were better trained and smarter.

Well, I argued, if they were smarter, why had we won the war? Equipment, he always retorted, equipment. Despite dozens of spirited discussions, we never resolved the issue to either's satisfaction. One of his favorite boasts was that I could be in a flat field with a machine gun and he could approach me with no cover whatsoever and take me out. How we argued this point! But no matter how heated the arguments became, he never forgot he was the prisoner and I was the victor. We always became angry with each other but always wound up laughing in the end.

Partially because of the food he was receiving, he wanted badly to join the American army, even if it meant being transferred to the CBI (China-Burma-India) Theater of Operations as had been rumored for the 84th. He was regular army and fighting was all he knew or wanted. Every German I spoke to expressed shock and disappointment that the Americans were halting at the Elbe River and giving Berlin to the Russians. It was indeed a political decision that sentenced the world to more than four decades of Cold War and military tension between Russia and the United States. At the rate we had been pushing eastward, we could have made it first to Berlin in a day—two at the most. Most Germans emphasized over and over that Germany was not America's real enemy, Russia was. The decision to give Berlin to the Russians after so many men had died fighting so long and hard to reach it didn't sit very well with most of us either.

The streets of Trebel were becoming clogged with armies of Germans trying to make their way to the west. We were told that at a certain time the next day, American forces would fire a green flare out over the river. If the Russian troops had reached the other side, they would answer with a red flare.

It was May 2 and tension was growing by the hour.

We all journeyed to the river to watch. The hours dragged to 1100 when someone yelled, "There it is," and we all stood silently watching the graceful arc of the Red Army signal. The war, although not officially over for another six days, had ended. As tears started to roll down my cheeks, I dropped to one knee and gave thanks for being spared. Then I sat under a tree to meditate. I wanted to be alone in those final few moments.

Joe Everett joined me and in his Oklahoma drawl said softly, "God was good to us, Bluntie old boy." I just nodded. Nothing I could say would express my feelings more eloquently.

It was not a time of vigorous backslapping but of quiet reflection during those initial moments when we first fully realized we had fired our last shot and that the final shot had been fired at us. Each of us had our own private thoughts of what we had seen, what we had done and what the future held for us. It took some time to accept the fact that we would go home alive again and someday resume a normal life. We would all need, each in our own ways, considerable reacclimation to civilian life.

We had been deprived of that jewel of all Germany, the capital city that had been our dream and goal for so many months, but there were other considerations, namely our lives. Still the disappointment and resentment were deep; what we considered the error of the political decision allowing the Russians to take Berlin would not be easily forgiven.

Before us, the river was clogged with refugees still trying to escape to freedom. The 84th had taken 61,392 prisoners during its charge across central Europe, a major accomplishment. I excused myself from Everett and walked away until I found a small stream leading to a wooded area. I followed the brook to a pine grove where I lay down and looked up at the sky as I had done so often in civilian life. I listened for the songs of birds but there were none. There were so many questions for which I had no answers. Of one thing I was sure: I had to push the horror of the past behind me and rebuild my life. I would have my memories. The notes I had jotted down every day would assure that. I knew it would be almost impossible to relate to anyone what I had seen, felt and done.

But all that mattered now, questions notwithstanding, was that the war was over and I was still alive.

17

Combat Withdrawal

The end of hostilities meant I would have to undergo the transformation from violence and fear to peace and security, but I didn't realize on that calm day in May 1945 just how difficult it would be for me, or how long it would take.

First, I would be separated from buddies with whom I had endured so much. Friendships would end abruptly, probably never to be shared again. These wartime relationships were akin to family love and were nurtured by months of shared deprivation and hunger, of survival-threatening cold and excruciating anguish, of stark terror and sensitivity-shattering horror, crippling exhaustion and personal triumph. And never again would there be the nonsensical hilarity and crazy escapades that had forged bonds among us that would be emotionally difficult to break.

I pondered these thoughts as I tried to catch my breath in Trebel from the vagaries of war. I dreaded the inevitable separations and the adaptation to the boredom of civilian life back in the States. But despite the dread of severed friendships, the overriding emotion was an optimistic anticipation of the future.

A company notice was posted that we had earned battle stars for the Rhineland, The Ardennes and Central Europe campaigns. Three miniature pieces of bronze on our ETO ribbon could hardly exemplify so much suffering, but the symbolism of the battle stars was extremely important to all of us. Each star had been earned the hard way, with considerable pain and blood.

Bowen told us the 84th had taken the most prisoners—more than

70,000—of any other infantry division in the ETO. The division had also covered more ground, more quickly during the breakthroughs to the Roer, Rhine, Weser and Elbe rivers than any other unit and had captured and destroyed 112 German pillboxes and bunkers. In addition, we had been on the line for 171 continuous days, an almost unbelievable feat.

The refugees continued to stream across the Elbe in their desperate flight from the Russians. On one day, May 2nd, the day the rockets were fired, it was estimated that more than 60,000 Germans successfully crossed to the American side of the river.

The next day, Everett and I rowed across the Elbe and joined in the Russian festivities that had been going on non-stop for two days. There were mandolins and concertinas and dancing and vodka—lots of vodka. Russian soldiers and GIs were passed out drunk everywhere sleeping it off. Weapons, money, souvenirs, pictures, watches, cigarettes, helmets and uniforms were being exchanged in a spirit of good will and comradery.

Female Russian MPs made passes at us and laughed heartily when some of us shrank back. Cossack troops put on brilliant displays of horsemanship while others in the Red Star Army were drunkenly firing their weapons into the air to accentuate the music and the whirling dervish dancers. I swapped a P-38 pistol with a Russian MP for her rifle and kept it for many years. The superiority of ours over theirs was immediately apparent, but they had won their battles with what they had and so had we.

But the celebratory merriment was short-lived. It was replaced by military reality even before the last dance was danced, the last drink downed. On VE Day + 1, when we returned to our company area, a bulletin had been posted that henceforth boots would be shined, pants cleaned and pressed, close order drills would commence, hair would be cut, beards would be shaved, neckties would be worn and first bugle call would be at 0615, followed by reveille at 0625, mess at 0700, drill call at 0725 and taps at 2200. Also, saluting of officers would resume immediately.

The "chicken shit" had begun, as we all knew it would, but we hadn't expected it quite so soon. We had underestimated the Army in thinking it would give us a reasonable period to savor our victory. We had all gotten out of the habit of saluting officers in combat. To do so would have marked them as prime targets for snipers who might be deciding which of us to shoot.

One morning, I was dispatched to pick up supplies from a rear area, and on the way I passed a POW pen holding more than 8,000 German prisoners. Most of them slept on the ground for they had surrendered with only what they could carry on their backs while swimming across the Elbe. A more perfect picture of Germany's total collapse couldn't have been taken.

Arriving back in Trebel, I found a fistful of letters and several food packages from home waiting for me at the CP. At every mail call overseas, I inevitably received more mail than anyone in the company, a testimony to my parents' capacity for love.

Orders had been received to remain in the company area; a move was forthcoming at any time. The only others left to tell were the German prisoners working in my stead in the company kitchen. But for them, I had the good news that they were going with us. They were delighted for, as the saying goes, they had never had it so good. They had three square meals a day, no one treated them as prisoners and they were free to come and go as they pleased.

The one element they were having trouble adjusting to, however, was the democracy in our army. Officers were called by their first names and, before the end of hostilities, were seldom saluted. The Kraut prisoners were also quick to pick up on the fact there were no outward displays of rank-has-its-privileges, for the officers ate with the enlisted men while privates walked together talking and laughing with senior officers.

This was difficult for the Germans to comprehend. In their army, the caste system, even between junior officers and the enlisted ranks, was absolute. It had been established for generations. Theirs was an unbelievably strict and harsh military hierarchy that never could have been imposed successfully on American soldiers born and raised in a democratic society. American personalities allowed for obedience but only when it was to the advantage of the person being ordered.

Before we left Trebel, I applied for a transfer to Anti-Tank Company. I was still carried on Army records as being in LOVE Company and if we were to see more action in the China-Burma-India Theater of Operations (CBI)—and that was the persisting rumor confirmed by our brass—I wanted no part of an infantry line company again. The law of averages might smile upon someone once, but never twice. Ernie Pyle, the war correspondent, had proven the principle, surviving the bitter Italian campaign only to be killed later by a Japanese sniper in the Pacific Theater.

The orders came suddenly and our departure was melancholy for I had become quite fond of picturesque Trebel. It held so many memories—the end of the war and the gradual rebuilding of my personal world. Picking up speed, the convoy churned westward on Adolf Hitler's autobahns and, as usual, we had no idea where we were going or what our next duty would be. But at least while heading west, we were also at the same time moving closer to home.

By the time we finally stopped for the night, the convoy had traveled 183 kilometers back through Hannover and Braunschweig to the small, untouched village of Wenigstens. This gave me a chance to pack up my Russian rifle and mail it home, hoping some rear echelon hero would not requisition it first.

The town was a picture of the real rural Germany, complete with costumed inhabitants, ox-drawn carts, immaculately "sauber" (clean) houses and grassed-in yards, The next day, I spent most of the morning writing letters home, pre-dating them back to the last time I had written. I knew that my letters meant as much to home front morale as those I received meant to mine.

The convoy loaded up and started rolling southwest again, eventual destination still unknown. But it really didn't matter; I couldn't do anything about it anyway. It was normal in the Army to resign yourself completely to whatever fate and circumstances bounced your way.

In the middle of the night, we pulled into Rolfshagen bei Minden, where my Kraut prisoner-friend grabbed two couches in a farmhouse parlor for us to spend the night. The company set up a temporary kitchen in the courtyard for breakfast. I hadn't had a C- or K-ration in weeks and I hadn't missed them either. Hot food, even though still only Army slop, was infinitely better. My prisoner, whose name I unfortunately never recorded and time has since erased, searched the house for loot with me and found a pistol in the attic. When he gave it to me, I knew then I had nothing to fear in our relationship. In the attic I found a dress Wehrmacht uniform which I mailed home. Climbing together up a steep hill behind the farmhouse, the German and I were treated to a magnificent view of a broad valley.

The company remained in Rolfshagen several days and I came up with what I considered an adventuresome idea. I set up an office in the farmhouse living room and had a desk brought in. I placed flowers, a Colt .45 pistol, some cigars, a walkie-talkie and a pile of official-looking papers and books on it.

With all the impressive trappings in place, I declared myself the area's war criminal investigator and tribunal, on May 25, 1945. We spread the word in the town that I was interviewing any DPs still in the area about war crimes perpetrated against them by local Nazis. A few slave laborers came singularly and reluctantly at first, but eventually they came in groups to my makeshift courtroom.

My Kraut prisoner assisted me with the many dialects, and for those speaking foreign languages I sought the aid of GIs in the company who spoke French or Polish. The stories of horror I listened to were incredible, each more heart-wrenching than the one before it. The most emotional one involved a 10-year-old boy who had been taken to Dachau at age seven, had been castrated and then forced to watch his mother and sister raped and murdered. Later, he watched German camp guards bayonet his father.

The boy stood mute before me, expressionless eyes cast on the floor, unable to retell the memories he held locked up inside him. I tried bribing him with candy and soft words but he never spoke, as others in the room recited his story for him. I gave him a chocolate bar and dismissed him. I could do nothing; Dachau was hundreds of kilometers from my unofficial jurisdiction.

As the boy was led from the room by the villagers, I had momentary pangs of conscience, for this was a game I was playing and this small tyke's world was real. I considered, for a moment, ending the charade as a travesty against human suffering. But I reasoned that even though I might be accused of playacting, I was still in a position to do some good, to subject war criminals to American justice. I also knew that G-2 and the MPs would welcome any assistance they could get from any source, even me.

Another DP told of floggings by a local school master. Other Polish forced laborers told of cruelties committed by the Rolfshagen burgermeister who was a member of the SA, Hitler's Sturmabteilung. These were Hitler's infamous "brown shirts," Germany's bullyboys. He had allegedly beaten "auslander" (foreigner) women and children as a regular practice, forced them to work inhuman hours and then, when they were of no further use to him, had them deported to Rehren, the concentration camp we had visited during the push to the Elbe some weeks earlier. I took signed depositions from as many of these people as I could and turned them over to regimental G-2 for further investigation and possible prosecution.

But the local burgermeister was mine and mine alone. My German prisoner and I promptly jumped onto a confiscated motorcycle we had found and headed for the village to "arrest" the schoolmaster and the burgermeister. In the schoolmaster's office, we found several snake whips and a quantity of Nazi flags and propaganda leaflets. I arrested him at gunpoint and marched him out before the entire school before turning him over to a group of DPs waiting and watching outside.

Then we headed for the town hall, where the burgermeister had his office. We learned that somehow he had been warned we were coming and had fled minutes before we arrived. We biked to his home where a housekeeper told us he had just fled to a friend's house. We couldn't figure out how he always managed to keep one jump ahead of us. But it was interesting to note that at each location there was always someone there who wanted to inform on him and see him arrested for his past crimes. The DP from whom I had taken a statement was right. This man was hated by the whole village.

We cycled all over town after him before learning he was trying to escape to a nearby settlement that was considered by the locals as a temporary haven for war criminals. On the way there, we found our prey peddling furiously along a country road on a bicycle.

He spotted us and swerved across a field, eventually falling from his bike and legging it toward a wooded area. We cut him off with our motorcycle and I jumped off and tackled him. I shoved my .45 against the side of his head as a group of forced laborers came running from a nearby field. We dragged him to the motorcycle, draped him over the sidecar and drove directly back to the G-2 headquarters in Rolfshagen. I felt that this Kraut was too dangerous, too important, and too wanted, to trust to an MP directing traffic in a country town. In my mind, this burgermeister's crimes had put him in the big time.

The G-2 investigators winced when they saw my prisoner's bloody face but when I filled them in on his case history, they called for a medic. They too wanted him alive.

After about an hour, I drove back to the group of DPs who had been wreaking their vengeance on the schoolmaster and took him to the military police headquarters. The slave laborer punishment was an integral part of my self-styled judicial process. The medics had their hands full that day.

By the time we returned to the farmhouse, we had missed supper and had to make do with the contents of my packages from home. That night I pondered over the hotbed of Nazism we had uncovered in this small, tranquil German village. My German prisoner found a Hitler Jugend (Hitler Youth) knife inscribed "Blute und Ehre" ("Blood and honor"). I promptly packaged it up and mailed it home. It was almost a relief when we loaded up the trucks and struck out for Lauenau. When we arrived, I dressed my prisoner in a GI uniform and put him to work in the kitchen for he always complained of being hungry.

It was in Lauenau that the bombshell hit. I received word on May 30 from battalion that I was being transferred to the division's Special Services unit as a bandsman. It was a day that would "live in infamy" for me. My crated-up bass drum from home had followed me all over Europe and finally, I was going to get a chance to bang on it.

But thinking more upon my transfer, I began to fume when I realized that stupid rear echelon ignoramuses should have noticed my bandsman classification before I was sent into combat with a line company and subjected to months of suffering and danger.

While trying to locate my bass drum, I was told a trailer transporting musical instruments had been hit by artillery, and everything except my drum had been destroyed. The only damage was a small tear in one head from shrapnel.

As soon as I could put together a group, we started "woodshedding" some arrangements. Officially, we were designated the 333rd Regimental Band, but we billed ourselves The Tophatters. Pizzazz was in during the '40s and Tophatters had a lot more pizzazz than Regimental Band.

The music, as ragged as it was, was all I needed to snap me out of the sleep-robbing nightmares and the grubby existence I had been forced to endure for nine months. The resiliency of man, and the ability to adapt to new environments, soon made the war only a memory.

During the band's developmental period, I wrote a comical article about inventing a new style of music. After passing it around the band for laughs, I threw the story away. Imagine my surprise when the next issue of *The Railsplitter*, our division newspaper, ran my story, word-for-word under the byline of a special services officer, who had found the discarded story, plagiarized it in its entirety and used it for his own purposes.

The story described how my new style of music had "brought the house down" at Doughboy Schloss (castle) where we first performed it. My fictitious idea was to take the sugary, melodious sounds of Guy Lombardo's band and combine them with the swinging rhythmic beat of Count Basie's orchestra, thereby pleasing everyone's taste in music. I didn't know whether to be amused or angry about the newspaper article. So much, I figured, for journalistic integrity, especially from officers.

The Tophatters consisted of Charles Berg of South Dakota on piano; Leonard "Jiggs" Ackerman of California on guitar; Sgt. James Carroll of Indiana or Roy Henthorn of Ohio, alternating on bass; William Kimmel of Pennsylvania and Joseph "Koko" Annicciarico of New Hampshire, on alto saxes; Harry Brickell of New Jersey, on tenor sax; John "JB" Shaw of Ohio, on trombone and Robert Eyer of Pennsylvania and Frederick Barnette of West Virginia, on trumpets; and me on drums. Musicians were given deferential treatment (justifiably, I might add). We ate only the best of food, in a factory about a quarter mile from our billet.

One day, the band was told to prepare a program for a special event the next day at the noon meal. We set up on a makeshift stage and started to swing for about 200 GIs eating there. As we played, I noticed something strange about the men eating in the tent: they were all wearing ties. I glanced over at the entrance and spotted Major General Bolling and Colonel Louis W. Truman, Bolling's chief of staff, filing into the dining room. So that was the special event, a visit by Bolling, who by now had his second star. But I was stunned when I saw they were being followed by President Harry S. Truman, General of the Armies Dwight D. Eisenhower and Secretary of State James F. Byrnes.

We immediately swung into "Missouri Waltz," upon which Truman left the visiting entourage, came over to the band stand and thanked us. Without thinking, I put out my hand. He shook it vigorously with a grin. Bolling and Colonel Truman, the president's cousin, glowered at my breach of etiquette but nothing was said. What could they say?

We continued the concert as the delegation of Army brass and politicians disappeared again, without even sampling the food. Most of the troops appeared totally uninterested in what was going on, for this meal was the best chow they had had in a long time. The special meal had been prepared in case the dignitaries sampled it.

The Tophatters went on the road and relocated in the small town of Rinteln for one night. As always, I wandered around exploring as soon as duty-free time allowed. I was surprised to hear music in the distance, since there was little or no music in Germany in those early post-war weeks. The country was a long way from recovering from the devastation of war. Following the sounds, I came upon a carnival in all its gaudy glory, which had attracted a huge crowd. I rode the hobbyhorses and airplane swings and mingled unnoticed with all the civilians and their children. For a couple delightful hours, I was a kid in another world again.

When I returned to my billet, I found that Joe Everett and all my other squad mates had been transferred back to their respective line companies, and we had not been given the opportunity for proper good-byes. I knew full well our paths would never cross again. In Everett's case, it saddened me deeply for we had shared so much together.

Soon, the band moved out again, this time passing through the Pied Piper's famous town of Hameln, southwest of Hannover. It was another quaint, stone-housed village with an arched bridge over a river at the center of town.

Whenever possible, the convoy picked up speed and headed south, barreling along a mile a minute through Kassel, Paderborn, Frankfort, Darmstadt and finally to Lamperheim bei Mannheim, where we stopped after a grueling 400-kilometer drive. Consulting a map, I found we were located in the southwest corner of Germany near both Switzerland and France. The trip, slowed continually by war destruction and only the last part of which was on smooth autobahns, had taken 25 hours of almost continuous bouncing around.

We were told we would remain in Lampertheim for several days.

On one occasion, I discovered a 14-year old boy stealing from our rooms. I held him against a wall and shoved my .45 under his nose. He broke down and sobbed for forgiveness. Slapping him across the face, I cocked the pistol and threatened to shoot him if I ever saw him again. He ran away crying and never reappeared.

Because I could speak German, I was occasionally ordered by company officers to find booze and bed partners for them. I turned over to them any liquor I could confiscate, and made it a practice to round up the homeliest, least desirable, most desperate, shopworn, over-the-hill women that no one else wanted. The officers never complained; in fact, they seemed rather grateful that I was pimping so successfully. Many officers, I was rapidly finding out, were generally without shame.

The band was booked at a Red Cross-USO club in nearby Mannheim. I had seen utter devastation in five war-torn countries but none to surpass Mannheim. As far as one could see, nothing was left standing higher than eye level. Wherever I looked, civilians were scavenging through the ruins to find morsels of food. There was no life in the city; it was a desert of death.

On our last day in Lamperheim, I became violently ill, fainting and vomiting repeatedly. My speech slurred and my skin became jaundiced. I was carried to a weapons carrier that would transport us to our next destination—Leutershausen, only a few kilometers away. The truck, encountering human traffic jams on roads clogged almost solid with German civilian and military refugees migrating to points unknown, inched its way along for about an hour before it reached our new destination.

As sick as I was, I wondered whether the price of war had been worth it for these mostly innocent victims, the majority of whom were women, children and the elderly. In most cases, their men had not yet returned, and perhaps never would, from battle.

18

Occupation of Southern Germany

We rolled into the picturesque village of Leutershausen where I would spend the next seven months. By the time we arrived, I could no longer stand up and several band members carried me to the home of the Musselknautz family where I was put to bed. I'm not sure whether I lapsed into unconsciousness or sleep but when I came to, it was the next morning and a stern-looking, buxom German woman with black leather boots and hair pulled back in a tight bun was standing over me. "Sie sind sehr krank" ("You are very sick"), were her first words when I opened my eyes.

"Guten Morgen," I wheezed. She didn't respond but went on to say she had stayed up all night trying to reduce my fever. She offered me an egg and a sip of water which I immediately threw up. After about a week, Army doctors administered heavy doses of belladonna, a narcotic used to calm an upset stomach. It didn't help much. When the woman attending to me slept, she was relieved by her aged mother. They were straight-laced Nazis of the first order, but I was too sick to care. All I wanted was someone to mother me back to health.

When weeks passed and my condition worsened, another doctor was called in but he too was unable to diagnose my illness, saying only that I was suffering an apparent complete physical breakdown brought on by so many months in combat. He prescribed total rest. For days, I drifted in and out of consciousness as my weight dropped to about 100 pounds. After a month, my appetite returned and I kept down a bowl of potato soup, a German staple the women claimed was a cure-all. Sick as I was, I remembered the taste of the soup from my brief capture by the SS tankers during the Bulge. Only this time there were actually potatoes in it.

Occasionally, some of the band members dropped by with food from the company kitchen which I shared with the women. As my condition improved, I tried to talk to the women who had cared for me but they remained steadfastly distant the whole time I was in their home. Between the food being brought to me by the other musicians and the goodies from home that arrived almost daily, my recovery was gradual but steady. It was almost as if the loving hands of my family were reaching across the ocean.

To recuperate, I sunned myself on a vine-covered terrace where I watched the village's children on their way to and from school. Growing stronger, I began sitting on the street curb outside my billet every afternoon and sharing my chocolate from home with the children as they came by. Like wildfire in the village, I became known as the "Soldat mit Schokolade."

From the villagers I learned that Leutershausen was midway between Weinheim bei Mannheim and the university city of Heidelberg, which had been declared an open city during the war to preserve its priceless history. Both armies honored the edict during the fighting and no bombs or shells had fallen on it.

But as peaceful as Leutershausen was, the few returning Wehrmacht soldiers straggling into the village always posed a potential threat and forced me to wear a shoulder-holstered Luger at all times and sleep with it at night under my pillow. The woman who had cared for me in my illness finally told me she had a son my age killed in France during the Allied invasion. I could only imagine what thoughts she harbored about Americans and Hitler's senseless war.

With me eventually back on my feet, the Tophatters started gigging nightly in Mosbach, Weinheim, Aberbach, Mannheim, Stuttgart and every village and town in between. We were in constant demand. The grind of being on the road almost constantly was taxing, but our schedule allowed us to sleep until noon each day and we were required to pull no other duty than to perform.

On one occasion, we were rousted out of our sacks about 0200 and told that Colonel Gomes, regimental commander, wanted music at his castle headquarters immediately. He was throwing a party that would last all night, and when we arrived the place was crawling with top brass, most of them already quite drunk. After setting up my makeshift drums, I disappeared into the kitchen where the most sumptuous meal I had ever seen was being prepared. No delicacy known to man was missing from the menu prepared by the woman cook who had been with the colonel since the Elbe River. Every time she turned her back, I helped myself to the buffet.

Never being very good at protocol or working within military regulations, I cornered General Bolling during an intermission and registered a complaint about the runaround I had been getting from a certain major at Special Services command. He had sets of drums, still in crates, but had refused to issue one to me. I reminded the general that I couldn't perform very well for officers' parties without decent drums.

I showed him the Hitler Jugend snare drums I was using as tom toms wired to a bass drum and confiscated cymbals wired to makeshift stands. He assured me the problem would be rectified immediately. I was notified to pick up a new set of Leedy drums the next day. The troublesome major treated me like a VIP when I arrived and it was obvious that Bolling had been true to his word. The next time we played for the general, I gave him a friendly wave, though he acted as if he had never seen me before. We soaked the officers $5 for these engagements, even though our normal rate for such functions was $3 a man.

The band, which had originally been formed with 13 men, was constantly being decimated by musicians being shipped home and soon it was reduced to nine. The tensions of the war were slow to subside in southern Germany and the people of Leutershausen remained sullen and distant. I continued to carry my pistol at all times. I was careful to abide by all the customs of the villagers and even went to their church on Sundays. Slowly, they accepted me with a casual nod on the street and I started to relax. I found I could bargain cigarettes and chocolate with local farmers for eggs, milk and meat I could share with the old female Nazis with whom I lived, for I was determined to repay their kindness and, at the same time, break down their anti-Ami attitude. Whenever I went to the local barbershop for a haircut and shave, I was accompanied by another gun-toting bandsman. I didn't want to tempt a barber armed with a straight razor at my throat. But he was a friendly sort and was always astonished when I paid him for his services.

"You won the war. We lost," he argued. I paid him the going rate for his services—seven cents for the haircut, three cents for the shave and a two-cigarette tip. When he saw me glancing at his noticeable limp, he said he had lost a leg on the Eastern Front and that he was pleased that if Leutershausen had to be occupied, it was by Americans, not "Ivan." Each time I went to his shop, he cautioned me that someday America would be at war with Russia. This was a theme I heard everywhere I went, from everyone I talked to. The distrust between the two countries was deep.

Other GIs were frequenting the barbershop and throwing money indiscriminately at him without even asking what the standard village rate was. Within a week, the barber had become Americanized because shave and haircut prices quadrupled. But to me, haircuts and shaves were free, providing a few cigarettes were given as a tip.

While driving to a job one night, our jeep ran into a thin cable strung across the road but no one was injured and the windshield was only slightly damaged before snapping the cable. Civilian "were-wolves" had not all given up the fight.

One afternoon while sitting on the curbstone waiting for my flock of children to stop by for their daily chocolate ration, I became aware of a well-developed golden blonde in her late 20s standing over me and smiling. In perfect English she said, "You like children, don't you?" I peeked into her carriage at six-week-old Deiter. When she saw me admiring her child, her motherly pride took over. She told me her name was Friedel Volz, that she lived only two houses from my billet and had seen me before on the street. I asked whether I could visit her. She nodded and when I told her I had to play in Lampertheim that night, she said she would sit up and wait for me.

When the band finally returned to Leutershausen, it was almost 0100 and I was sure this vision I had met had already forgotten about me. I rapped softly on her window and, sure enough, the wooden shutter opened and I crawled into a darkened kitchen. While she lit a candle, I made myself comfortable. As I looked around the sparsely furnished room, she cooked two eggs and a small piece of meat on a wood-burning stove. After apologizing for the humble meal, she served me my king's banquet.

I shall never forget what she wore that first night: a soft dirndl blouse open at the neck with a loose-flowing flowered skirt and a black leather belt pulled tightly around her trim waist. She truly was a vision in the candlelight.

As we sat and talked, she told me she had been burned out of homes in Mannheim, Freudenheim and Neckarsteinbach before migrating to Leutershausen to escape Allied bombs. She and her infant son had moved in with her parents in a three-room house. Her father, before the war, had been a representative for an American corporation. She said she was a widow, that her husband, a Wehrmacht soldier, had been killed on the Eastern Front. I found out later he was actually an anti-tank sergeant with the 1st SS Panzer Division, the Leibstandarte Adolf Hitler. Friedel took me to Heidelberg to tour the famous university and the centuries-old castle containing a gigantic, two-story high, 221,726-liter wooden wine cask in the cellar. We ambled through dank, moss-covered passages, wet by water trickling from arched ceilings, studying ancient artifacts, museum pieces, dungeons and subterranean chambers from the medieval period.

Later, we enjoyed a cup of coffee at a sidewalk cafe before going to a theater. The shops were open and the streets crowded as if the war had never happened. Actually, there it hadn't. When I returned to Leutershausen, I received the shocking news that a train had rammed a truck full of GIs on their way to leaves in Paris and one of our band members had been killed. It was difficult to accept the unnaturalness of death in peacetime. As the unofficial leader of the Tophatters, I was chosen to write to his wife telling her of the happiness he had brought to so many with his musical talent. Afterwards, regiment sent in a replacement almost immediately and the beat went on.

One afternoon, I went to Heidelberg alone and met by chance a retired professor from the university standing alone on the Neckar River bridge. I struck up a conversation with him that ended many hours later at night in his home where his very prim wife served us tea and biscuits.

He had taught at the university for 40 years and told me, in almost flawless English, of the Hitler years and of the Hindenburg Republic that had preceded the Nazis. He had refused to submit to Nazi indoctrination, and consequently had been imprisoned for a year. He described the brainwashing of Germany's youth, the mindwarping pageantry of Hitler's many political rallies, the persecution of Jews, the denying of religion, the book burning, the betrayal of parents and neighbors by children, and the enslavement and destruction of an entire nation's people and culture. He told of Gestapo raids in the middle of the night and the "final solution" extermination of the Jews. The old professor held nothing back and in several hours I received a crash course on German history during the previous 40 years.

I told him of Ohrdruf and other camps I had visited. He, in turn, told me of 18 boys hung by the SS from lampposts in Heidelberg itself for refusing to fight the advancing Americans when the cause had already been lost. He tried to explain to me the philosophies, beliefs and mentality of the German people and to prophesy the future of his country, if, in fact, it had any.

He quizzed me about the Russians and what America thought of them. As I talked, he painted a picture of the Russians and the Communist threat to the world as quite different from what we had been taught. He predicted our alliance would not last. The Russians, he said, had a treacherous government. I had trouble believing him, for all I knew of the Russians was the fun-seeking bunch, a little wild maybe, I had met on the Elbe River only weeks before. Still, he gave me a fascinating education, and I was sorry to have to excuse myself because I needed to return to Leutershausen to play a job.

The gig was another officers' party, which soon turned into a drunken brawl, for these "Gentlemen by Act of Congress" reverted to their primitive instincts faster than any group we ever played for. They slopped around like snobbish animals, lewdly grabbing every woman they could lay their hands on. As they staggered around, I was sure that I had been correct in refusing a commission during the Bulge because had I accepted it, I would probably be dead or, worse still, associating socially with these boorish degenerates.

But most of my time was spent with Friedel. Packages from home were arriving more frequently during peace time and usually included toys for the baby and yarn and other goods to knit him clothes. But one thing that was always in short supply in the town, and consequently rationed severely, was milk for the children. To obtain two cups a week for her baby, like other mothers in Leutershausen, Friedel had to stand in line at a local farmhouse for two hours and then hope the farmer was in a sharing mood. I gave her cigarettes to use for bargaining purposes, and she always got her quota, and then some.

I was also able to obtain coffee, flour, butter, milk, bread, pineapple juice and other staples for Friedel's family by bribing the company cooks with liquor and cigarettes. I never ate a single meal in the chow line, but brought each one back to her house to share it. We divided it into small portions and everyone in the family got a taste of food they had not had in years. Even hash, baked beans and pineapple slices were better than potato soup, kraut (cabbage) and black bread. American coffee, replacing the ersatz version made from apple leaves during wartime Germany, was the ultimate luxury for the family. The one item that Friedel and her family never touched was the chocolate I shared with them—that invariably went to Dieter.

Every Sunday, I attended church with Friedel despite the resentment and disapproving looks of the townspeople. She didn't fear their opinions of her fraternization, nor did I. Soon it was July and I continued to sun myself on my second-floor balcony, my own private corner of the world to be alone with my family's letters and packages.

Secretly one day, we were told every house in the town was to be searched at a prearranged time for illegally stashed weapons or Nazi propaganda materials, all of which would be confiscated and destroyed. At 0400 on the designated day, the rifle butt pounding began simultaneously at every door. The townspeople were herded onto the streets while individual searches were conducted. Dozens of pistols, rifles, bayonets, knives, Nazi flags, propaganda books and pamphlets, swastika armbands, ammunition and even potato masher grenades were seized. Such items had been prohibited by the Provost Marshal's office. Those found with weapons and subversive materials were held for questioning.

At one house where I was acting as an interpreter for a team of officers, we heard strange sounds from within. We edged closer to a bedroom door, guns drawn, and listened to pained groaning sounds. On signal, we burst in and found a girl about 12 wiping an older woman's brow with a wet towel by candlelight. The groans, which had sounded like utterances preceding death, turned out to be the warnings of impending life. We were about to assist in the birth of Leutershausen's newest citizen.

A doctor was needed but when I asked a group of people standing around grumbling outside in the night air, I was told the closest one was in Weinheim, too far to be of any immediate assistance. I jumped into the officers' Jeep and in five minutes, I was standing in the middle of a Weinheim street yelling for a "Doktor." An older man appeared at a window and, when told the situation, climbed into the jeep and returned with me to Leutershausen.

The bloody, wiggling baby boy was beautiful.

No sooner had the band gotten a few hours sleep after the search than we were informed Colonel Gomes was having another party on his front lawn that required our attendance to entertain his guests. Never mind soup to nuts—this affair was pheasant to ice cream cake. The parties were crashingly boring but the food was great.

On August 1, exciting news hit the town. A USO show featuring the Shep Fields all-reed orchestra, comedian Jack Benny, screen actress Ingrid Bergman, harmonica virtuoso Larry Adler and vocalist "Lilting" Martha Tilton would be appearing that afternoon in Heidelberg. Bergman did a segment from her latest movie, "Joan of Arc," and then, in a comedy skit, picked up Benny and threw him bodily into the band's sax section. The others each did their routines to the roaring approval of nearly 30,000 GIs at the outdoor amphitheater atop a mountain across the Neckar River from Heidelberg.

When Fields asked for volunteer musicians to sit in with his band for a feature number, Blunt was the first on stage. The band swung through a couple up-tempo numbers and then I took off on an extended solo. I returned to Leutershausen floating on air. Band jobs were coming in almost faster than we could schedule them, and we found ourselves on the road in practically every city and town in southwestern Germany.

On August 8, I was offered and accepted a three-day pass to Paris. The pass stipulated that I could be absent from the company from 0515 August 8 to 2025 August 11, a total of 87 hours and 10 minutes—an extra bonus of 15 hours and 10 minutes. That 10 minutes always puzzled me because in the Army everything usually had to come out even.

In Karlsruhe, I boarded a rinky-dink train and was off on a journey that took three times what the distance called for. The only accommodations were boxcars with standing room only. But Paris offered more excitement than Leutershausen, so I tolerated these conditions willingly. It was soon apparent that most of the leave time would be spent getting to and returning from Paris. I registered at Le Moderne Hotel just off the Place de Concorde. The hotel had been taken over by the armed forces and broken up into barracks-style accommodations for American military personnel. With a family letter in my pocket telling me that my lieutenant colonel uncle was stationed there with G-4 Section (supply), I found his office in a hotel overlooking the Arc of Triumph. I was allowed to cool my heels outside his office for 30 minutes before being shown in. I walked in as any combat-weary nephew would but was promptly told that I was addressing a colonel, that all military procedures would be followed and that I was to salute and stand at attention during the visit.

After a few pleasantries, most of which seemed to be an attempt to get rid of me as fast as he could, he offered me a candy bar, but I was so incensed by my treatment I told him I already had one and declined his offer. Relieved that I hadn't accepted it, he quickly shoved it back in his desk drawer. With that, I was dismissed.

Armed with a city map, I visited the Eiffel Tower, the Louvre Museum and Napoleon's tomb, Notre Dame Cathedral, the Latin Quarter, the artists' Left Bank of the Seine River, The Opera House and all points in between. It may have been known as the City of Love but I found it dingy and dirty with communal sidewalk toilets shared by all, usually in plain sight of everyone else. After returning to the cleanliness of Germany, I had no further desire to visit Paris.

The next day I took a subway ride through the city and found the underground system simple to negotiate, despite the signs written in French. It was much easier, I thought, than those in London, where every train, from my experience, seemed to wind up at Waterloo Station. I stopped at a combination PX and department store to buy perfume for my sister June, who had been so faithful about sending peanut butter fudge to me in the family food packages. On a spur of the moment, I sent a telegram home: "Greetings from Paris. Feeling wonderful. Seeing everything. Worcester is nicer. Keep happy. Bud."

Later, I visited the acclaimed ancient Egyptian obelisk and found it to be like everything else in Paris: disappointing. I'm afraid that at the age of 19, I wasn't very sophisticated in the appreciation of ancient arts and artifacts. Next, it was to the Place de Republique with its ornate statues and gargoyles. In a matter of minutes, my curiosity about ancient architecture was completely satisfied. But as is true of all gifts the Army gives its men, the end comes too soon, and with hardly a backward glance I headed for the train station.

August 15, not long after my return from Paris, a flurry of rumors were rampant that the Japanese had surrendered in the Pacific. If that were true, the 84th would not be going to the CBI Theater of Operations after all. But it was not until some time later that we received the word officially—in the third stall at the company latrine, where else?

The last inter-divisional football game of the season was in Berlin on October 22, 1945 and I had to pull some strings to be included on the team trip, for the 84th was in contention with the 82nd Airborne Division for the ETO football championship.

The trip to Berlin involved 20 grueling hours in an uncomfortable, cold, two-and-a-half-ton troop carrier but the discomfort was worth it, I figured, for I didn't want to go home without first seeing the German capital. Temporary billets had been set up in advance in civilian homes but I had other plans: to deliver a message from Friedel to her brother's family in the Spandau section of the city. After taking a trolley and hiking more than a dozen blocks, I located the address.

After vigorous knocking, the door opened a crack, allowing a woman to peek out before slamming it shut again. I knocked more authoritatively and a stern-looking woman stood in the doorway demanding to know my business with them. I told her I had a message from her in-laws in Leutershausen. The door was flung open wide and I was literally yanked into the woman's apartment. After accepting my identity, a beautiful girl about my age cautiously appeared from hiding. Her name was Irmgard, and she radiated an innocence I had not often seen in Germany before.

Irmgard, thinking I was a Russian soldier, had fled, as she always did when Russians appeared, to a potato bin in the cellar where she had buried herself for fear of being raped. Mass ravaging of Berlin's women had been part of the plundering perpetrated by the conquering Russian troops when they entered Berlin.

I brought them up to date about everyone in Leutershausen and about new baby Dieter. Invited to stay for dinner, I reluctantly accepted the only piece of meat I am sure this family had seen in weeks, for to decline the offer would have been, as in most European countries, insulting. We talked of the war and America long into the night. Then Irmgard produced a beat-up Victrola and I clumsily tried to dance a German waltz with her. How they all laughed at my awkwardness.

The time came for the game and I decided to bring Irmgard as a date. I gave her my full-length GI overcoat, while I made a thin field jacket suffice for the trolley car trip to the Berlin Reichssportfeld, the sight of the 1936 Olympics. As we waited for the trolley to come, I became aware of the scornful looks of Berliners waiting near us who, I was sure, considered Irmgard just another shack-up job. I couldn't stand still for this; she was one of the sweetest, most innocent girls I had met in Europe. "Meine Frau," I nodded to the crowd knowingly. Embarrassed, they turned away. We were barely able to stifle our giggles through all this, but after we got on the trolley to the stadium, we both let it all out. It was great fun to laugh again for surely I had shed enough tears the past year. The 84th Division won the game, 23-13 and was crowned European champion.

After the game, she and I went to a theater to see a German version of "Showboat," but the jokes that broke up the audience were lost on me. I sat and listened to the music. We next went on the grand tour of what remained of Berlin and visited the Reichstag, Brandenburg Gate, Joseph Goebbels' home, the Luftwaffe and Propaganda ministries, the Berlin Opera House, Hitler's death bunker site, Templehof Airport, the Unter der Linden Park and even the once beautiful Berlin train station.

When I entered the Russian Sector on the other side of Brandenburg Gate, I was besieged by Russian soldiers bartering for watches, cigarettes, anything they could bring back to Mother Russia. Beforehand, I had set the hands to the correct time on my Telegram & Gazette $2 Ingersall carrier's watch that hadn't worked in months, and sold it instantly to a Russian soldier for $75, and a carton of American cigarettes for another $100.

Before leaving, he tried to con me into buying one of the 20 or so watches he wore strung up his arm under his army overcoat and which he obviously had lifted from German prisoners or corpses. While this swapping was taking place, Irmgard stood firmly on the other side of the towering archway a considerable distance away, for she feared even being on the same street with the Russians.

As soon as I could, I sent the cash home, for $175 in those days was big money. I more than made up for the money stolen from me by the Army as punishment for the crime of having my uniforms laundered by a German woman in Rheinhausen. I was told later the

Russians were not allowed to bring large sums of money back home for it would upset the country's fragile economy. They could, however, bring back as much war plunder as they could carry.

It was a marvelous testimony to the German will and resilience that we could make our way at all through Berlin for, like much of the country, this city of nearly four million people had been practically turned to rubble.

The truck convoy back to Leutershausen had already left without me but that didn't phase me at all for I decided to go AWOL for a day or two to enjoy more of Berlin. I could always make up some excuse when I got back to Leutershausen. After another day of sightseeing, I bade farewell to my host family and started hitchhiking west to Hannover and then south to Frankfurt, where I paused long enough to briefly visit General Eisenhower's SHAEF headquarters.

Then it was back on the road again to Mannheim where I took a trolley to Heidelberg and another to Leutershausen. Somewhat sheepishly, I walked up the main street, trying not to attract attention. When I arrived at my billet, I found that even after being two days late, no one had missed me—except Friedel. I gave her a letter her brother had asked me to deliver and she was overjoyed for she had had no word from him since the Russians had occupied the city. Christmas packages started arriving, filled with food, toys, sweaters and other presents for Deiter. These were happy days filled with love and sharing.

Word came down that most of my former outfit was being transferred to the 78th Infantry Division in Kassel, above Frankfurt, for rotation home. The rest would follow in December. Because my name was not on the shipping lists, I could only watch as the trucks loaded and pulled away, happy for those going home but disappointed that I was not among them. I had not built up sufficient rotation points to go home with the others in November, but my time would come four months later.

No sooner had the trucks pulled away and the Tophatters disbanded than orders came transferring me to the Seventh Army, 12th Armored Division band in Seckenheim, a suburb east of Mannheim on the Mannheim-Heidelberg highway. The curtain on my odyssey was slowly being lowered.

I returned to Leuterhausen as a European tourist 39 years later to find that cars had replaced the ox carts and asphalted streets covered the cobblestones of the '40s. With my wife and son, Richard, I had left the tour group in Heidelberg and taken a taxi to Leutershausen for a sentimental pilgrimage back in time. As I walked along the main street leading into town from the trolley line and began searching for familiar landmarks from the past, an elderly woman in a babushka carrying a wicker shopping basket, spotted me and started shouting, "Der Amerikanishe Soldat mit Schokolade!" ("The American soldier with the chocolate").

As fast as her advanced age allowed, she ran toward me and grabbed me in a smothering bear hug. Then, in her excitement, the torrent of words were flowing out of her so fast I couldn't understand what she was trying to tell me. I turned to my wife and son and saw tears on their cheeks as they realized what was happening to me. It was truly an emotional moment and as happy as I was to be remembered, I was, at the same time, deeply saddened that my visit could only be so brief.

There was so much I wanted to do and say to her and so many questions about Friedel. Yes, she said she remembered her but she had moved away years before. Friedel's parents, the old woman said, had died long ago. She said Friedel had had another child, Klaus, so I assumed she had weathered the attitudes and gossip of the town and remarried. The woman promised to get word to Friedel that I had returned and that I now had a family of my own.

Still excited, she said her daughter had been one of my chocolate babies and now, with children of her own, they would want to meet me. Sadly, I told this wonderful old grandmother that I had no time. She insisted that the whole town be told I was back so they could throw a party for me. Again, I had to beg off, all the while working my way back to the waiting cab. She pleaded with me to stay but I was forced to turn my back on her and drive away, leaving her standing in the street waving as we turned the corner and headed back to the tour bus. She would surely have a story to tell the town that night. I couldn't tell whose disappointment was greater, hers or mine.

Even before I could accept the fact that I was, in one sense, being left behind by my division, I was sent confusing signals about my next duty station. I had orders to join the 60th Army Ground Forces Band, but before I could even determine where they were located, the orders were changed. Instead, I was being transferred from the 9th Army to the 7th Army, from the 84th Infantry Division to the 12th Armored Division and from a swing band to a music school in Seckenheim, about 15 kilometers from Leutershausen.

The rotation of troops out of the ETO raised havoc with the forces left behind. Units remaining overseas were being broken up, fragmentized, dissected and decimated as the Army's logistics coordinators tried to find available troop deployment ship space and still keep remaining units up to strength. For example, when I was finally sent home, I was transferred to a forestry unit I never was a part of and, in fact, never even went to. These were only transfers on paper going on all over the ETO after the war.

What was transpiring was like trying to fit all the pieces of a jigsaw puzzle together at the same time. The only constant was that the Army was trying to get us all out of Europe as fast as it could—and this would eventually work to my advantage.

Upon arriving in Seckenheim, I found housing was on a catch-as-catch-can basis, so I quickly grabbed an attic room a short distance from the Special Services Music School. The room had a potbelly stove to keep me warm during the harsh German winters, a window offering a panoramic view of the town and a built-in bunk bed large enough for two people. As barren as it was, the room had everything I needed. Being on the top floor, it afforded me the privacy I always sought. Having spent most of my formative years in nature's solitude, I wanted to keep it that way. It was obvious I was going to be happy there with everything I had been craving: hot food, almost total solitude, convenience to everywhere, and music all day and night.

There were no classes held at the music school and our Army chores consisted solely of performing on demand. Also, the town had a civilian post office where I could send letters home and to German girlfriends without being subject to Army censorship.

No sooner had I settled in than I called my brother-in-law back in England. I posed as "Colonel Blunt," the same ruse I had used before. The call was routed to Frankfurt, then Paris, on to London and several minutes later to Parmenter's Air Force base at Hanley, Staffordshire. As each operator came on the line, I kept repeating, "military urgent priority." The ploy worked like a charm and the next voice I heard was, "Pfc. Parmenter speaking." He said afterwards that as soon as he was told a Colonel Blunt was on the phone for him, he started to play-act his part on the other end. "Don't say a word, don't even smile, Whit. It's me, Buddy," I cautioned him.

All he kept saying on the other end was, "Yes Colonel, no Colonel, yes Colonel." We both loved every minute of it. We chatted about home and where and what we had been doing. He informed me that he was being rotated home in a few weeks for he had been in the ETO a year longer than me. He had been told of my combat in the Bulge and Germany and he had been concerned. After five minutes, our luck pressed as far as we dared without risking court-martials, we ended the "military urgent priority call" with urgent priority haste. What a horse laugh we both had after we hung up and what a moral victory it was to beat the military again at its own game. I was able to call him several other times using the same method. It worked every time, and he was even able to place a "military" call to me on one occasion.

I soon drifted into the company of Paul Smith from San Diego, California, a pianist formerly of the Ozzie Nelson band who, after his military stint, would join Tommy Dorsey's band. Smith's musical star continued to rise after his discharge: he became the head arranger for the Andrews Sisters, a super nova in West Coast jazz circles and finally accompanist and music director for world-renowned jazz vocalist Ella Fitzgerald.

Smith, also known as "Long Drink Smitty" because of his six-foot-four build, his Lil' Abner resemblance and his ill-fitting uniforms, spent tireless hours developing furious jazz duets on twin pianos at the school with another piano player. It was not uncommon for these sessions to go all day without interruption and into the night. I often accompanied them and some of the wildest, most innovative and creative jazz piano ever to come out of Germany emanated from the Seckenheim music school halls. For the almost nightly gigs we were playing all over southern Germany, Smith and I would find a bass player and off we would go. It was the most exciting period of my musical career.

Rumors kept circulating about our being rotated home, and this kept most of us on edge, for the number of overseas service points needed to be shipped home was constantly being lowered. Time erased each rumor as it usually does and we continued our daily routines—but getting home was quickly becoming uppermost in our minds.

To break up some of the routine at the music school, I took to hanging around the military airport at Mannheim where I met a warrant officer pilot from an artillery unit who took me for a spin in an L-5 observation plane. When he offered to take me along on a 90-mile trip to Frankfurt, I jumped at the chance.

The next day we took off and headed north for SHAEF headquarters, about an hour's flight away. These flights were the first times I had been in the air since 1937 when I flew in an old barnstorming Curtiss Condor tri-motor biplane with pioneer-aviator Clarence Chamberlin who had piloted the monoplane "Columbia" from New York to Germany a decade earlier. Part of the way into the Frankfurt trip, the warrant officer yelled back to me, "Take it!" Without hesitation, I grabbed the joy stick and soon had the gentle touch needed to fly these delicate, canvas-covered birds.

"Keep the nose on the horizon and your eyes on the autobahn and you can't miss it," he said, referring to Frankfurt. I remained at the controls for most of the trip. As his guest, I had coffee and a sandwich at the officers' club while he shopped for silk stockings for a girlfriend back in Mannheim. I flew the plane back to Mannheim and, following his instructions, managed to settle the aircraft into an approach pattern. Just before we touched down, I took my hands off the controls so he could land the plane. We bumped down rather hard and rolled to a stop.

"That wasn't too bad except the landing was a little rough," he commented. Only when I told him I had given control of the plane over to him at the last moment did I learn he had not taken it and the plane, a slightly larger and heavier version of the classic Piper Cub, had landed itself and lived up to the factory publicity claims that Piper planes practically flew themselves.

Having family pictures of myself wearing aviation goggles at the age of four, I felt I had been destined to fly almost since birth. When it had been time at the Fort Devens Induction Center to choose a branch of the service, I had been guided by my father's advice. Navy? "They would never find your body if the ship sank." Marines? "The death rate is too high." Air Corps? "Flying is too dangerous." Army? "OK." The choice had been made that simply.

The Frankfurt flight plus what I had seen at Parmenter's Air Corps base left little doubt in my mind—the Air Corps would have been far more desirable than what I had endured during seven months of combat. It was one of the few times in my life that I felt my father had been wrong. After the trip in that little L-5, I was solidly hooked on aviation. I got my private license October 22, 1948, less than two years after my first at-the-controls flight in Germany.

Word was posted on the school bulletin board that rotation points were being shaved to 50. The Army was stepping up its redeployment schedule as fast as travel arrangements could be made. Points were based on time overseas and the number of battles and decorations. I had only 45 points and would have to sweat it out a while longer.

Shortly after New Year's, the Army perpetrated one of the great con jobs of the century on me. If offered to swap a week of rest and rehabilitation in Switzerland for a 12-month extension of duty. Like a gullible fool, I jumped at the opportunity. I was eager to ship home but, at the same time, I realized I was getting the opportunity of a lifetime traveling throughout Europe, an opportunity that might never again be offered.

While waiting for my travel orders, word was received that General George S. Patton had been injured in a Mannheim traffic accident. He died several days later of what had been reported as minor injuries. The day of his funeral, I stood on a Heidelberg sidewalk and watched Germans weep openly as the procession passed by. Although a former enemy, he had been a great general and if there was anything the German people respected, it was a victorious military officer.

Former German soldiers who had fought against his Third Army saluted as Patton's body was taken to the castle and then later to the train station. Thousands along the route fell silent as the horse-drawn caisson carrying his body passed in review. Often, I heard Germans remark that if the Fatherland had had Patton and Eisenhower on its side, they would have won the war. Invariably they added, after all, that Eisenhower was German.

My travel orders for the Switzerland furlough came in for the week of January 16–23 and upon arriving in Basel we were offered three alternate tour routes—one for ski enthusiasts, another for mountain climbers and a third for sightseers wanting to visit as many cities and towns as time allowed.

I chose the most comprehensive routing, for I was an explorer by nature and wished to absorb as much Swiss culture and scenery as possible in only seven days. The next day, we arrived at the mountainside resort at Chateau-d'Oex. Almost silently the train had rolled through long, winding mountain tunnels that eventually blossomed into brilliant bursts of sunlight sharply accentuating tile awesome Swiss landscapes, each an artist's rendering of exquisite beauty. I had reservations at LeGrande Hotel, a majestic wooden resort clinging luxuriantly half way up a mountain slope and offering breathtaking views of the Swiss mountain ranges.

Three days into my Swiss trip, a phone call I had placed to America was ready. Fortunately, I had given the hotel a forwarding address where I would be. I waited as Swiss, French and New York operators patched me through to Narragansett Avenue, Worcester Massacusetts. My mother's excited voice sent a chill through me for a moment. My family had gathered around the phone for they had been alerted a day in advance that a call from Switzerland was coming through in the early afternoon. The three minutes went by as one, but the purpose of the call, to reassure my loved ones that I was alive and well, had been achieved.

Most of the cities in Switzerland, and especially the towns, were an interesting mixture of historical and contemporary architecture and cultures. Modern buildings were scattered amongst those centuries old as if both styles were fighting for society's acceptance. Side by side sat the world of yesteryear and the world of tomorrow. From Chateau-d'Oex we traveled to Montreux and Lausanne, where we checked into a hotel on the shores of Lake Geneva. I climbed a nearby hillside and was rewarded with an awesome view of snow-mantled mountains and shimmering, placid lakes. The scenery held me in its grasp. After drinking it all in, I reluctantly returned to the world of reality below.

19

Long Journey Home

Arriving back in Seckenheim, I found Smith had a long list of gigs waiting to be played. It was back to the grind immediately. The money was piling up, for engagements paid $4 to $8 a night, depending on how much the traffic would bear, the importance of the event and how much money we felt the party hiring us had.

Rumors were rampant that 45-pointers were to ship home soon, but this didn't apply to me since I had signed on for the one-year extension of duty. But my bags were packed, just in case. As time went by, rumors about redeployment back home grew more prevalent. Each rumor brought on a euphoria; each delay a depression for those with enough points. But every day more transfers were posted on the school bulletin board. Cautiously, I let myself feel optimistic and kept checking the board.

Then, one day, the wait was over; my orders were posted. I was being transferred to the 1391st Engineer Forestry Company and sent to Bremerhaven, a seaport on the North Sea.

The big question in my mind, however, was what a forestry company had to do with occupying post-war Germany? Upon asking questions of the brass, I was told my transfer was to a unit headed Stateside in a matter of days. Suddenly, it became clear. The Army had screwed up my records, perhaps by the same clerk named SNAFU who had missed my bandsman classification months earlier, and my extra year's commitment was apparently lost in the shuffle of paperwork. Far be it from me to tell them they didn't know how to do their job correctly.

Orders came through saying I would ship out for the States February 14, Valentine's Day. This meant I would be home for my mother's birthday on St. Patrick's Day, March 17. If I had planned it, I couldn't have given her a better present.

I notified my family to stop writing and sending packages for I would be home soon. This could have been a foolish move for I had seen Army orders screwed up before, such as my acceptance to Fort Benning OCS before I was relegated to the 84th Division.

Told that only one souvenir gun could be brought home and that we would be searched at the point of embarkation, I started selling my pistol collection with a heavy heart. I took the trolley to Leutershausen for what I knew would be a very sad and difficult farewell. When I arrived, I was told that Friedel was ill at Heidelberg Hospital and would not be home before I shipped out. I left as quickly as I could without looking back. Next came farewells to Smitty and all the other musicians.

When the orders were finally cut, we moved out by truck, but instead of driving due north to Bremerhaven, the driver took us to Aberbach and then 150 kilometers south to Esslingen bei Stuttgart. No one seemed to know just exactly where we were supposed to go and I started to get the sinking feeling that we would miss the boat in another classic example of an Army foul-up.

Finally, we did a turnaround, winding up in Rotenberg where we were told we would be moving out again in the morning. After dumping my gear in a small castle tucked away in the hills, I started exploring the town for I knew this was to be my last few hours in Germany and I wanted to be sure that I had seen everything. Questioning the first civilians I met, I learned that Rotenberg, with 70 houses and 380 inhabitants, was the second smallest town in Germany.

I retrieved my gear from the castle and moved into a private home where I was offered hot milk and a feather bed. I still slept with a pistol under my pillow for it was a difficult habit to break. As long as I remained in a potentially hostile country, it seemed like a prudent course of action.

The next morning I sold most of my stash of cigarettes to civilians in the town and later was able to send home money orders totalling $550. What was supposed to be a one-night stand in Rotenberg turned into a delay of several days for a reason that only Army mentality understood. I knew then that the boat had left days earlier for America without Blunt.

On March 1, we finally started heading north toward Bremerhaven. Some made the trip by freight cars, others by truck convoy. In terms of comfort, it didn't matter much one way or the other. Exhausted by the continuing delays, I volunteered to accompany the baggage to the port in advance of the convoy.

The weather was cold and the truck was uncomfortable but at least I was on the move again, going somewhere in the general direction of home. From the back end of the truck, I watched the convoy pass through Mannheim, where we had started from. After two days on the road, we pulled into a bomb-ravaged city and I yelled to the first civilian I saw, "Wohin Sind Wir?" ("Where are we?")

"Bremerhaven beim Nord See" ("Bremerhaven by the North Sea"), a stevedore replied.

We were hustled off the trucks and taken to a former German Army post consisting of a parade ground and apartment-like brick barracks. The post had miraculously been untouched by the Allied bombings and we were assigned almost lavish accommodations. From our windows we could see an entire flotilla of Liberty ships, Victory ships, troop transports and freighters. Somewhere on the waterfront was a ship with my name on it, but which one?

We were told that it could take up to two weeks to be processed. All we could do was watch the bulletin board daily for our unit name, ship designation and departure date. The first person I bumped into on the post was Smitty, who was also sweating out his shipping orders. We celebrated at a local Red Cross club, feasting on coffee, cokes and doughnuts. I walked around the city the next day sightseeing but not getting too far away from the bulletin board.

Because of the layout of the installation in which we were stashed, it was easier to skip meals and live off what remained of packages from home rather than walk the 10 blocks to the dining hall. During free hours, Smitty and I managed to play a few jam sessions together. Even though I had no drums, I was never very far away from a pair of sticks. Our German occupation marks were converted to uncirculated gold-seal American bills, something unseen for many months. With the bills in my hands, I was finally convinced I was going home. Fog, dampness and the cold wind blowing in across the North Sea, normal for Bremerhaven in March, kept us mostly confined to our billets.

Finally, the notice we had all been waiting for was posted. The 1391st Engineer Forestry Company would ship out on the *Frostburg* Victory ship on March 10. I ran into the city and sent a cablegram home: "Sailing Sunday 10th Victory Frostburg Bremerhaven Happy Birthday Mom Love." Reluctantly, I accepted the fact I couldn't make it home in time for my mother's birthday, but there was still the delayed Christmas celebration they had planned.

Remaining close to my billet, fearing that some foul-up still could, and probably would, occur, my mind had trouble accepting the fact that the Army actually was sending me home. I was certain that something had to go wrong at the last minute. But this time my pessimism was misplaced. On the assigned departure date, formations of impatient GIs lined up early on the docks and began snaking their way to a gangplank a block away. I looked at the prow of the ship to make sure it said *Frostburg*. It did.

"Blunt," someone barked out.

"Roscoe C. Jr.," I yelled back at the voice.

"Company E 54, Bunk 125," the voice growled again.

Blunt was one of 911 men being crammed onto the makeshift troop transport. Deep in the bowels of the ship, I found Ship's Company 54, Compartment E and finally bunk number 125. Flopping into it, I closed my eyes and gave thanks to whoever had put me there.

Even as the Victory ship was tied to the pier, my stomach started reacting to the harbor swells. I was becoming seasick and we hadn't even left the pier yet.

The first sounds I heard was a loudspeaker blaring out Les Brown's "Sentimental Journey." How sweet it sounded the first time I heard it. But the same record droned on and on, never stopping, day and night for the entire voyage home until I wanted to throw the automated disc jockey overboard. As I settled into my bunk and waited for the ship to get underway, I vowed that if there was to be another Army SNAFU, they were going to have one helluva battle getting me off that ship again, or even finding me, for that matter.

Exhausted from the months of anticipation, the two weeks of traveling and the hours of preparation, I fell asleep only to awaken some hours later to the familiar rolling and creaking of the ship. But, there would be no anti-submarine evasive routing this time, only flank speed, due west through the North Sea and the English Channel to New York City.

For months I had patiently waited for my rotation points to accumulate, and now that I had reached the quota and was actually headed home, I was plagued by intense impatience, for the ship seemed to be only plowing its way through the sea at a few knots an hour.

When seasickness allowed, I watched a GI I knew parlay $1 into several hundred in an improvised crap game on a blanket. As a favor to me, he asked for $5 so he could multiply it to $200 for me. He was on a roll. A New England conservative, I declined but when he continued to win, I thought for a fleeting moment that perhaps I should have taken him up on his generous offer. Still I was not willing to risk my money on rolls of the dice.

The crapshooter persisted and eventually wore me down. He returned minutes later with my $5 and also a $195 profit. I was almost converted then and there to the life of a gambler.

I attended a simple church service aboard ship on Easter Sunday, my mother's birthday. Even though still thousands of miles apart, I could at least celebrate with her in spirit. I knew she would be thinking of me. My seasickness increased and soon I was bunk-ridden. Misery loves company. Smitty, in a bunk near me, was even sicker.

The ship passed through a violent storm and the pitching and rolling made life below deck abominable. Seasickness is insidious; it robs you of food, of rest, of strength and it even strips you of will. And before it is through, it finally takes away everything else and leaves hopelessness in its wake. We were reduced to relieving ourselves in tin cans that others threw away for us. Each day, to stave off the hunger that exacerbated our unsettled stomachs, I tried to eat Saltine crackers, or candy bars, or an orange or anything that anyone offered me. But nothing stayed down more than a few seconds.

It was only after eventually reaching the calmer waters of outer New York harbor that the seasickness abated and I was finally able to eat a varied meal of baked ham, mashed potatoes, celery, lettuce, tomatoes and ice cream the merchant mariners offered us. Crew members, apparently aware of what many of us had gone through, couldn't do enough for us, even insisting that we have seconds and thirds at the ward room table. I had not seen or eaten fresh vegetables since leaving the States 18 months before.

As I lay in my bunk one morning, I became aware of a strange shipboard sound, even louder than the pulsing engines. It was the distant roar of men cheering. Shakily, I made my way to the deck and there it was, the distant New York skyline and the Statue of Liberty I had missed on the way overseas.

There were no hose-spraying harbor fireboats to greet us, no reception crowds, no hero's' welcome, just the near-silent approach of the ship plowing through the outer harbor between New York and New Jersey. Soon a harbor pilot launch pulled alongside and tugboats started nudging our ship toward a slip

We were finally home and all the horror and devastation was behind us, gradually becoming only a memory. Every inch of the starboard railing toward the city was filled with GIs drinking in the New York skyline. Each was deep in his own private thoughts.

The earlier jubilation at the first glimpse of America had calmed down to solemn reflection, overwhelming relief and, I'm sure, more than a few prayers of thanks. We dragged our barracks bags topside in wild anticipation of what we thought would be a mass, mob-like exodus. But as always in the military, natural impulse was not meant to be. We soon were reminded that we were still in the Army and everything, I mean everything, had to be done by the numbers.

Picture 911 eager, impatient, equipment-laden GIs trying to form into alphabetical order lines according to unit designation. It was total confusion bordering on mass hysteria. After an hour of shuffling and reshuffling, some semblance of order was established and we started to file towards the gangplank. On solid ground once again, many men went to their knees to kiss the American soil—or, more accurately, the rotted New York harbor pier. I just wanted to be away from the ship, the other men, the docks, the motion of the sea, everything.

For many years after the war, I described my shipboard ordeal as becoming seasick in Bremerhaven two days before getting on the damn *Frostburg* Victory and staying that way for three days after getting off it. It was not much of an exaggeration.

Red Cross coffee and doughnut wagons were on the docks and, as long as it was free, we accepted as much as our stomachs would tolerate. Surely I had suffered enough in Europe to deserve free eats, so I had no qualms whatsoever about accepting seconds.

We were herded passively onto trains, caring little whether it was the right one, for at least it was in America and any place it transported us would be OK, as long as it was far away from the bilge-smelling rust bucket that had brought us home.

Reminiscent of September 1944, the rail cars were stacked high with barracks bags and men were sprawled everywhere. A few were even lucky enough to have seats. I lay my head back and closed my eyes, letting my thoughts rumble around in my head. Somehow, I felt like a stranger in my own country. The cars seemed more streamlined than I remembered and so many people in mufti rather than olive drab looked unnatural.

The train began to slow and I saw a sign on a siding: "Camp Kilmer," the same camp from which we had departed 18 month previously. We were assigned to a temporary barracks and told our time was free until the next morning. I legged it for the nearest phone but found long lines already formed at each one so I diverted to the nearest PX to find some American ice cream while waiting for a phone to become available.

When I dialed 56264, the phone rang only twice before my mother answered. "I'm home," I stated simply. She could not comprehend immediately what I was saying and then, when she did, she couldn't contain the excitement in her voice.

"Where are you? Are you safe? Are you in this country?" the questions tumbled over each other.

"I'm fine and in New Jersey and should be home, I hope, in a couple days," I explained quickly, trying to calm her down. Then I could hear her crying softly on the other end.

They had received my telegram and she said my father had anticipated the phone call after reading in the *New York Times* that the forestry company to which I had been transferred had sailed from Bremerhaven with another forestry company, a field artillery battalion and three anti-aircraft battalions. I hadn't realized how closely he had been following my every movement.

She put my dad on and he was a lot calmer, at least from the sound of his voice. He informed me that all my souvenir packages had apparently arrived for he had been keeping an inventory and comparing each arrival with my letters telling him what to expect. Before hanging up, he promised, we would resume our man-to-man talks. One of the things that I had missed the most overseas were the quiet, meditative talks we had shared as I grew up. Now, I would have so much to tell him, but there would also be so much that I couldn't.

Everything was moving quickly; as fast as the Army had wanted to ensnare me, it now seemed just as eager to get rid of me. The 12-hour train trip was long and tedious and extended into the night. When I awakened after napping most of the way north, the train was stopped on a siding overlooking a broad street and a diner.

"Where are we?" I asked the conductor.

"Worcester, Massachusetts," he answered, bored. I sat up straight and looked out the window and as my eyes became accustomed to the dark, I recognized the intersection of Southbridge Street and Quinsigamond Avenue. Without thinking, I sprinted down the aisle and bounded out the car door to search for a phone. "We'll only be here a few minutes," the conductor yelled after me.

I scrambled blindly down a steep embankment and ran across the street to a nearby railroad roundhouse. "I need a phone," I yelled to the first person I saw. "Over there," he mumbled without looking up from his newspaper.

I dialed hurriedly and again my mother answered. "Are you still in New Jersey?" she asked, her voice rising.

"Nope, in Worcester on Southbridge Street," I answered laughing. I told her we were on our way to Fort Devens and I would call her from there as soon as I could. I headed back through the darkness to the train, and as I approached it I could see it was already pulling away slowly from the siding. My heart was thumping as I scrambled slipping and clawing back up the embankment and started galloping down the tracks after it. I managed to catch the platform at the rear of the very last car just as it matched my top running speed.

Laughing as I settled back into my seat, I hoped that that would be the last of the close calls I would experience in my soon-to-end Army career. After arriving at Devens in the middle of the night, I sat up until dawn outside the barracks, just smelling the clean, fresh New England air and looking at the silent stars in the sky. The night passed slowly. I was eager to get it all over with, to graduate to civilian and reunite with my family.

At 0600, the discharge processing started with a haircut and physical, dental and "short arm" inspections, presentation of earned medals and ribbons, inoculations and travel pay disbursement, military record checks and proper hygiene movies, mustering-out back pay and bonuses and reclassification from 1-A, military fit, to 4-A, no longer militarily desirable.

Part of the separation ritual included a persistent effort to convince us to re-enlist for another tour of duty, or at least join the Army Reserve. Having as much Army life as I could stomach in one lifetime, I respectfully declined. The other discharge-processing procedure before we were pushed out the gate was an unannounced, sneak search of our belongings to see if we had any contraband war souvenirs. From others who had already gone through it, I got wind of what was coming and hurriedly hid all my loot above the barrack's ceiling. When the brass arrived, my barracks bag was there for inspection, as bare as Mother Hubbard's cupboard. By the time I finally walked out Fort Devens' main gate for the last time however, my bag was so heavy again I could hardly carry it.

I called Parmenter to arrange a meeting and picnic with my mother and father. Then I retired to the USO club on the base to wait and have a chocolate frappe. But first, I put on a juke box record, "Slide Hamp, Slide" by Lionel Hampton's band. If I had to wait, at least I could get the joint jumping. No sooner had the record started, than I heard a voice, "Hey Bud." It was Parmenter and he said the family was in the car outside.

I walked rather apprehensively towards Parmenter's old black 1937 Pontiac that had been jacked up in my father's driveway for the duration of the war. I wondered if I had changed much. Had they changed? What would they think of me? But the reunion turned out to be much simpler than I had envisioned. My father jumped out of the back seat and embraced me with tears in his eyes and whispered in my ear how much he had missed and feared for me. I climbed into the car where my mother was sitting. She reached over, patted me on the knee and softly said, "My baby's home."

Then we drove to a nearby pine grove to enjoy a quiet picnic of ham-on-rye sandwiches, potato salad, chocolate milk, potato chips, celery, tomatoes and ice cream. My mother hadn't forgotten a thing.

Not much was said; there would be plenty of time for that later. The happy homecoming lasted until evening when I returned to the fort for one more night before my discharge became final and I would be officially designated "civilian" on March 28.

The next morning, when the last detail had been resolved and the "ruptured duck" pin awarded, I started dragging the souvenir-laden bag toward the gate. Seeing me struggling with it, a civilian truck driver stopped and gave me a lift.

As I waited by the gate, I stared at passing officers. The uniform didn't fool them, for I'm sure they knew that despite the beribboned Eisenhower jacket and combat infantry badge, I was a brand new civilian. I especially enjoyed the freedom of giving officers only a glance instead of a highball. Still, not feeling comfortable that close to the fort and everything it represented, I dragged the bag across the highway and waited there. Soon, Parmenter came wheeling by and the car door swung open. An hour later, I was home.

My odyssey was over, my duty done.